THE PAST
AS LEGACY

LUKE–ACTS
AND
ANCIENT
EPIC

MARIANNE PALMER BONZ

FORTRESS PRESS ✠ MINNEAPOLIS

THE PAST AS LEGACY
Luke-Acts and Ancient Epic

Library of Congress Cataloging-in-Publication Data
Bonz, Marianne Palmer, (   )
  The past as legacy : Luke-Acts and ancient epic / Marianne Palmer Bonz.
    p.   cm.
  Includes bibliographical references and index.
  ISBN 0-8006-3225-7 (alk. paper)
  1. Bible. N.T. Luke—Criticism, interpretation, etc.   2. Bible. N.T. Acts—Criticism, interpretation, etc.   3. Bible, N.T. Luke—Criticism, Textual.   4. Bible. N.T. Acts—Criticism, Textual.   5. Virgil. Aeneid.   I. Title.

BS2589 .B66 2000
226.4'-66—dc21

                                                            99-056275

Manufactured in the U.S.A.   AF 1-3225

04   03   02   01   00   1   2   3   4   5   6   7   8   9   10

To the memory of my father,
William Henry Palmer III,
who was my first and best teacher.

CONTENTS

PREFACE

It is widely acknowledged that Luke-Acts, the largest single literary work in the New Testament, has incorporated a number of stylistic elements and literary motifs from the Septuagint. The precise manner and underlying significance of this appropriation of the Israelite past, however, are issues that have yet to be convincingly resolved. Indeed, although a broad consensus of current scholarship categorizes Luke-Acts as Hellenistic historiography, no major interpretive advances have developed from this hermeneutical model since the work of Hans Conzelmann in the 1950s. Conversely, more recent attempts to relate Luke-Acts to historical fiction have foundered on the problem of the inherently trivializing literary perspective of the ancient Greek novel.

This study addresses the genre and interpretation of Luke-Acts in the light of its historical, social, literary, and ideological milieu, particularly as these elements are reflected in the Latin epics contemporary with Luke-Acts and in their famous Augustan prototype, Virgil's *Aeneid*. Literary evidence indicating that Virgil's works had been translated into Greek prose by the middle of the first century makes this line of inquiry especially promising. Interpreting Luke-Acts as a prose adaptation of heroic or historical epic provides a hermeneutical model that is both universal in its theological message and essentially popular in its narrative presentation.

Beginning with the question of literary occasion, this study introduces the particular configuration of historical circumstances that produced the great foundational epics of *Gilgamesh,* the *Iliad,* and the *Odyssey,* as well as the *Aeneid,* and suggests that the historical situation for the composition of Luke-Acts was closely analogous in certain key respects. After a detailed examination of the salient elements of dramatic presentation, function, and interpretation of the *Aeneid* and its direct literary descendants is provided, the generic paradigm of epic is applied to the composition of Luke-Acts, beginning with a detailed exegetical analysis of Acts 2 and ultimately comprising a survey of Luke's two-part work in its entirety.

The study concludes that, in his dynamic narrative presentation of a divinely ordained mission, which begins with Jesus in Nazareth and ends with Paul in Rome, Luke has endeavored to interpret the underlying meaning of the whole of Christian history—and in a manner surprisingly analogous to Virgil's interpretation of the meaning of Roman history. Indeed, at the center of Luke's theological reflections is the conviction that the divine solution for human salvation involves not only the death of the beloved Son but also the reformulation of the people of God.

This book is the product of a long and sometimes circuitous intellectual odyssey begun nearly ten years ago. Many people contributed to defining its course and enabling its progress. After expressing special thanks to Wendell V. Clausen, who generously agreed to read and critically evaluate my chapter on Virgil, I would like to acknowledge my particular indebtedness to four outstanding teachers: William C. Robinson Jr., who first introduced me to the critical issues of New Testament inquiry and who always encouraged me to seek innovative solutions; David Gordon Mitten, who provided expert guidance into the worlds of archaeology and classical antiquity; François Bovon, who shared his considerable expertise on Luke-Acts and the field of Lukan studies; and especially Helmut Koester, whose expert critical guidance has brought this study, as well as several smaller literary projects, to successful completion.

I am also grateful to K. C. Hanson and the editorial staff at Fortress Press for their helpful advice and patience in the preparation of this manuscript.

Last but by no means least, I would like to thank my husband, Richard, whose encouragement and generosity of spirit set this entire undertaking in motion.

ABBREVIATIONS

Adv. Jud.	*Adversus Judaeos*
ANRW	*Aufstieg und Niedergang der römischen Welt*
BEThL	Bibliotheca ephemeridum theologicarum lovaniensium
Bib	*Biblica*
CBQ	*Catholic Biblical Quarterly*
CNT	Commentaire du Nouveau Testament
CP	*Classical Philology*
CRINT	Compendia rerum iudaicarum ad Novum Testamentum
Decal.	Philo, *De decalogo*
EThL	*Ephemerides theologicae lovanienses*
HSCP	*Harvard Studies in Classical Philology*
HTR	*Harvard Theological Review*
HTS	Harvard Theological Studies
HZ	*Historische Zeitschrift*
ICC	International Critical Commentary
JBL	*Journal of Biblical Literature*
JRomS	*Journal of Roman Studies*
JSJ	*Journal for the Study of Judaism in the Persian, Hellenistic, and Roman Period*
JSNTSup	Journal for the Study of the New Testament Supplement Series
L	Luke's Special Source
LCL	Loeb Classical Library
LEC	*Les études classiques*
LSJ	Liddell–Scott–Jones, *Greek-English Lexicon*
LXX	Septuagint
NedThT	*Nederlands theologisch tijdschrift*
NovT	*Novum Testamentum*
NovTSup	*NovT Supplements*
NT	New Testament
NTS	*New Testament Studies*
OBO	Orbis biblicus et orientalis

OT	Old Testament
PW	Pauly–Wissowa, *Real-encyclopädie der classischen Altertumswissenschaft*
PW Sup	Supplement to PW
RB	*Revue biblique*
RHPhR	*Revue d'histoire et de philosophie religieuses*
RSV	Revised Standard Version
SBL	Society of Biblical Literature
SBLDS	SBL Dissertation Series
SBLMS	SBL Monograph Series
Sir	Sirach
SM	Sermon on the Mount
SNTS	Society for New Testament Studies
SNTSMS	SNTS Monograph Series
SP	Sermon on the Plain
SANT	Studien zum Alten und Neuen Testament
SUNT	Studien zur Umwelt des Neuen Testaments
TAPA	*Transactions of the American Philological Association*
TDNT	G. Kittel and G. Friedrich (eds.), *Theological Dictionary of the New Testament*
ThZ	*Theologische Zeitschrift*
TS	*Theological Studies*
WMANT	Wissenschaftliche Monographien zum Alten und Neuen Testament
ZNW	*Zeitschrift für die neutestamentliche Wissenschaft*
ZPE	*Zeitschrift für Papyrologie und Epigraphik*
ZThK	*Zeitschrift für Theologie und Kirche*

1

CURRENT PROBLEMS OF GENRE AND INTERPRETATION IN LUKE-ACTS

DOUBLE VISION IN TWENTIETH-CENTURY LUKAN STUDIES

Without excluding the significant contributions of their predecessors,[1] Henry J. Cadbury and Martin Dibelius may arguably be regarded as the seminal figures in Lukan research for this century. Each of these men, by virtue of his distinctive perspective concerning Luke as author, historian, and theologian, framed lines of future inquiry that have continually intersected but seldom truly converged. Cadbury's approach was primarily comparative and literary, finding its locus in questions of style and genre; Dibelius's approach was essentially organic, emphasizing the historical and theological development of kerygmatic tradition. Played in these rather different interpretive and stylistic keys, it is perhaps not surprising that the relative values that each assigned to Luke's role as author, historian, and theologian were also at variance.

Cadbury assigned his highest values to Luke as author and historian. With respect to Luke's skill as an author, it was Cadbury who argued that the speeches, letters, and canticles were all Lukan,[2] Cadbury who noted and defined a distinctive Lukan style and vocabulary,[3] and Cadbury who observed that Luke had introduced certain unifying themes serving literary as well as theological ends.[4] Furthermore, because of Luke's double prologue and the

---

1. Eduard Norden (*Agnostos Theos: Untersuchungen zur Formengeschichte religiöser Rede* [Leipzig, Tübner, 1913; reprint, Darmstadt: Wissenschaftliche Buchgesellschaft, 1974]) merits special mention in this regard.

2. Henry J. Cadbury, *The Making of Luke-Acts* (1927; reprint, London: SPCK, 1958), 184–93.

3. Ibid., 213–38; see also, Henry J. Cadbury, *The Style and Literary Method of Luke* (Cambridge: Harvard Univ. Press, 1920), 1–38.

4. Ibid., 303–6.

numerous instances of parallelism between the Gospel and Acts, he was convinced that Luke intended a unified work: Luke-Acts.[5]

In Cadbury's opinion, however, all of this acknowledged literary creativity was within the acceptable limits of the style and methods of Greco-Roman historians, particularly the style and methods of the rhetorical historians. Indeed, even though he readily acknowledged that the quality of Luke's sources was less reliable than that of the better historians of antiquity, his detailed analysis of Luke's incorporation and adaptation of his Markan source was meticulously carried out, primarily to illustrate the considerable degree to which Luke's use of sources paralleled generally accepted Greco-Roman historical method.[6]

In Cadbury's mind, the importance of Luke as historian was closely related to the importance of Acts as "the only bridge we have across the seemingly impassable gulf that separates Jesus from Paul, Christ from Christianity, the gospel of Jesus from the Gospel about Jesus."[7] Somewhat surprisingly, therefore, although he ultimately concluded that Luke-Acts "is nearer to history than to any other familiar [Greco-Roman genre] classification," Cadbury emphasized that this did not imply that its author should be considered as "a successor to Polybius or a precursor of Eusebius."[8] Indeed, in this respect he echoed the sentiments of one of his contemporaries, Karl Ludwig Schmidt;[9] while emphasizing that Luke had considerably more literary interests, skills, and ambitions than the other evangelists, Cadbury also argued that Luke's work was prevented by the nature and quality of its sources from fully rising above the category of popular literature. Whatever his reservations concerning the quality of Luke's sources, however, Cadbury's classification of Luke-Acts as history not only conveyed his assurance of its underlying evidential value to the New Testament historian but also his assumption that Luke's primary intention was to transmit faithfully the traditions of the past.

5. Ibid., 8–9. With respect to unity, Cadbury himself expresses his debt to Eduard Meyers, *Ursprung und Anfänge des Christentums*, 3 vols. (1921–23; reprint, Stuttgart: Magnus-Verlag, 1983).

6. Cadbury's study of Luke's redaction of Mark is the subject of part 2 of *Style and Literary Method*; the conclusions drawn from this earlier study are subsequently applied in *Making of Luke-Acts*, esp. 158.

7. Cadbury, *Making of Luke-Acts*, 2.

8. Ibid., 134.

9. Karl Ludwig Schmidt, "Die Stellung der Evangelien in der allgemeinen Literaturgeschichte" in *Eucharisterion*, ed. H. Schmidt (Göttingen: Vandenhoeck & Ruprecht, 1923), 50–134. Schmidt's distinction between popular literature and the formal literary genres of Greco-Roman high culture was in turn indebted to the earlier work of Franz Overbeck ("Über die Anfänge der patristischen Literatur," *HZ* 48 [1882]: 423, 432–37, 443).

The form of his work is narrative, and narrative carries with it the intention of supplying information. No matter how much Luke differs from the rhetorical historians of Greece and Rome and the pragmatic historians of Israel, his narrative shares with them the common intention of informing the reader concerning the past.[10]

Cadbury adds that although Greek historians often describe their intention to entertain or to edify, and Jewish historians seek to inculcate religious values, "artist or advocate, the historian is still historian."[11]

A somewhat different approach to the study of Acts in particular was subsequently developed by Martin Dibelius. Firmly rooted in the form-critical approach pioneered by Hermann Gunkel,[12] Dibelius's evaluation of Luke as author, historian, and theologian was tied very closely to his study of Luke's place in the history and development of the traditions concerning Jesus and the disciples. Furthermore, because this approach could not be so readily applied to Acts, Dibelius determined that the Gospel and Acts should be considered as separate literary types.[13]

According to Dibelius, even though Luke's style is somewhat richer and his elaboration exhibits a greater ability for creative reflection with respect to form and composition, Luke's Gospel does not differ radically from that of its predecessor Mark. The restrictions imposed by the traditions concerning Jesus, however, were not a constraint for Luke when composing his narrative of the early church. Dibelius attributed Luke's relative freedom in composing this sequel to the Gospel to two basic factors. First, in this new endeavor Luke no longer had to bow to precedent. Second, and more importantly from Dibelius's perspective, Luke had considerably fewer literary sources with which to work, having to rely primarily upon isolated stories and legends of little historical value.[14] Indeed, Dibelius argued that the original sources on which Acts depends consist of "small units, the individual saying or story" which, when combined into a unified composition, resemble a mosaic; much depends upon

10. Cadbury, *Making of Luke-Acts,* 299–300.

11. Ibid., 300.

12. Gunkel was most noted for his pioneering form-critical studies of Genesis and the Psalms.

13. Martin Dibelius, "Der erste christliche Historiker," in *Aufsätze zur Apostelgeschichte* (Göttingen, Ger.:Vandenhoeck & Ruprecht, 1951), 108.

14. In this opinion Dibelius may still remain in the minority. Speculation on the sources of Acts, however, has had a long and unproductive history. Of the many theories put forth over the years, Adolf von Harnack's is perhaps the most often cited and the most frequently modified. According to his theory, Acts 2–5 is composed of two parallel sources. The more important of the two (Acts 3:1—5:16) also continues into

the author's arrangement of the pieces, as well as the type of filler he supplies.[15]

While Dibelius conceded the basic truth of this conclusion for both the Gospel and Acts, he assumed a far greater degree of creativity (arrangement and filler) in the composition of Acts. Because of the presumed paucity of Luke's sources for this second book, the evangelist was not only forced to fill in the gaps between sources, he was also free to transform his existing sources to suit his overall theological purpose. Luke's purpose, as Dibelius understood it, was "to illuminate and to somehow present the [underlying] *meaning* of events."[16]

For Dibelius, Luke's primary contribution to the recording of early Christian history was not to convey historical information through the consciously stylized but nonetheless faithful transmission of his sources, as Cadbury had asserted. Rather, Luke's primary contribution was his nuanced interpretation of what he regarded as the tradition's true meaning. Although, therefore, both Cadbury and Dibelius would agree that Luke's composition of the speeches in Acts conforms with the custom of Greek historians to highlight important events by the incorporation of such speeches, only Dibelius emphasizes the primarily symbolic significance of Lukan speeches, especially when they are inserted by the author into material that is essentially nonhistorical. In his opinion, Paul's speech on the hill of the Areopagus in Athens is one such instance of a purely symbolic occasion.[17]

Thus, although Dibelius is aware of Luke's literary skills, he consistently assumes their subordination to the evangelist's theological interests. In the Areopagus scene, for example, Dibelius links Luke's stylized depiction of the Athenian audience to his theological intention for that particular segment of the narrative, which is "the emphasis of this symbolically important scene, the encounter of the gospel with the Greek spirit."[18]

---

the middle of the book (Acts 8:5-40; 9:29—11:18; 12:1-32), originated in Jerusalem or Caesarea, and is highly reliable. The other main source for the opening chapters (Acts 2:1-47; 5:17-42) is largely legendary and essentially worthless. A third source, the Antiochene source (Acts 6–15) has been supplemented by a number of smaller sources with more localized interests. Although a number of scholars still accept all or part of this theory or one of its many variations, as Jacques Dupont (*Les sources du livre des Actes: État de la question* [Paris: Desclée de Brouwer, 1960], 159) has succinctly concluded: "Despite the most careful and detailed research, it has not been possible to define any of the sources used by the author of Acts in a way which will meet with widespread agreement among the critics."

15. Dibelius, "Historiker," 112.

16. Ibid., 110 [my emphasis].

17. Martin Dibelius, "Paulus auf dem Areopag," in *Apostelgeschichte,* 70; ("Paulus auf dem Areopag—das bedeutet nicht eine historische, sondern eine symbolische Begegnung").

Moreover, according to Dibelius, even where Luke had access to reliable knowledge of historical situations, he frequently chose to suppress it if this material differed from his basic theological perspective. Thus, although Paul's own letters suggest considerable tension between his perspective and that of Peter, Luke intentionally typifies his portrayal of both apostles so that they become essentially interchangeable in outlook. Although Dibelius is aware that the portrayal of characters as typical, general, or ideal is a common technique of ancient historians, he emphasizes that Luke uses this technique to convey the underlying meaning of the mission as being determined not by the personalities or qualities of individual apostles but by the power of God alone.[19] This utilization of literary technique for theological ends applies especially to the miracle stories, where, for example, in the narrative of Peter's or Paul's imprisonment, the divine miracle of their release is the main point of the story. Likewise, Paul's speech in a synagogue in Asia Minor parallels earlier speeches by Peter.

Dibelius further suggests that Luke's intentional use of parallelism and repetition is designed to depict the true unity of Christian proclamation, despite disparities of time and geography. Indeed, he argues, even Paul's trials are narrated to convey underlying truths rather than historical information.[20] Dibelius continues by suggesting that the trials have been introduced by Luke primarily as a further vehicle for Christian assertions concerning the divine nature of the mission to the Gentiles and to proclaim that Jewish eschatological hopes find their fulfillment in the Christian message. To the extent that Luke wishes to "convey historical information" at all, therefore, this desire is governed not by a concern for what has taken place in the past but for what is taking place in the evangelist's own time. Thus it was Dibelius's belief that Luke's understanding of history is fundamentally theological and, as such, has little need or interest in superfluous historical information.

If the scholarly studies of successors such as Ernst Haenchen[21] tended to obscure the subtle differences between the approaches of Cadbury and Dibelius to the multiple problems regarding compositional unity, literary and theological expression, and the importance of history in Luke-Acts, Hans Conzelmann's work represents a more profound attempt to reconcile them. In Conzelmann's opinion, as in Dibelius's, conveying the underlying meaning of early Christian tradition is of primary concern to Luke. Thus, in his Gospel,

18. Dibelius, "Historiker," 117; (" . . . der Hervorhebung dieser symbolisch bedeutsamen Szene, der Begegnung des Evangeliums mit dem griechischen Geist").

19. Ibid., 115–16.

20. Ibid., 117.

21. Ernst Haenchen, *The Acts of the Apostles: A Commentary,* trans. B. Noble and G. Shinn (Philadelphia: Westminster, 1971).

Luke rearranged the geography of his Markan source in order to advance his own theological motives.[22]

Likewise, Conzelmann believes that Luke conceived of his project as narrating the concluding segments of an Israelite salvation history marked by three distinct periods: the time of Israel (to which Luke briefly alludes in the opening chapters of his Gospel), the time of Jesus, and the time of the church. This geographical and temporal schematization of history for the enhancement of theological understanding is also evident within the book of Acts. In this second book, for example, Luke deliberately deviates from Paul's account of the apostolic council in order to have it serve as the narrative bridge between the earliest church, which was bound by the law, and the church of Luke's own time, a predominantly gentile church, free of the law.[23] Moreover, because Conzelmann's hermeneutical principles of geographical and historical periodization span both books, his interpretation appears to reconcile the division caused by Dibelius's methodological differentiation of the Gospel and Acts. Accordingly, Conzelmann, albeit in a minimal way, embraced Cadbury's conclusion concerning the unity of Luke-Acts.

Nevertheless, despite Conzelmann's formidable efforts to bridge the gap between the theological orientation of Dibelius and his successors and the literary orientation of Cadbury and his successors, his work has received its most severe criticism for its failure to achieve this very goal. For example, his refusal to recognize the importance of the birth narratives in Luke's overall literary scheme has justifiably earned the criticism of many.[24] Furthermore, because he keys all three of his historical divisions to passages in which Luke has edited his Markan source, Conzelmann's redaction-critical method has the effect of treating the whole of Acts as an afterthought of no structural consequence. Finally, his exaggerated emphasis on the importance of the delay of the parousia in Lukan theology is also attributable to his "Mark-centered" hermeneutical method and has come under some criticism over the years.[25] Thus, although

22. Hans Conzelmann, *The Theology of St. Luke* (1961; reprint, Philadelphia: Fortress Press, 1982), 18–60.

23. Hans Conzelmann, *Acts of the Apostles,* Hermeneia (Philadelphia: Fortress Press, 1972), xlv–xlvi.

24. For example, Augustin George, "Le parallèle entre Jean-Baptiste et Jésus en Lc 1–2," in *Études sur l'oeuvre de Luc* (Paris: Gabalda, 1978), 43–65; Paul Minear, "Luke's Use of the Birth Stories," in *Studies in Luke-Acts,* ed. L. E. Keck and J. L. Martyn (Nashville: Abingdon, 1966), 111–30; Raymond E. Brown, *The Birth of the Messiah* (New York: Image Books, 1979), 250.

25. Oscar Cullmann, *Salvation in History* (New York: Harper & Row, 1967), 240; J.-D. Kaestli, *L'eschatologie dans l'oeuvre de Luc, ses caractéristiques et sa place dans le développement du christianisme primitif* (Geneva: Labor et Fides, 1969), 81–83, passim.

Conzelmann's interpretation has the great virtue of revealing a strong theological message that is consistent and developmental throughout the whole of Luke-Acts, his analysis is somewhat weakened by his failure to illuminate the more significant literary elements discernible in Luke's composition, which also have a bearing on interpretation.

Despite significant differences among Cadbury, Dibelius, Haenchen, and Conzelmann regarding the relative importance of the literary and theological concerns of the author known as Luke, none of these interpreters questioned his role as historian. And in the intervening years since Conzelmann, newer studies continue to offer revised perspectives on Luke-Acts as exemplifying some subgenre of Hellenistic historiography. In addition to Eckhard Plümacher's major study published in the early 1970s,[26] the most formidable of these works to date is Gregory Sterling's comparative study of Luke-Acts and Josephus's *Antiquities*.[27]

It was, however, the innovative work of C. H. Talbert, one of the heirs to Cadbury's remarkable literary legacy, which launched an entirely new phase in Lukan research in two significant respects. Talbert's studies represent a genuinely creative and comprehensive attempt to rethink the issues of genre and of Luke's literary links with the wider Greco-Roman world, even as they build upon a number of Cadbury's observations regarding Lukan stylistic techniques and literary motifs. For example, whereas Cadbury had simply noted the parallels between Jesus and Paul, Talbert attempts to show that the detailed and systematic use of correspondence between them is part of a carefully worked-out system of parallels and contrasts that extends throughout the entire composition.[28] He further argues that this intentional stylistic scheme extends from the corresponding prefaces to the parallel conclusions, each of which ends on the victorious note of the fulfillment of scripture.[29]

Beginning with Virgil's *Aeneid* as the clearest and most skillfully executed contemporary example of this stylistic approach,[30] Talbert traces the manner

---

26. Eckhard Plümacher, *Lukas als hellenistischer Schriftsteller: Studien zur Apostelgeschichte*, SUNT 9 (Göttingen: Vandenhoeck & Ruprecht, 1972). The great strength of this extremely learned work is not so much in the originality of its insights as in the comprehensiveness of its scope.

27. Gregory E. Sterling, *Historiography and Self-Definition: Josephos, Luke-Acts, and Apologetic Historiography* (Leiden: E. J. Brill, 1992). Sterling's work will be discussed in more detail in the concluding section of this book.

28. However, many of Talbert's parallelisms are rather forced, and Talbert has been justly criticized on this account.

29. Charles H. Talbert, *Literary Patterns, Theological Themes and the Genre of Luke-Acts*, SBLMS 20 (Missoula, Mont.: Scholars Press, 1974), 16–17.

30. Ibid., 67–70.

in which many of its formal conventions and literary devices had gradually insinuated themselves into various prose genres, including the one that he seeks to advance: biography. Bearing in mind that in antiquity the image of the popular philosopher was that of a religious or semidivine figure, Talbert has endeavored to pursue the suggestion that Luke sought to develop his Markan source in a manner similar to that of the Hellenistic biographies of ancient philosophers.[31] He accomplishes this by means of a comparison between Luke-Acts and Diogenes Laertius's *Lives of Eminent Philosophers.*

In his comparative analysis, Talbert seeks to offer a fresh interpretation of Luke-Acts embracing form, content, genre, and historical situation. With respect to form, he concludes that Luke-Acts is a two-part work consisting of a life of the founder and a narrative of his successors. Its content also parallels that which is observable in Diogenes Laertius's *Lives,* in that it narrates the complete life of a founder of a religious community, a list of the founder's successors and selected other disciples, and a summary of the proclamation of the community.[32] Finally, Talbert contends, even the underlying purpose of Luke-Acts brings it in line with that of the genre of biographies of founders and their successors, inasmuch as the author is seeking to pass on an account of the true Christian way.

Despite the originality and comprehensiveness of his hypothesis, Talbert's study has met with minimal acceptance and significant criticism. Some criticism challenges Talbert's genre designation, questioning the suitability of his description of Acts as the narrative of a founder's successors and pointing out that Acts does not supply even the most salient details characteristic of this genre category.[33] Nevertheless, by illustrating the degree of literary creativity and compositional control exercised by its author, Talbert has been successful in forcing open the question of genre and in highlighting its importance for the overall understanding and interpretation of Luke-Acts.

Talbert's study also has been severely criticized by some because its literary analysis ignores the constraints of source and redaction criticism, and because it seriously diminishes Luke's role as a historian and theologian.[34] As a result of this perceived lack of rigor, Talbert has failed to convince a significant number of New Testament scholars, for whom source, form, and redaction criticism

---

31. This suggestion originated with Hans von Soden, *Geschichte der christlichen Kirche,* vol. 1: *Die Enstehung der christlichen Kirche* (Leipzig: Tübner, 1919), 73.

32. Talbert, *Patterns,* 129–30.

33. See Mikeal C. Parsons and Richard I. Pervo, *Rethinking the Unity of Luke and Acts* (Minneapolis: Fortress Press, 1993), 36.

34. François Bovon, *Luke the Theologian: Thirty-Three Years of Research* (Allison Park, Pa.: Pickwick, 1987), 65–68.

remain important tools for the understanding of early Christian texts. Nevertheless, his work has made a significant contribution to Lukan studies by its insightful suggestion that Luke did not simply *craft* his composition to give the impression of literary unity but did to a considerable extent *conceive* of this major New Testament work in terms of a cohesive and carefully structured narrative whole.

Talbert's renewed emphasis on Luke-Acts as a literary composition has been instrumental not only in reopening the genre question, but also in helping to activate a more focused literary-critical approach to Lukan studies, an approach that has gained a considerable degree of momentum in recent years. In contrast to proponents of historical criticism, who seek to understand a text by fixing its location within a particular historical, social, and cultural grid, and by understanding its organic development from earlier sources, literary critics focus on various elements of the text as a narrative and formal unity. Thus, for the majority of New Testament interpreters, who view Luke-Acts as one extended text, such a compositional approach should be enthusiastically welcomed as a useful balance to the more analytical methods of historical criticism. Indeed, Robert Tannehill's major study on the narrative unity of Luke-Acts[35] has yielded a wealth of new insights as well as the most comprehensive new perspective on the composition and theological interest of Luke-Acts since the work of Conzelmann.

In terms of its basic approach, narrative criticism, as exemplified in the work of Tannehill and in the more recent study by William S. Kurz,[36] eschews questions of historical context, preferring to concentrate on the specific narrative elements of the text itself—elements such as plot, story line, narrators, characters, and significant formal and stylistic patterns. If, however, Tannehill's work reveals the interpretative possibilities of narrative criticism, Kurz's work exposes its limitations. Relying solely upon a method with no external historical markers cannot validate the text's historicity, as Kurz seeks to have it do; nor can it even position a text within its particular historical world.

An alternative synchronic approach to the study of Luke-Acts is the structuralist analysis of Robert L. Brawley.[37] While many narrative critics simply ignore questions of historical context, Brawley actually argues for their irrel-

---

35. Robert Tannehill, *The Narrative Unity of Luke-Acts: A Literary Interpretation,* 2 vols. (Philadelphia/Minneapolis: Fortress Press, 1986–94). A number of references to details of his study appear in chapters 4 and 5 of this book.

36. William S. Kurz, *Reading Luke-Acts: Dynamics of Biblical Narrative* (Louisville: Westminster John Knox, 1993).

37. Robert L. Brawley, *Centering on God: Method and Message in Luke-Acts* (Louisville: Westminster John Knox, 1990).

evance on grounds that (1) one can never possess more than a fraction of the requisite historical knowledge in any given situation calling for such knowledge, and (2) such knowledge affects interpretation in only a comparatively few number of passages.[38] Leaving historical-critical considerations aside, therefore, and drawing instead on the methodological theories of modern literary critic Roland Barthes, Brawley focuses on "certain structural elements" revealed by the Lukan text that he perceives as working to "constrain interpretation."[39] Brawley's structural analysis, however, requires the atomization of the text into minute linguistic parts that may then be incorporated into complex formulae—a process that even Brawley admits is "time-consuming and bulky."[40] As Beverly Gaventa has rightly noted, Brawley's study does contain a number of interesting and provocative insights.[41] It should be added, however, that these insights do not appear to have a direct relationship to the application of his complex literary method.

Nevertheless, the renewed attention to literary concerns in general and the emphasis on the text as a compositional unity in particular are decidedly positive developments in Lukan research. If, however, all historical constraints are ignored, and critical nuance as well as common sense is subordinated to the rigors of aggressive methodologies, the results yield little of value. Indeed, as Meir Sternberg has rightly emphasized, for optimum interpretative results, historical and literary approaches must be applied in tandem.[42]

In the intervening years since Talbert's early work, Richard I. Pervo has again challenged the prevailing assumption that Acts, the second part of Luke's work, be characterized as historiography. Leaving aside the question of Luke's Gospel, Pervo proposes that serious consideration be given to the novel as the genre that best illuminates the style and literary perspective of Acts. He contends that it was not uncommon for popular Greek novels to imitate the outward form

---

38. Ibid., 160–62.

39. Ibid., 62.

40. Ibid., 78.

41. Beverly R. Gaventa, "Review of Robert L. Brawley, *Centering on God: Method and Message in Luke-Acts*," in *Critical Review of Books in Religion,* ed. Elden J. Epp (Atlanta: Scholars Press, 1991), 184.

42. "Historical and literary inquiry thus fall into an unhappy symmetry. In their concern with whatever frames or anteceded the text, the historians tend to overlook the chief body of historical evidence that awaits proper interpretation. In their concern with interpretation, the [literary] critics tend to overlook the extent to which their goal involves and commits them to the quest for frames and antecedents." (Meir Sternberg, *The Poetics of Biblical Narrative: Ideological Literature and the Drama of Reading* [Bloomington: Indiana Univ. Press, 1987], 11.)

of historiography, even if romance or adventure was their central focus.[43] Xenophon's *Cyropaedeia,* an early Hellenistic work, is Pervo's primary example of a literary paradigm for Acts. At the other end of the temporal spectrum, Pervo cites Heliodorus's *Aethiopica* (fourth century CE) as a more sophisticated example of a historical novel, most likely modeled on Homer's great epic, the *Odyssey.*[44]

In response to some literary critics who contend that true Greek novels exhibit considerable consistency of form as well as plots that invariably center on the separation and reuniting of lovers,[45] Pervo argues for a much broader genre definition, asserting that novels need not have love as the central plot, only a "problem to resolve, a goal or object to attain, an identity to find."[46] Elements of history, biography, and romance mingle in the *Cyropaedeia* (early fourth century BCE). From this important prototype can be traced the *Alexander Romance* (second century BCE) and Philo's *Life of Moses* (early first century CE). In addition to this historical biographical type, there were several novels of an apologetic or ethnic type. In works such as *Joseph and Aseneth,* for example, Pervo contends that the author seeks to extol the ideals and ethical way of life of a particular people through the medium of an interesting story. After careful review, he suggests that Acts belongs somewhere within these admittedly broad parameters of edifying narrative fiction.[47] Arguing that even on stylistic grounds the composition of Acts is closer to narrative fiction than to historiography, Pervo concludes that, given the semiliterate audience whom Luke was addressing, "the edifying historical novel was . . . the genre most appropriate to his purposes and most available."[48]

In his analysis, Pervo is able to demonstrate that Acts exhibits in abundance many of the literary characteristics found more often in works of fiction than in works of history. His argument for the selection of the Greek novel as a paradigm for Acts is somewhat undermined, however, because his most relevant examples sparsely range over a period spanning nearly eight hundred years. Even the work that he selects as his prototype, the *Cyropaedeia,* was written

---

43. Richard I. Pervo, *Profit with Delight: The Literary Genre of the Acts of the Apostles* (Philadelphia: Fortress Press, 1987), 92.

44. Ibid., 90.

45. Gian Biagio Conte, *Latin Literature: A History* (Baltimore: Johns Hopkins Univ. Press, 1994), 459–60. Other critics of ancient novels, however, support Pervo's claim for a broader definition of the genre. See, for example, J. R. Morgan, "Introduction," in *Greek Fiction: The Greek Novel in Context,* ed. J. R. Morgan and R. Stoneman (London: Routledge, 1994), 1–3.

46. Pervo, *Profit,* 104.

47. Ibid., 121.

48. Ibid., 137.

four hundred years prior to the composition of Acts. Pervo's hypothesis is further weakened because he adheres to the increasingly untenable position that Luke's Gospel and Acts are separate literary entities. In agreement with Pervo is Mikeal Parsons, who offers a detailed attack on the unity of Luke-Acts.[49] Although seemingly impressive, Parsons's objections do not withstand careful scrutiny.[50]

49. Parsons distinguishes two levels in which the narrative must be defined: as discourse and as story. While he is willing to concede a degree of unity on the story level, he notes five ways in which Luke differs from Acts on the level of narrative discourse: (1) whereas in the Gospel there is a clear distinction between the voice of the narrator and that of Jesus, in Acts there is no such distinction between the voice of the narrator and that of Peter or Paul; (2) even though Lukanisms appear in both the Gospel and in Acts, the style of Acts is decidedly more Hellenic; (3) the journeys in Luke and Acts, although parallel in structure, function differently; (4) whereas Jesus as a character is portrayed as omniscient in the Gospel, Peter and Paul do not appear that way in Acts; and (5) whereas in the Gospel Luke employs narrative asides with great frequency, in Acts he does so only rarely (Parsons and Pervo, *Rethinking the Unity*, 51–75).

50. First, contrary to Parsons's assertion, in Luke's Gospel there are a number of examples of Jesus' speaking that cannot be differentiated from the viewpoint of the narrator. Even within the parables, which are arguably the closest equivalent to the apostolic speeches in Acts, there are many examples in which Jesus speaks in Lukan language and idiom. Two notable examples are the parable of the lost coin and the parable of the prodigal son. In both of these parables, Lukan terminology and theological perspective appear throughout. Even if one rejects Luise Schottroff's conclusion ("Das Gleichnis vom verlorenen Sohn," *ZThK* 68 [1971]: 27–52) that Luke composed this parable *de novo,* it is far more difficult to reject the detailed and very cautious analysis of François Bovon (*L'évangile selon Saint Luke 15–24,* CNT 3c (Geneva: Labor et Fides, 2000]). Bovon attributes crucial verses of this parable to Luke's own hand, and he also suggests that the evangelist was probably the author of the parable of the lost coin. (See the discussion in chapter 5.) In response to Parsons's second point, the more decidedly Hellenic tone of Acts—which is most pronounced in the second half of the book—complements the movement of the Christian mission into the gentile world and, therefore, may simply represent another aspect of Lukan literary artistry. Moving to the third point of Parsons's argument, the slow pace of Jesus' journey as compared with the journeys of Paul in Acts is mandated by the traditional sources that Luke has inherited and wants to incorporate. Fourth, although the Jesus of Luke's Gospel is more consistently omniscient than are the apostles in Acts, Peter does recognize the duplicity of Ananias and Sapphira, with a display of supernatural omniscience that is remarkably similar to numerous instances of Jesus' prescience. In addition to this example should be added the continuous supply of divine guidance that enables both Peter and Paul frequently to appear omniscient. And in response to Parsons's fifth and last point, the extensive use of narrative asides in the Gospel may be explained as a literary device introduced by Luke to strengthen the sense of narrative distance between the reader and this chronologically early and geographically distant part of the story.

Finally, as was the case with Talbert's proposal, Pervo's hypothesis lacks persuasiveness because, in the minds of many proponents of historiography, it fails to offer an interpretation that is theologically substantive. For example, David Balch has argued, somewhat unfairly, that acceptance of Pervo's hypothesis would lead to an excessively individualistic interpretation of Acts because novels are typically concerned with the private world of extraordinary individuals.[51] David Aune rejects Pervo's hypothesis in a more sweeping manner, arguing that such a genre designation would fatally compromise Luke's reputation, both as a theologian and as a historian.[52] Whatever the merits of Pervo's specific proposal, however, his major contribution to the field rests on his recognition that, despite the somewhat misleading wording of the Lukan prologue, the evangelist's dramatic presentation of the Christian story does not really aspire to serve as an accurate portrayal of the significant events of Christian history. Rather, it creates an imaginative and schematized historical story in order to provide a memorable and definitive interpretation of the underlying meaning of Christian history.

Seeking to reach a more convincing and more widely acceptable resolution to the genre problem, two other recent studies endeavor to build upon the foundation established by Pervo's research.[53] These recent studies by Lawrence Wills[54] and Christine Thomas[55] are reasoned attempts at solving the genre question for works such as Luke-Acts, 2 Maccabees, and the apocryphal Acts by further blurring the distinctions between history and the novel. In this regard, the work of Wills and Thomas has been aided by a flood of recent studies on the nature of fiction and its relation to history in antiquity.[56]

51. David L. Balch, "The Genre of Luke-Acts: Individual Biography, Adventure Novel, or Political History?" (SNTS Seminar Paper, Bethel, Germany, July 1991), 1.

52. David E. Aune, *The New Testament in Its Literary Environment,* Library of Early Christianity (Philadelphia: Westminster, 1987), 80; William H. Shepherd Jr., *The Narrative Function of the Holy Spirit as a Character in Luke-Acts* (Atlanta: Scholars Press, 1994), 112.

53. Prior to Pervo, however, Rosa Söder (*Die apokryphen Apostelgeschichten und die romanhafte Literatur der Antike* [Stuttgart: Kohlhammer, 1932]) had compared the apocryphal Acts with the novel.

54. Lawrence M. Wills, *The Jewish Novel in the Ancient World* (Ithaca: Cornell Univ. Press, 1995), 30.

55. Christine Marie Thomas, "The Acts of Peter, the Ancient World, and Early Christian History" (Ph.D. diss., Harvard Univ., 1995).

56. G. W. Bowersock, *Fiction as History: Nero to Julian,* Sather Classical Lectures 58 (Berkeley: Univ. of California Press, 1994); A. Billaut, *La création romanesque dans la littérature grecque a l'époque impériale* (Paris: Presses Universitaires de France, 1991); B. P. Reardon, *The Form of Greek Romance* (Princeton: Princeton Univ. Press, 1991); F.

Both Wills and Thomas, however, eschew Pervo's effort to define the novel on the basis of specific stylistic criteria, a task that they believe is essentially artificial and anachronistic, since, as Wills justifiably observes, the novel was a wholly derivative genre in antiquity.[57] As a result of careful textual analyses, these scholars do, nevertheless, develop three basic characteristics that they agree are common to all novelistic texts, whether of a quasihistorical character or not: (1) they are characterized by fluidity in their textual transmission, including variations in entire story structures;[58] (2) their narratives are episodic, featuring themes of love, adventure, or both;[59] and (3) they employ formulaic story types and characters, which are thereby amenable to endless parochial variation and easy adaptation.[60] Based upon the work of Thomas and Wills, therefore, one may conclude that the salient feature of this type of novelistic literature, and what distinguishes it from historiography, is not the level of its historical reliability nor the degree to which it seeks to entertain as well as to edify. Rather, the underlying characteristic of a "historical novel" or a "novelistic text" is its generic ability to provide, in virtually endless repetition or variation, a narrative featuring commonplace themes of a moral, ethnic, historical, or romantic type, adaptable to virtually any particular time, place, or occasion.

Given these conclusions, however, it should be emphasized that even if novelistic texts do feature personages of historical, communal, or cultic importance, the fact that they do so in an inherently trivializing manner would seem to exclude Acts from placement among these genre categories. Therefore, although the conclusions of Wills and Thomas have the unintended effect of further diminishing the possibilities that the Greek novel might serve as an instructive paradigm for Luke-Acts, or even for Acts alone, their studies nonetheless advance Pervo's groundbreaking efforts in questioning the extent, as well as the definition, of the divide between historiography and fiction as generic categories.

Létoublon, *Les lieux communs du roman: stéréotypes grecs d'aventure et d'amour*, Mnemosyne Supp. 123 (Leiden: E. J. Brill, 1993); Morgan and Stoneman, *Greek Fiction*.

57. Wills, *Jewish Novel*, 20. In this opinion Wills is supported by Mikhail Bakhtin (*The Dialogic Imagination*, ed. M. Holquist, trans. C. Emerson and M. Holquist [Austin: Univ. of Texas, 1981]), who states (p. 39) that "the novel, after all, has no canon of its own. It is, by its very nature, non canonic. It is plasticity itself."

58. Thomas, "Acts of Peter," 79.

59. Wills, *Jewish Novel*, 22.

60. Thomas, "Acts of Peter," 175–76; Wills, *Jewish Novel*, 36.

HISTORIOGRAPHY VERSUS "HISTORY-TELLING": THE GREAT EPICS OF ANTIQUITY

Approaching this problem from a somewhat different perspective is an important study by Meir Sternberg. In his *Poetics of Biblical Narrative,* Sternberg argues for the classification of the narratives of the Hebrew scriptures as historiography, albeit historiography that has as much in common with Homer and Hesiod as it does with Thucydides.[61] Not only do biblical narratives strain the conventional category of historiography in the multiple levels on which their stories can be interpreted,[62] but they also depart from historiographical norms in their penchant for omniscient narrators.[63] Moreover, Sternberg acknowledges that for biblical narratives to be considered historiography, the interpreter must draw a clear distinction between "history-telling," which has to do with the *truth claim* of the discourse, and "historicity," which has to do with its *truth value.* "For history-writing is not a record of fact—of what 'really happened'—but a discourse that claims to be a record of fact. Nor is fiction-writing a tissue of free inventions but a discourse that claims freedom of invention."[64]

According to Sternberg, therefore, to say that biblical narratives ought not to be classified as fiction is not an endorsement of their historicity (or "truth value"), but rather an assertion that the inspiration for what is being narrated transcends the creative control of the author. Thus, the Greek novel is rightly classified as fiction because it is acknowledged by both author and reader to be the free invention of the author.[65] On the other hand, Homeric epic would qualify as historiography (or "history-telling"), because it conveys the truth about the past—even if that truth is expressed in mythological language. Indeed, as Rosalind Thomas has observed, "the Homeric bard is portrayed as repeating what he and his audience know to be true."[66] Thus, Homeric epic is not the fictional creation of the poet, but the inspired narrative of history in its truest sense. "It is the Muses in this society—and therefore the bards as mouthpieces of the Muses—who are the guarantors of truth; and truth is intimately linked to memory."[67]

---

61. Sternberg, *Poetics of Biblical Narrative,* 10, 77–78.

62. Ibid., 10.

63. Ibid., 12.

64. Ibid., 25.

65. Ibid. See also, J. R. Morgan, "The Greek Novel: Towards a Sociology of Production and Reception," in *The Greek World,* ed. Anton Powell (London: Routledge, 1995), 130. See also, Bakhtin, *Dialogic Imagination,* 39.

66. Rosalind Thomas, "The Place of the Poet in Archaic Society," in *Greek World,* ed. Powell, 114.

67. Ibid.

The great epics of antiquity were considered the repositories of genuine wisdom concerning the meaning of the past and its implications for the present. But, whereas Sternberg stretches the category of historiography in order to include the literary "grey area" posed by the biblical narratives, Burton L. Mack embraces the category of ancient epic as the more logical location for the same biblical scriptures.[68] Moreover, inasmuch as Luke-Acts is written as a continuation—albeit a redirection— of the ongoing biblical narrative, Mack suggests that Luke-Acts must also be considered as part of Israel's national epic.[69] Thus, whether one calls Luke-Acts historiography, historical fiction, or even historical epic, the common assumption on which all of these recent studies rests is that Luke the historian need no longer mean Luke the purveyor of historical information or historicity. Indeed, the time would seem auspicious for a reconsideration of Luke's triple role as author, historian, and theologian, as well as for renewed attention to the particular type of dramatic presentation that he adopted to unify all three aspects of his work.

As Conzelmann's interpretation suggests, it was Luke's vision to create a dramatic narrative that would interpret the history of Christian beginnings, not only in relation to the life and death of Jesus of Nazareth but also in relation to the message of the Israelite prophets of the distant past and to the Christian believers of Luke's own time. Furthermore, Luke envisioned a Christian tradition both ancient and venerable, one that pointed to the Christian present and celebrated it as the beginning of God's fulfillment of the promise of history and, indeed, not just of Israel's history but of universal human history. In this effort, the evocative moments of the Israelite past had to be appropriated for the new community of faith, not only by the redirecting of ancient biblical prophecy for Christian kerygmatic ends,[70] but also by linking the new community's founder to Israel's royal Davidic lineage.[71] This essential—albeit admittedly parochially significant—pedigree had then to be incorporated into a universal historical perspective that begins with the tracing of Jesus' ancestry back to Adam (Luke 3) and ends with the tracing of Paul's progress to Rome, the world capital of Luke's own time (Acts 28).

The boldness of Luke's historical vision, therefore, consists of two key elements. Not only does it contain his appropriation and redirection of Israel's salvation history, as Conzelmann's interpretation has rightly emphasized, but it

---

68. As Burton L. Mack (*Who Wrote the New Testament?* [San Francisco: HarperCollins, 1989], 14) has observed, "epic is a rehearsal of the past that puts the present in its light."

69. Ibid., 13–15.

70. A process begun long before the time of Luke, as can easily be inferred from the genuine writings of Paul (Gal 3:15-18; 4:21-31; 1 Cor 10:1-11; Rom 15:21, etc.).

71. As, indeed, Matthew had already done.

also includes, as Cadbury had observed, Luke's perception of the gradual unfolding of Christian proclamation as the divinely initiated and directed fulfillment of a universal human destiny.[72] Both of these key Lukan elements of appropriation and universalization find their fullest and most complete expression in the great foundational epics of Mesopotamia and, subsequently, the Greco-Roman world. Indeed, unlike the various categories of Greek novels, for example, whose most significant characteristic is their flexible adaptation to an infinite variety of parochial circumstances and occasions, the great epics of antiquity have tended to appear only at significant inaugural moments in a community's or a society's corporate life.[73]

Over a thousand years prior to Homer, the *Epic of Gilgamesh* was composed by an anonymous Babylonian author who had created this poetic narrative from an assortment of smaller literary compositions of Sumerian origin, dating back to the middle of the third millennium.[74] The Babylonian epic had taken an earlier series of heroic tales and had transformed them into an ethical and philosophical reflection on the meaning and purpose of human existence. Although the epic's initial formation can only be dated in broad terms to the first half of the second millennium, it is very likely that it was created during the early period of Babylonian ascendancy, which eventually culminated in Hammurabi's illustrious reign.[75] Inasmuch as the moral and ethical focus of the *Epic of Gilgamesh* complements the idealization of the principals of Babylonian rule captured in the famous Hammurabi law codes, it is possible that what became Babylon's national epic[76] was created to give artistic expression to the values and common identity of this early phase of the Babylonian empire.

The Babylonian epic, which continued to be adapted over time, spread throughout the region and beyond and was translated into several languages,

---

72. Cadbury, *Making of Luke-Acts,* 303–6.

73. J. B. Hainsworth, *The Idea of Epic* (Berkeley: Univ. of California Press, 1991), 3; see also, Gregory Nagy, *The Best of the Achaeans: Concepts of the Hero in Archaic Greek Poetry* (Baltimore: Johns Hopkins Univ. Press, 1979), 7.

74. According to Jeffrey H. Tigay (*The Evolution of the Gilgamesh Epic* [Philadelphia: Univ. of Pennsylvania Press, 1982], 243–44), it is possible that these early Sumerian tales, seven of which are now known, began to take written form already by the twenty-fifth century BCE.

75. For a detailed analysis outlining the broad parameters of the epic's creation, see ibid., esp. 39–72. For historical reasons why the epic should be dated to the early centuries of the second millennium, see Alexander Heidel, *The Gilgamesh Epic and Old Testament Parallels* (Chicago: 1946; reprint, Chicago: Phoenix, 1963), 14–16.

76. Heidel, *Gilgamesh Epic and Old Testament Parallels,* 14.

its influence possibly extending even to the early Archaic period in Greece.[77]
Detailed thematic correspondences have prompted some interpreters to suggest that the *Epic of Gilgamesh* may have been a significant influence on early
Greek epic.[78] Primarily, however, the Homeric epics were shaped by indige-
nous artistic and historical forces. The oldest levels of the oral composition of
these epics are the catalogues composed and perhaps sung by late Mycenaean
storytellers, who passed on their narrative accounts by song or word-of-mouth,
as Mycenaean civilization slipped into total eclipse.[79] Although the next several centuries were marked by economic disintegration, social instability, and
severe cultural decline, a new configuration of Greek peoples gradually
emerged as the survivors of this Dark Age.

Even before the beginning of colonization and the birth of the *polis* (city)
in the eighth century,[80] Greeks had begun to form associations reflecting a new
sense of corporate identity.[81] Although the universalizing of idealized Greek
experience and values would perhaps only achieve its full civic, social, and religious expression in the great Panhellenic festivals of the seventh and sixth
centuries,[82] it was the *Iliad* and the *Odyssey* of the late eighth century, through

77. According to one recent study, the stories of Apollo, Demeter and Persephone,
Aphrodite, and Athena, as presented in the seventh-century Homeric Hymns, appear
to have been constructed, or perhaps reconstructed, in light of parallel stories of Near
Eastern deities taken from the literature of Mesopotamia. See, for example, Charles
Penglase, *Greek Myths and Mesopotamia: Parallels and Influence on the Homeric Hymns and
Hesiod* (London: Routledge, 1994), 241.

78. For this assessment, see John V. A. Fine, *The Ancient Greeks: A Critical History*
(Cambridge: Harvard Univ. Press, 1983), 20–21. On the other hand, Thomas van
Nortwick (*Somewhere I Have Never Travelled: The Second Self and the Hero's Journey in
Ancient Epic* [New York: Oxford Univ. Press, 1992], 40) has cautioned against attribut-
ing "the many genuine parallels to any influence more direct than a shared mythical
substratum."

79. Although many critics assume that Homeric epic evolved naturally from earlier
Mycenaean poetic tradition, G. S. Kirk (*Homer and the Oral Tradition* [Cambridge:
Cambridge Univ. Press, 1976], 20–21) is careful to point out that these early Mycenaean
accounts found embedded in the Homeric epics *Iliad* and *Odyssey* "may have survived
for a time in a non-poetical tradition."

80. Fine, *Ancient Greeks*, 51.

81. Already by the ninth century, twelve communities of Ionians settled in Asia Minor
had united in a loosely formed confederation, the League of Ionians. See ibid., 32.

82. Although the establishment of the Olympic Games dates to the early eighth century (776 BCE), most literary historians argue that the full development of Panhellenic
identity and sentiment took at least another hundred years. Gregory Nagy (*Pindar's
Homer: The Lyric Possession of an Epic Past* [Baltimore: Johns Hopkins Univ. Press, 1990],
52–53) appears to extend the parameters of the development of Panhellenism the farthest. Arguing for its definitive beginning in the eighth century, with the institution of

Homer's critically nuanced appropriation and inspired adaptation of the now-distant heroic past, that gave authoritative artistic expression to the values and aspirations of the newly emerging Greek world. Possibly because the composition of these epics gave poetic voice to the early development of the new realities of Greek life,[83] the *Iliad* and the *Odyssey* became its foundational histories,[84] celebrating Greek culture and defining the corporate identity of its widely scattered people. Through its critically nuanced appropriation of the heroic past, Homeric epic enabled the newly emerging society of Archaic Greece to see itself as history's chosen and worthy heir, rather than merely its accidental survivor.

Similarly, Virgil's *Aeneid* was created during the hopeful period of Augustus's early reign, when the Princeps sought to assuage the bitter social divisions that were the legacy of years of civil war. This practical political goal was brilliantly achieved through the poet's unifying vision of Rome's eternal destiny, as revealed in the mythologized blessings and achievements of its archaic past. Because, however, Rome had no substantive record of its past that was suitable for poetic elaboration, the *Aeneid* represents Virgil's resourceful adaptation and appropriation of Greece's epic tradition, newly transformed so as to celebrate Rome's divine election and elevate *Romanitas* (the Roman way) to ascendancy as the universal human ideal for the new millennium of Roman power. Virgil's appropriation of the Greek past was achieved through the incorporation of Aeneas as the protagonist of his story, thereby creating his own epic as a continuation of the story line of Homer's *Iliad*. Although Aeneas was a relatively minor character in the *Iliad,* a Trojan warrior whose life had been spared by the gods before Troy's destruction, through Virgil's ingenious literary invention the *Aeneid* became the surprising fulfillment of its revered Greek predecessor, at a time when the Homeric epics continued to enjoy the status of sacred texts throughout the Hellenized world.[85]

the Olympic Games, the establishment of the Delphic Oracle, and the creation of Homeric poetry, Nagy further contends that Panhellenism must be viewed as an evolutionary communal consciousness even "extending into the Classical period."

83. Indeed, according to John Alvis (*Divine Purpose and Heroic Response in Homer and Virgil: The Political Plan of Zeus* [Landover, Md.: Rowman & Littlefield, 1995], 3–4), Homer's acceptance of the end of the age of heroes is because he anticipates a new social and political order that will set restraints on heroic excess and place a new emphasis on communal responsibility. See also, van Nortwick, *Somewhere I Have Never Travelled*, 62.

84. Kirk, *Homer and the Oral Tradition*, 3; Fine, *Ancient Greeks,* 1. See also Charles Segal, "Bard and Audience in Homer," in *Homer's Ancient Readers: The Hermeneutics of Greek Epic's Earliest Exegetes*, ed. R. Lamberton and J. J. Keany (Princeton: Princeton Univ. Press, 1992), 3–29.

85. Nagy, *Pindar's Homer*, 215.

On the one hand, the Babylonian epic *Gilgamesh*, the ancient narrative cycles of the Hebrew Bible, and Homer's *Iliad* and *Odyssey* may all be classified as epic in the broad, generic sense of an idealized and extended saga of a people's past, through or against which the present may be interpreted and understood. On the other hand, only within the Greek world did epic develop a long and rich literary history that stretches all the way from Homer, in the dawn of the Archaic period, to the final flowering of Latin epic narrative in the late first century of the common era. It is this rich developmental history of the epic that generated a number of literary innovations and stylistic refinements that ultimately influenced the entire range of literary genres in Greco-Roman antiquity. Moreover, throughout its extended literary evolution, the epic genre generally has been characterized by an ability to address the more profound and universal questions of human existence as well as by its relatively wide audience appeal.

Greek epic poetry has its origins in the hoary mists of primordial time, developing from the poetry of communal hymns sung in celebration of the gods. From this hymnic poetry of praise evolved the narrative songs celebrating heroic deeds, which achieved full artistic development in Homeric epic. The *Iliad* and the *Odyssey* were the earliest and most profound expressions of Greek identity, sung from the eighth-century perspective of early Panhellenic aspirations. From its inception, therefore, Greek epic incorporated religion, drama, history, and even politics. In Homeric epic, praise of the hero provides the narrative basis for a rich blend of drama, pathos, and the expression of profound human aspiration that transcends narrow social and regional bounds.[86]

Praise of the hero continued in attenuated form in the fifth-century lyric poetry of Pindar. As the latest expression of Panhellenic poetry, Pindar's odes retained an element of continuity with its Homeric predecessor,[87] but was also the most relevant precursor of the debased, patron-generated praise epics of the late classical and early Hellenistic periods.[88] Indeed, after the great poets of Panhellenism had receded into history, the grand themes of transcendent human aspiration found their clearest expression in Greek drama, as epic sank into a period of extended decline.

At this point Aristotle issued his famous critique of the epic of his day, but he also attempted to rescue the revered genre from further decline by redefining its purpose and essential characteristics. In his essay entitled *Poetics,* Aristotle

---

86. According to Bakhtin (*Dialogic Imagination*, 13), the essence of epic is its narration of the transcendent world of "the national epic past . . . a world of 'beginnings' and 'peak times' in the national history . . . a world of founders . . . of 'firsts' and 'bests.'"

87. Nagy, *Pindar's Homer*, 53, 146, passim.

88. Hainsworth, *Idea of Epic*, 10–12.

devoted several sections to outlining the generic criteria for epic poetry. First of all, he reasoned, epic ought not represent the confused disorder of everyday life, which was, after all, the primary concern of historians. Epic was intended to provide the insight and clarity lacking in historiography by representing history as an orderly typology. Indeed, with respect to historical epic, its central concern was with the transformation of mere historical facts into the unifying and universal level of poetic myth.[89] Dramatically speaking, the epic story must be centered on a single action (περὶ μίαν πρᾶξιν), whole and complete in itself, with a beginning, middle, and end (*Poetics* 23.1; 26.14). Thus, the focus of historical epic differs from that of the historical monograph, in which what is required is an exposition, not of a single dramatic action but of a single period of time, showing all that befell one or more persons within that given period (*Poetics* 23.2). According to Aristotle, therefore, the essence of Homer's greatness lay in his interpretation of the Trojan War, which focused on one particular part of that historical event while incorporating many incidents from other parts of the wider history (*Poetics* 23.5–6). In this manner, the poet gave variety and interest to his work without sacrificing unity of theme or dramatic intensity.

Beyond this basic objective, epic requires several other literary elements. Its plot construction may be simple (like the *Iliad*) or complex (like the *Odyssey*) and may hinge on either character or calamity (*Poetics* 24.3). Furthermore, the epic plot should also incorporate the dramatic elements of reversal and recognition, and it may represent several parts of the story as going on simultaneously (*Poetics* 24.6).[90] Finally, after stipulating that the poetic meter of epic should be heroic hexameter, Aristotle concludes with the somewhat enigmatic judgment that epic is the genre that affords the greatest scope for the inexplicable (*Poetics* 24.15). By this, he apparently means that the epic convention of gods interacting with human beings as central to the poem's dramatic motivation and plot narration gives the poet more ways of explaining what in historiographical narratives is generally left unexplained or dismissively attributed to τύχη or *fortuna* (chance, fortune).

It is easy to see that the style characteristics of Greek epic as delineated by Aristotle serve to distinguish this genre markedly from the contemporary development of the Greek novel, on the one hand, and from Greek history, on the other. Indeed, despite their occasional incorporation of epic motifs and mannerisms, novels are inherently antithetical to epics in their conception, presentation, and especially in their function. The worldview of the novel is typ-

---

89. Ibid., 64.

90. That is, the narrative device generally known as "divided action" or "interlacement."

ically parochial; the perspective of epic is predominantly universal. More importantly, although epics may contain episodic tales designed for their audiences' edification, their salient literary characteristic is one of a tightly drawn and strictly imposed dramatic unity, with the story focusing on a single dramatic action in the form of a battle, journey, or quest.

As the essential characteristic of the genre, this dramatic unity may be further emphasized through a variety of literary means. It may be highlighted structurally by carefully controlled thematic and dramatic divisions. Epic unity may be accomplished also by a number of stylistic devices. Epics frequently employ literary parallelism to illustrate the relation of different characters to the unifying theme of the narrative or to depict different phases of the plot as symbolic repetitions of the central action. Epics also frequently employ prophecies, dreams, visions, or other aspects of divine guidance to prefigure later events. These events, in turn, may be described in terms that allude to the earlier prophecies. This complex synthesis of prophecy and fulfillment thereby enhances the unity of the composition.

Moreover, it is on this level of literary and dramatic unity that the epic genre is most clearly distinguished from that of historiography. Although general or antiquarian histories may exhibit certain unifying themes or connecting motifs, they do not exhibit compositional unity to any discernible degree. For example, although the *Jewish Antiquities* of Flavius Josephus contains the unifying thematic thread of God's providence, and the *Roman Antiquities* of Dionysius of Halicarnassus resonates with the theme of the dynamic growth of Rome, neither work was designed as a compositional unity. On the contrary, in each of these histories, stories and events of the past—arranged in chronological, geographical, or topical order—are simply knit together, much like a large and colorful afghan. In both works, one has the sense that the endings are arbitrary and that other stories could well have been added had the authors been so inclined. Even historical monographs, which tend to focus on a specific period of time or even on a specific historical event, do not feature a unity of dramatic action as the salient characteristic of their literary composition. Moreover, these shorter historical works make no universalizing claim, nor do they attempt to encompass the whole of history within their deliberately limited focus.

Despite Aristotle's critique of the entire poetic enterprise, it was not until early in the third century BCE that Callimachus of Cyrene, the talented poet who had come under the patronage of Ptolemy II, initiated a series of stylistic reforms aimed at producing lyric poetry of great polish and artistic beauty. These reforms represented a literary refinement of Homeric poetic technique and a concentration of aesthetic vision in poetic works of a much smaller scope than that of conventional epic. A generation later, Apollonius Rhodius, believed by many to have been Callimachus's pupil, wrote an epic, the *Argonautica,* in which he attempted, with limited success, to merge the new artistic refinements of Callimachus's Alexandrian school with the mythical themes and grand scale of Homeric epic. About the same time that Apollonius was composing his mythologically inspired epic poem, Latin literature was beginning to develop its own epic tradition based on the Homeric prototype.[91] Characteristic of these early Latin works was an intensely nationalistic concern with historical themes.

Virgil, the great Roman poet of the early Augustan era, was heir to all of these traditions. His work strongly reflects Homeric and Alexandrian influence, as well as a traditional Roman concern for national history. Moreover, the years in which he wrote the *Aeneid* corresponded to the beginning decade of Augustus's accession to the pinnacle of world power.[92] Thus, whereas both *Gilgamesh* and the Homeric epics are treated as almost purely self-contained narratives, "drawing on mythical patterns paralleled elsewhere, but divorced from the dynastic history" of any specific contemporary community, this is not the case with the *Aeneid,* both because more is known about early Roman history and because the essence of Virgil's creative genius was to read Rome's early history back into the Aeneas legends, "making it [i.e., the history] a part of the hero's burdens" and further diminishing "the prominence of the hero's personal evolution in favor of the progress toward Rome's founding and eventual glory."[93] Through the literary device of prophecy, the *Aeneid* brings the Augustan present directly into contact with the heroic past. To the degree that Virgil thereby appears to violate the ancient stricture regarding "absolute epic distance,"[94] the *Aeneid* represents a new developmental stage in the epic genre.[95]

Because he was one of the brilliant young poets of Augustus's inner circle and a self-proclaimed prophet (*vates*) of this watershed epoch of human history, it became Virgil's task to use the poetic art to interpret the meaning of the origins and implications of Rome's rise to world power. His epic incorporated a

---

91. Of these early Latin writers, Ennius is the most frequently mentioned because of his development of Latin hexameter verse. Of equal or more importance, however, was the earlier work of Naevius, who combined elements of myth and history into his Hellenistic tales of Roman origins.

92. Virgil began writing the *Aeneid* in 29 BCE and continued to work on it until his death in 19 BCE. Octavian became Augustus in 27 BCE. The *Aeneid* was published posthumously, at the emperor's behest.

93. Van Nortwick, *Somewhere I Have Never Travelled,* 127.

94. Bakhtin, *Dialogic Imagination,* 13.

95. The contemporary world of Augustus and Rome is linked directly to "the world of the fathers, the beginnings and peak times—canonizing these events, as it were, while they are still current" (ibid., 14–15).

complex synthesis of patriotic, moral, and religious themes in its mythologizing history of archaic Roman origins and of the divine prophecies that would reach their eschatological fulfillment in the Golden Age of Augustan rule. It is perhaps no wonder, therefore, that among those who considered themselves to be Roman not only in the capital city but throughout the empire, the *Aeneid* so quickly achieved a status equal to that which Homeric epic continued to enjoy throughout the Hellenized world. Moreover, Roman epic maintained a widespread popularity and a somewhat attenuated vigor throughout the first century of the common era.

Although some of the literary successors to Virgil used historical themes and others employed mythology, all of the epics of the later first century may be characterized as responses to the profound social, political, and ideological message of the *Aeneid* and to the challenge that this powerful message posed for a later generation. Lucan's *De bello civili,* written during the despotic reign of Nero, is virtually a mirror reversal of Virgil's patriotic tale of the guiding role of divine Fate in Rome's destiny. Statius's *Thebaid,* possibly begun at the end of Vespasian's reign in order to justify the legitimacy of Flavian rule, was also an implicit rejection of the *Aeneid*'s salvific claims, at least to the extent that these claims involved the Julio-Claudian dynasty. Two other epics written during Domitian's reign,[96] however, continued to view Rome as divine Fate's chosen city. In the case of Valerius Flaccus's *Argonautica,* and even more pointedly in Silius Italicus's *Punica,* the Virgilian themes of Rome's divinely ordained destiny and the eschatological promise of the Golden Age are reaffirmed, even if their ultimate realization is postponed to the indefinite future.

All of these epics, from the *Aeneid* to the *Punica,* were intended to be recited publicly as well as to be read and enjoyed privately. Moreover, in the case of the *Aeneid,* it must even be assumed that this work was read and admired by the empire's Greek subjects—at least by the time of the apostle Paul—for the Roman philosopher Lucius Annaeus Seneca wrote a letter to the imperial slave Polybius, in which he notes the important tasks that Polybius has undertaken in translating Virgil's poetry into Greek and Homer's works into Latin. That Polybius's translation of Virgil was, in fact, a paraphrase in Greek prose is certain based upon Seneca's wording:

> Agedum illa, quae multo ingenii tui labore celebrata sunt, in manus sume utriuslibet auctoris carmina, quae tu ita resolvisti, ut quamvis structura illorum recesserit, permaneat tamen gratia—sic enim illa ex alia lingua in aliam

---

96. At least one more epic was also begun during Domitian's reign, Statius's *Achilleid.* The poet died during the early stages of its composition, however, and only one book survives in its entirety.

transtulisti, ut, quod difficillimum erat, omnes virtutes in alienam te ora-
tionem secutae sint.

Consider now those poems of both authors, which have become famous by
your brilliant effort, and which you have set loose with such skill that, even
though their form has disappeared, their charm still remains—for you have
translated them from one language to another so that all their merits have
followed them into a foreign mode of speech, which was most difficult.[97]

Although the *Aeneid's* fame and popularity are widely attested, it is difficult
to gauge the extent of the popularity and influence of the later Latin epics
beyond the vicinity of Rome itself. Nevertheless, the quantity of epics produced, especially during the eighties and nineties of the first century CE, as well
as the public nature of their intended presentation and promulgation, indicates
the importance of the epic genre and its influential place in the culture of the
Roman empire throughout the first century of the common era.

LUKE-ACTS: A FOUNDATIONAL EPIC FOR THE EARLY CHRISTIAN CHURCH

As was the case in the writing of the *Iliad,* the *Odyssey,* and the *Aeneid,* the creation of Luke-Acts reflects a critical combination of circumstances comprising its dramatic occasion and social context. By the end of the first century, the
Christian mission had grown from its inauspicious beginnings to a point at
which the author of Colossians, a slightly older Lukan contemporary, could
claim that the gospel had been proclaimed to every creature under heaven (Col
1:23). Furthermore, this proclamation had met with a surprising degree of success, particularly among the pagans of the Greek-speaking provinces of the
Roman empire. So impressive was this success that, writing just a few years later
in his capacity as acting governor of the province of Pontus and Bithynia, the
younger Pliny found it necessary to consult with the emperor concerning the
political and economic problems caused by extensive Christian conversions
(Pliny, *Epistulae* 10.96.9–10).

Equally as stunning as the rapid success of the Christian mission among
Gentiles, however, was the finality of the rupture of the church with its religious past. The church was frequently on the defensive as a sect within Israel
during its earlier years, and the combination of internal tensions and external
calamities, culminating in the Roman destruction of Jerusalem and its temple,
ultimately overwhelmed those from all sides who had sought accommodation
and compromise. A significant break, probably occurring in the latter half of

97. Seneca *Consolatio ad Polybium* 11.5; see also, 8.2; 11.6.

the eighties, coupled with the continued growth of the gospel among gentiles, greatly intensified the need to define Christian identity and to affirm the status of the new community as the true Israel.

At about the same time, however, the Christian community began experiencing its own crisis of vision.[98] What was already being mythologized retrospectively as the heroic period of the original disciples and the subsequent mission of the great apostle to the Gentiles was now definitively over. The charism of the spirit and the inspiration and diversity that it apparently had engendered were beginning to lose their vitality and authority among those who now guided the church. Indeed, the church itself was beginning to succumb to a more institutionalized communal life under the guidance of spiritual and ethical teachings that were already in the process of becoming standardized and codified.[99]

It may be argued that Luke's solution to the historic problems presented to the predominantly gentile Christian communities of his generation was remarkably similar to that applied by Virgil to the problems and challenges of Augustan society. Just as Virgil had created his foundational epic for the Roman people by appropriating and transforming Homer, so also did Luke create his foundational epic for the early Christian community primarily by appropriating and transforming the sacred traditions of Israel's past as narrated in the Bible of the diasporan Jewish communities, the Septuagint.[100] Through this process of appropriation and transformation, Luke sought to confer a noble identity and an aura of destiny upon the Christian present, raising the designation "Christian" to the level of universal human aspiration. More than any

98. C. K. Barrett (*The Acts of the Apostles*, ICC, vol. 2 (Edinburgh: T & T Clark, 1994–1998], xl–xli) speaks of this later time as one of resolution and harmony in the church and contrasts it with the tensions of the earlier period. Although there is an element of truth in his interpretation, in my opinion the dominant perspective from which Luke writes is one of nostalgia for the heroic past and a longing to connect himself and his audience to an idealized version of those early days.

99. For example, the widespread appearance of the so-called Household Codes in the church correspondence of this post-Pauline generation (cf. Col 3:18—4:1; Eph 4:21—6:8; 1 Pet 2:13—3:7).

100. It was Thomas L. Brodie who first suggested that Luke's appropriation of the Septuagint was analogous to Virgil's appropriation of Homer. See especially his excellent article, "Greco-Roman Imitation of Texts as a Partial Guide to Luke's Use of Sources," in *Luke-Acts: New Perspectives from the Society of Biblical Literature Seminar*, ed. C. H. Talbert (New York: Crossroads, 1984), 17–46. On the other hand, the biblical traditions of Israel are not the only traditions that Luke appropriates. In a series of articles, still mostly unpublished, Dennis R. MacDonald has shown that as the story of Acts moves into the gentile world, Luke begins to incorporate a number of extended literary allusions to Homeric epic. See the discussion of Acts 27 in chapter 5.

other New Testament author, Luke composed Luke-Acts as a continuation of the story line of Israel's scriptural past. In Luke's narrative, the story of Jesus and the birth of the church become the surprising and miraculous fulfillment of God's long history with Israel.

Nor was the adaptation of the ancient biblical message to contemporary Greco-Roman epic form entirely without precedent. In the second century BCE, fragments from two epic poems and one Greek tragedy have survived, all of which are now attributed to Hellenized Jewish writers. These relatively obscure literary works were recorded by the Greek historian Alexander Polyhistor in the middle of the first century BCE. Fragments of Polyhistor's transmissions were subsequently preserved by the fourth-century church historian Eusebius.

Early in the second century BCE, a Jewish writer, probably living in Alexandria and known to posterity only as Philo, produced an epic poem entitled *On Jerusalem*. Because only six short fragments have been preserved,[101] the subjects of which range from the utterly sublime to the faintly ridiculous,[102] it is difficult to speculate on the precise themes and purpose of the original composition beyond George W. E. Nickelsburg's surmise that the epic poem was probably composed to celebrate Jerusalem and the history of its people.[103] In full compliance with the classical rule of the genre, this Philo composed his epic in hexameter verse. The outcome of this poetic experiment, however, was decidedly unpromising. Nickelsburg finds the language "flowery" and "bombastic," and Harold A. Attridge adds that "much of the poetry is barely intelligible."[104] Nevertheless, the work is interesting for its imitation of Homeric poetic mannerisms, such as Homer's fondness for descriptive epithet, and its attempt to combine these elements of Greek epic presentation with biblical and apologetic themes.

A technically superior epic poem, Theodotus's *On the Jews,* was probably also composed in Alexandria in the mid to late second century BCE. Of this work, eight somewhat longer fragments survive, again recorded by Alexander Polyhistor and preserved by Eusebius.[105] This work is clearly the product of a very well educated Hellenistic Jew and follows the literary reforms laid down

101. Eusebius of Caesarea *De praeparatione evangelica* 9.20.1; 9.24.1; 9.37.1–3.

102. While the first few fragments refer to the dealings of God with the patriarchs, the last few discuss Jerusalem's water system.

103. George W. E. Nickelsburg, "Hellenistic Jewish Poets," in *Jewish Writings of the Second Temple Period*, CRINT, ed. Michael E. Stone (Philadelphia: Fortress Press, 1984), 120.

104. Nickelsburg, "Jewish Poets," 118; Harold A. Attridge, "Philo the Epic Poet," in *The Old Testament Pseudepigrapha*, ed. J. H. Charlesworth, vol. 2 (Garden City, N.Y.: Doubleday, 1985), 781.

105. Eusebius *Praepar. evang.* 9.22.1–11.

by Aristotle and the later Alexandrian poet Callimachus. The plot focuses on a central action, the rape of Dinah and the sack of Shechem (Gen 33:18—34:31 LXX), and it appears to have been a defense of the practice of circumcision as well as of other aspects of Jewish exclusivism.[106]

Theodotus writes in a far more graceful and intelligible hexameter verse than does Philo, and he exhibits a knowledge of both Homer and Apollonius Rhodius, whose language and word usage he skillfully incorporates. However, because Theodotus is so successful in his imitation of Greek epic vocabulary and meter, his composition has, to a great degree, lost the linguistic and stylistic flavor of the Septuagint.[107] Artful and sophisticated though his poetry may be, therefore, it nevertheless represents another unsuccessful attempt at adapting biblical narrative to the uncongenial constraints of Greek poetic verse.

Also of interest as a possible literary precedent for Luke-Acts is the poetic drama of the Hellenistic Jewish playwright known as Ezekiel. This author was probably a contemporary of Philo the epic poet, and fragments of his drama *The Exodus* (Ἡ Ἐξαγωγή) have also been preserved in Eusebius.[108] Whether the play was ever actually performed is impossible to say, but several scholars have argued that it was clearly written for that purpose.[109] Ezekiel's drama centers on the events of Exodus 1–15, especially concentrating on the heroic figure of Moses, who delivers a long opening monologue in which he summarizes previous events and establishes the context for the story that is about to unfold. Complying with the genre requirements of Greek tragedy, Ezekiel has composed his drama in iambic trimeter, the execution of which is considered by literary critics to be competent, if somewhat prosaic.[110]

Taken together, these Hellenistic Jewish efforts to convey biblical themes and the ancient Israelite religious and cultural perspective in strict compliance with the metric conventions of Greek epic and drama demonstrate a marginal success at best. Although the most skillful presentation is probably that of Theodotus, the fact that his work shows the greatest linguistic and stylistic estrangement from its biblical roots indicates that transposing the spirit of Israel's scriptural heritage into the language and idiom of Greek poetry was an inherently problematic undertaking. Consequently, even if Luke had possessed

---

106. Nickelsburg, "Jewish Poets," 121–25.

107. F. Fallon, "Theodotus," in *The Old Testament Pseudepigrapha*, ed. J. H. Charlesworth, vol. 2 (Garden City, N.Y.: Doubleday, 1985), 787.

108. Eusebius *Praepar. evang.* 9.28–29.

109. B. Snell, "Ezechiels Moses-Drama," *Antike und Abendland* 13 (1967): 153–54; R. G. Robertson, "Ezekiel the Tragedian," in *The Old Testament Pseudepigrapha*, ed. J. H. Charlesworth, vol. 2 (Garden City, N.Y.: Doubleday, 1985), 806.

110. John Strugnell, "Notes on the Text and Metre of Ezekiel the Tragedian's 'Exagogé,'" *HTR* 60 (1967): 453.

the artistic skill and linguistic sophistication of a Theodotus, which he probably did not, it would have been exceedingly difficult, as well as counter to his particular literary and theological interests, to attempt an authentic Greco-Roman epic presentation in hexameter verse. Furthermore, as Seneca's letter to Polybius clearly implies, the version of the *Aeneid* that Luke is most likely to have known would have been a Greek prose version, much like the vast majority of modern translations of this ancient poetic work. Luke's literary presentation is, therefore, a compromise. Appropriating and adapting the biblical style and traditions characteristic of the Septuagint, while at the same time incorporating as many of the elements of Greco-Roman epic structure and dramatic presentation as were compatible with a prose narrative, Luke has composed a foundational epic for the early Christian communities of the Greco-Roman world.

That Luke aspires to narrate the saving history of the true Israel has been widely accepted ever since the efforts of Conzelmann first resulted in a detailed analysis elucidating that broad literary purpose. What remains open to discussion, however, is the *manner* in which Luke's vision of history and its meaning is presented. Is Luke's primary concern with the development of a sacred geography and chronology, as Conzelmann first articulated? Or are Luke's literary and theological interests centered on the enactment of a mission, divinely inspired and directed, and with the crowning success ultimately awaiting the mission's completion? Are Luke's political concerns primarily apologetic or accommodationist? Is he simply seeking a secure and respected place for the church within the Roman world? Or is the focus of Luke's concern with the divinely inspired proclamation of a new people whose mandated mission is universal in scope and whose eschatological kingdom is already in the process of realization? In short, is epic a better literary model than historiography, biography, or romance for understanding and interpreting the particular nature of the historical and theological vision that Luke seeks to express?

Indeed, could it be that, despite its popularizing style and relative lack of artistic refinement, Luke-Acts was composed as a foundational epic for the newly emerging Christian communities of the Greco-Roman world, written to confer ancient Israel's religious heritage definitively and exclusively upon the church? Did the author seek to affirm the church's identity as completely independent of contemporary Israel and its diasporan communities, and to legitimize and empower its missionary mandate, with its promise of salvation for all believers and its universalizing claim to represent the ultimate fulfillment of God's true plan for humankind? Only after an extensive analysis of the *Aeneid*, its immediate predecessors, and its late-first-century literary descendants can the manner and degree of Lukan imitation of the contemporary epic model be fully discerned and properly evaluated.

2

THE *AENEID:*
ROME'S SACRED HISTORY

ANTECEDENTS AND INFLUENCES

Writing toward the end of the first century of the common era, the Spanish-born rhetor and influential literary scholar Marcus Fabius Quintilianus praised Homer as the father of classical epic. Just as the ocean is the source of every stream and river, he wrote, Homer is the source of every significant literary genre. Quintilian goes on to say that of all the epic poets, Greek or Roman, Virgil most nearly approaches Homer, both in terms of artistic perfection and in terms of seminal literary influence. Indeed, he writes, in some respects Virgil surpasses Homer (Quintilian, *Institutio Oratoria* 10.1.46, 85–86). Many modern scholars echo Quintilian's judgment of Virgil's influence and importance. One even insists that it is the *Aeneid*, not the *Iliad*, that represents the technical perfection of the genre, the classical epic par excellence.[1]

This assessment of the *Aeneid* rests primarily on the fact that Virgil's poem represents a unique and profound synthesis of Homeric dramatic principles and Callimachean artistic techniques.[2] Originally developed in early third-century Alexandria, Callimachus's critical principles and artistic method quickly set the standard for poetic style throughout the Hellenistic world and eventually influenced nearly every other literary genre as well.[3] It is important, therefore, to

1. Viktor Pöschl, *The Art of Virgil: Image and Symbol in the* Aeneid (Ann Arbor, Mich.: Greenwood, 1986), 1–9. Not surprisingly, some Homeric scholars question Pöschl's judgment. See, for example, G. S. Kirk, *Homer and the Oral Tradition* (Cambridge: Cambridge Univ. Press, 1976).

2. Unless stated otherwise, the translations in this and the succeeding chapter are my own.

3. As noted in chapter 1, insofar as Callimachean principles were applied to later epic poetry, they were indebted to the earlier criteria established by Aristotle (*Poetics* 23–24; 26.14).

take note of these Callimachean or Alexandrian innovations in order to understand the way in which the *Aeneid* both emulates the epic poetry of Homer and also transforms it.

In the classical period it had been drama rather than epic that had become the true heir to Homeric poetry. Indeed, the epics of the fifth and fourth centuries BCE had degenerated into sycophantic and formulaic encomia. These works were written by poets of dubious talent, who generally contented themselves with imitating the superficial mannerisms of Homer. Although their aims were to make their productions sufficiently heroic and grandiose to please the wealthy and powerful patrons for whom they were written, their works had more in common with tedious annalistic histories than they did with Homeric epic.[4]

Typical of this class of poet was Choerilus of Samos, who, according to Plutarch, was hired by the great Spartan leader Lysander to accompany him on his military campaigns and to write a poetical panegyric of his achievements.[5] Choerilus, who reportedly had fled from slavery on the Aegean island of Samos and had come under the influence of Herodotus,[6] evinced a passion for historical detail. His epic work, *Persica*, is a lengthy chronicle of battles glorifying his illustrious and powerful patron. Somewhat later, Choerilus of Iassos wrote in a similar vein for his patron Alexander the Great. It was precisely this degeneration of epic poetry into personal glorification and propaganda that provoked Callimachus's strong reaction and prompted his efforts to restore poetry to the realm of art.

Considered by many to be the greatest poet of the Hellenistic age, Callimachus of Cyrene came under the patronage of Ptolemy II Philadelphus (285–247 BCE), for whom his primary task was to organize the Alexandrian royal library. This onerous work notwithstanding, Callimachus apparently was a prolific writer of both prose and poetry, although very little of his work has survived. Most important among his extant writings is a collection of *Hymns,* as well as fragments of the elegiac poem *Aetia* and the miniature epic *Hecale.* Callimachus set forth the motivations underlying his program of artistic reform in the preface written for a revised edition of the *Aetia* and published toward the end of his life. These goals, which stress artistic perfection rather than lit-

---

4. The epic of the Hellenized Jewish poet Philo (see the discussion in chapter 1) would doubtless have fit this category of inferior poetic style.

5. Plutarch *Lysander* 18.4.

6. Based on the fabled account of Suidas and cited in Albin Lesky, *A History of Greek Literature* (London: Methuen, 1966), 304.

erary volume, place a premium on insight and originality and, above all, eschew literary bombast and pomposity. Thus, in concluding his prefatory remarks, he makes this plea to his students and admirers:

ἑτέρων δ' ἴχνια μὴ καθ' ὁμά
δίφρον ἐλ]ᾶν μηδ' οἷμον ἀνὰ πλατύν, ἀλλὰ κελεύθους
ἀτρίπτο]υς, εἰ καὶ στεινοτέρην ἐλάσεις.
Τεττίγω]ν ἐνὶ τοῖς γὰρ ἀείδομεν οἳ λιγὺν ἦχον
. . . θ]όρυβον δ' οὐκ ἐφίλησαν ὄνων.

Do not drive your chariot on the common tracks of others, nor along a wide road, but on untrammeled paths, even though your course be more restricted. For we sing with those who love the clear-toned sound of the cicada and not the . . . braying noise of asses.

Aetia 1.26–30

True to his word, Callimachus sought to infuse poetic works with a new musicality and an elegance of style by means of the introduction of formal devices, such as parallelism and contrast, balance and repetition, and carefully selected detail. Refinement of form was accompanied by musicality of language and mood, by a return from history to myth, and by a new attention to private concerns and emotions. In its deliberate turning away from the grand scale and the heroic or elevated style that had become synonymous with the fawning celebration of great men and costly battles, Callimachean style reflected the new art of "a disillusioned Alexandrian world."[7]

In the poetry inspired by Callimachean principles, post-Homeric epic concerns were replaced by a new Alexandrian emphasis on love, a new focus on women, a greater interest in the unheroic and morally flawed character, a preference for realistic (even sentimental and trivialized) settings, and new emphases on romance and dramatic irony. This Callimachean interest in private concerns and diminished aspirations inspired the rise of the Hellenistic novel with its characteristic themes of love and adventure, its strong interest in female characters, and its emphasis on private emotions and on settings that depict ordinary daily life in sentimental and idealized ways.[8] Although the Hellenistic novel did also absorb some of the aesthetic refinements of form

---

7. John Kevin Newman, *The Classical Epic Tradition* (Madison: Univ. of Wisconsin Press, 1986), 183.

8. A recent discussion of the relation of the ancient novel to post-Callimachean epic may be found in Peter Toohey, *Reading Epic: An Introduction to the Ancient Narratives* (London: Routledge, 1992).

insisted upon by Callimachus and his students, it did not make principles of form and structure central characteristics of its genre, as did post-Callimachean epic poetry.

In his pursuit of stylistic perfection, Callimachus had deliberately cautioned against the continued production of full-scale epics, arguing instead for their replacement by the miniature epic, or *epyllion*. Nevertheless, it was Apollonius Rhodius, generally considered to have been one of his students, who subsequently did combine the artistic techniques and the more subjective literary motifs of the Alexandrian school with heroic themes and the grand scale of Homeric epic. Written about the middle of the third century BCE, Apollonius's *Argonautica* was to exert a major influence on Virgil's artistic expression. Although the story of Jason's journey in the first Greek ship, the *Argo,* to the outer reaches of the known world in quest of the Golden Fleece was of ancient origin, predating the works of both Homer and Hesiod,[9] it continued to be a popular literary theme well into the classical period. It was not, therefore, in the selection of its mythological plot that the *Argonautica* became a significant milestone in the developmental progress toward Virgilian epic; rather, it was in its artistic presentation.

Briefly told, it is the story of a young prince trying to regain his throne who is set the daunting task of traveling to the edge of the known world, to the mysterious land of Colchis, in order to bring back the prized Golden Fleece. Accompanied by a band of primordial heroes, Jason embarks on a lengthy journey that includes many adventures, some of which closely resemble incidents described in the *Odyssey*. One such incident is the romantic interlude that Jason enjoys with Queen Hypsipyle on the island of Lemnos. When Jason and the Argonauts finally arrive at Colchis, Athena and Hera persuade Aphrodite to use her powers to cause the king's younger daughter Medea to fall in love with Jason so that she will be moved to help him in his task. Although torn between her passionate love for Jason and her duty to her father, Medea eventually overcomes her scruples and provides Jason with a magical ointment necessary for the accomplishment of his mission. That night Medea joins the Argonauts, offering further help in obtaining the Fleece, after which they all flee on the *Argo,* with the Colchians in hot pursuit. During the long trip back to Thessaly, the crew of the *Argo* is harassed by pursuing forces and hostile storms. En route and under inauspicious circumstances, Jason and Medea marry. The epic ends with their return to Thessaly.

---

9. Cf. Homer *Odyssey* 12.71; Hesiod *Theogony* 992–1005.

In its adoption of heroic myth and its drama conducted on two levels (cosmic and earthly), in its adaptation of incidents from the *Iliad* and the *Odyssey*, and in its use of Homeric language and simile, the *Argonautica* represents a return to the world of Homeric epic. Yet closer examination reveals that the similarities between Apollonius's *Argonautica* and the Homeric epics are more apparent than real. The *Argonautica* is characterized by an elaborate emphasis on formal unity and balance, which finds expression in a tripartite structure (initial voyage, events in Colchis, homeward voyage), as well as a bipartite structure (evidenced by separate invocations for books 1 and 2 and books 3 and 4).

The *Argonautica's* extensive use of parallelisms and doublets also emphasizes the principle of balance and enhances the overall unity of the composition. An Alexandrian perspective is further betrayed by the epic's focus on love, its development of a complex and interesting female character, and its portrayal of the hero as morally flawed. Ironically, however, it is frequently by means of Homeric allusions and Homeric language that these unheroic and psychologically sophisticated Alexandrian themes are dramatized.

One example from the *Argonautica* is perhaps sufficient to suggest the way in which Alexandrian themes and perspectives are layered upon Homeric motifs, thereby also providing an example of the skillful complexities of the practice of emulation (μίμησις), which is distinctively characteristic of epic. As has already been mentioned, the adventures of the initial voyage of the *Argo* include an incident that appears to be drawn deliberately to call to the reader's mind Odysseus's encounter with Circe on the island of Aiaia (*Odyssey* 10.135–574). Jason and the Argonauts arrive on the island of Lemnos shortly after all of the Lemnian men either have been killed or have been driven from the island by the women. Their queen, Hypsipyle, has sent a messenger to the *Argo* to greet the crew and to summon Jason to a formal welcome at the palace.

As Jason dresses for the occasion, the allusions and motifs switch to those of the famous arming scenes from the *Iliad*. Jason places around his shoulders a divinely wrought mantle, a gift from Athena, and many lines are devoted to a detailed description of the various mythological scenes woven onto its luminous surface (*Argonautica* 1.721–68). This is clearly reminiscent of the Homeric description of the shield that Hephaestus made for Achilles (*Iliad* 18.478–615), which was to assure his victory in combat against Hector. The allusion to an arming scene continues with a description of the spear Jason carries, a gift from Atalanta who, so the text delicately suggests, was a previous romantic conquest (*Argonautica* 1.770–73). The simile that compares Jason's appearance to that of a bright star may be a further allusion to *Iliad* 22.25–31, in which Achilles, before the fatal duel with Hector, appears to Priam as like a star.[10] What is so strikingly ironic in these military allusions, however, is that Jason's preparations are intended to gain him mastery over the heart of Queen Hypsipyle, and his field of combat will be the palace boudoir.

Thus, the Homeric allusions in this passage operate on two levels. On the surface level relating to the narrative plot, Jason's landing on the island of Lemnos and his brief affair with Hypsipyle are paralleled with Odysseus's arrival on the island of Aiaia and his affair with Circe, thus bringing to the reader's mind the possible danger that the situation presents for the hero and for the successful completion of the voyage. More important, however, are the military allusions from the *Iliad*. Their effect is quite the opposite. Through them the reader is warned of Jason's predatory nature, particularly where women are concerned. This decidedly unheroic element of Jason's character is central to the interior, psychological drama that lies just beneath the surface of the story line. It is this focus on private emotion and interior psychology that makes the *Argonautica*, despite its Homeric scale, motifs, and language, so quintessentially Alexandrian.

VIRGIL AND THE HISTORICAL CONTEXT OF THE *AENEID*

In its discovery and analysis of the pervasive influence of Alexandrian principles on the poetry of Virgil, recent scholarship has greatly advanced and refined the more traditional analyses of his work, which tended to interpret the *Aeneid* wholly against its Homeric background.[11] As important as these Hellenistic literary refinements were, however, Virgil's work cannot be fully understood apart from the political and social context of the Augustan age.

The period in which Virgil wrote the *Eclogues*, followed by the *Georgics* and the *Aeneid*, was the culmination of an era of profound national crisis and change: the death of the Republic, seemingly endless civil war, social and reli-

---

10. A. W. Bullock ("Hellenistic Poetry," in *Greek Literature*, vol. 1 of *Cambridge History of Classical Literature*, ed. P. E. Easterling and B. M. W. Knox [Cambridge: Cambridge Univ. Press, 1985], 595), who passes over the sinister significance of Jason's encounter with Hypsipyle and cites this Homeric parallel in relation to a later scene between Jason and Medea (Apollonius Rhodius *Argonautica* 3.956–61).

11. Although an appreciation of Virgil's debt to Homer can be traced back at least to the early second century (cf. Suetonius *Vita Vergili* 21), in modern scholarship this appreciation has been pursued with great vigor and thoroughness, first by Richard Heinze, *Vergils epische Technik* (Leipzig/Berlin: Tübner, 1915); and more recently by George Nicolaus Knauer, *Die Aeneis und Homer: Studien zur poetischen Technik Vergils* (Göttingen: Vandenhoeck & Ruprecht, 1964).

gious decline, economic upheaval, private loss, and personal tragedy. After this turbulence, there ensued an equally dramatic reversal resulting in imperial triumph, restoration of peace (both internal and external), the return of material prosperity, and a renewed Augustan emphasis on social and civic responsibility and on dutiful religious observance.

Based on the evidence of contemporary biographers, as well as on indications within his own works, it is likely that Virgil shared personally in these national experiences of loss and reversal that characterized the years of his mature poetic reflection.[12] His first major work, a collection of ten small poems known as the *Bucolics,* or *Eclogues,* which were written between 42 and 38 BCE,[13] already suggests the poet's intention to weave the melancholy and disillusionment brought about by the continuing civil wars into the serene lyrics of these pastoral poems. The First and Ninth Eclogues allude to the land confiscations and evictions that occurred, particularly among the smaller landholders of the Italian gentry, as a direct result of the second triumvirate's defeat of Brutus and Cassius at Philippi in 42 BCE and the subsequent need of the victors to reward their troops for their services.

Because of the repeated references in the *Eclogues* to the plight of the small landholder, many scholars have accepted Suetonius's assertion that Virgil himself was a victim of this policy of land confiscation.[14] If, however, Virgil shared personally in the social disruption and loss of hope and innocence—of which the civil wars were both metaphor and reality—he also shared personally in the dramatic reversal of fortune that Octavian's rise to power ultimately brought about. Even before the publication of the *Eclogues,* Virgil had been invited to join the select coterie of poets maintained by the patronage of Octavian's close friend and confidante, the wealthy and highly cultivated Maecenas. Indeed, again according to Suetonius, it was in gratitude for his generosity and pro-

---

12. Suetonius *Vita Vergili* 20. However, Wendell Clausen ("Theocritus and Virgil," in *Latin Literature,* vol. 2 of *Cambridge History of Classical Literature,* ed. E. J. Kenney and W. V. Clausen [Cambridge: Cambridge Univ. Press, 1982], 304) cautions that Virgil's lamentations ought not be considered autobiographical.

13. The date of the completion of the *Eclogues* is much debated. Most commentators accept a date of 39 or 38 BCE. See Jasper Griffin, "Virgil," in *The Roman World,* ed. J. Boardman, J. Griffin, and O. Murray (Oxford: Oxford Univ. Press, 1988), 210–11. See also, Gian Biagio Conte, *Latin Literature: A History* (Baltimore: Johns Hopkins Univ. Press, 1994), 268. However, Wendell Clausen ("Theocritus and Virgil," 314) dissents. Arguing that the god to whom Meliboeus refers in the First Eclogue must be Octavian, Clausen places completion of the composite work in 35 BCE.

14. See n. 12 above.

tection that Virgil dedicated to this important patron his next poetic work, the *Georgics*, completed in 29 BCE.[15]

Maecenas, who was patron to Horace and Propertius as well as to Virgil, created a literary circle whose members, although too talented and too independently respected to be dismissed simply as court poets, nonetheless had close ties to the emperor. Octavian, acting indirectly through Maecenas, encouraged the creation of a new type of literature that was widely popular[16] and consciously Roman[17] in character. As a result of their brilliance and their proximity to power, these poets acquired a kind of national status and were entrusted with a poetic mission that was more than merely artistic.[18] Their task was to define Rome's moral and religious values and to inspire its people with a patriotic vision of a world whose eschatological fulfillment was embodied in the Augustan identification with the return of the Golden Age.

Virgil's next major work, the *Georgics,* suggests his increasing sense of commitment to the role of poet as interpreter and preacher.[19] What began as a celebration of pastoral life in the *Eclogues* becomes in the *Georgics* a nostalgic idealization of that life, primarily for the purpose of moral instruction.[20] For example, one of the work's most frequently analyzed passages is the description of the socialized habits and communal way of life of a colony of bees (*Georgics* 4). In their hard work, their selfless concern for the common good, and their unwavering loyalty to their divinely ordained sovereign, the bees bear a close correspondence to the Augustan ideal of the Roman people. They, like the bees, will have the reward of a corporate immortality in the continued survival and prosperity of their race.

15. Suetonius *Vita Vergili* 20.

16. It was popular in the sense that it was intended for a far wider audience than the rather select number who would actually read it.

17. Many of the works of this so-called New Poetry were intended to be read before public gatherings, and they were created for occasions that were both religious and patriotic. Certainly this was the case for Horace's *Carmen saeculare*, and it was probably also the case for major segments of the *Aeneid*.

18. Conte, *Latin Literature*, 255. See also, John Kevin Newman, *Augustus and the New Poetry* (Brussels: Revue d'Études Latines, 1967), 190.

19. R. O. A. M. Lyne, "Augustan Poetry and Society," in *The Roman World*, ed. J. Boardman, J. Griffin, and O. Murray (Oxford: Oxford Univ. Press, 1986), 188.

20. See especially Jasper Griffin, "The Fourth Georgic, Virgil, and Rome," in *Virgil*, ed. Ian McAuslan and Peter Walcot (Oxford: Oxford Univ. Press, 1990), 94–111.

The *Georgics*, which took between six and ten years to compose,[21] was completed just in time to be read aloud to Octavian on his return from war in the East in 29 BCE. It is, therefore, hardly surprising that it includes some words of glowing praise and earnest supplication to the young ruler who seemed to offer salvation and hope for a lost generation (*everso . . . saeclo; Georgics* 1.500). Even so, however, this encomiastic passage and others like it are offset somewhat by occasional expressions of reservation and concern, lest Octavian's desire for power and conquest prove harmful and excessive.[22]

The decade of the twenties, in which Virgil wrote the *Aeneid*, must have been an era of immense national relief and profound optimism for the future, feelings that there is every reason to assume Virgil would have shared.[23] Augustus's grasp of the levers of power had been effective but graceful,[24] and he appeared to be exercising that power with caution and tact. On the other hand, the forced suicide of Virgil's good friend Gaius Cornelius Gallus (26 BCE), who had fallen into disgrace while serving in Augustus's administration in Egypt, may have caused the poet to become wary of the excessive imperial prosperity and power that followed in the wake of the peace of the gods. Perhaps it was this restrained skepticism concerning the ultimate meaning of corporate power and glory—and its relationship to the fate of the individual— that engendered the poetic irony playing just beneath the surface of this otherwise very patriotic poem, an epic that exerted a profound influence on numerous writers of varying motives and skills over the next century and beyond. It is my contention that the author known to us as "Luke" was one of those authors upon whom Virgil's epic of Roman origins and divinely guided destiny had a profound influence. Accordingly, the analysis of the *Aeneid* that follows serves not only to illustrate the major themes of Virgil's work but also to isolate a number of the dramatic devices that he employed so effectively and that can also be discerned in the later prose epic, Luke-Acts.

---

21. If Clausen's dating of the completed *Eclogues* is correct, it would have been only six years, assuming that Virgil did not begin the *Georgics* until the *Eclogues* had been completed.

22. For example, *Georgics* 1.36–37.

23. Several recent studies, however, disagree with this supposition. See, for example, W. R. Johnson, *Darkness Visible: A Study of Vergil's* Aeneid (Berkeley: Univ. of California Press, 1976), 136–38.

24. "Julius Caesar tried to rape Rome and therefore failed. Augustus seduced Rome and therefore succeeded." Z. Yavetz, "The Personality of Augustus: Reflections on Syme's *Roman Revolution*," in *Between Republic and Empire*, ed. Kurt A. Raaflaub and Mark Toher (Berkeley: Univ. of California Press, 1990), 40.

OVERTURE: THEMES AND STRUCTURES IN BOOK 1

As noted earlier, Virgil's *Aeneid* reflects many literary influences, which have been recast to serve the historical circumstances of the Augustan age and transformed by the poet's own intellectual and artistic insight. Alexandrian attention to form has been heightened and perfected so that structure becomes a reflection of meaning,[25] as a brief analysis of the narrative development of book 1 will illustrate. At its most basic level, the *Aeneid* tells the story of the legendary migration of the Trojan hero Aeneas and a faithful remnant of the Trojan people as they make their way from the ruins of Troy to the shores of Italy. It narrates their journey and adventures en route and the bitter war that attends their arrival. Furthermore, Virgil emphasizes the crucial role of divine guidance, both in establishing their mission and in enabling them to fulfill it. Although several other historians, both prior to Virgil and contemporary with him, had included various elements of this story in their own writings, Virgil's version seems to be essentially his own synthesis of a number of traditional sources, which he crafted to suit his political, religious, and artistic purposes.[26]

> Arma virumque cano, Troiae qui primus ab oris
> Italiam fato profugus Laviniaque venit
> litora — multum ille et terris iactatus et alto
> vi superum, saevae memorem Iunonis ob iram,
> multa quoque et bello passus, dum conderet urbem
> inferretque deos Latio; genus unde Latinum
> Albanique patres atque altae moenia Romae.

> Arms I sing and the man who first, banished by Fate from the coasts of Troy, came to Italy and the Lavinian shores—he, severely tossed about on land and

25. Pöschl, *Art of Virgil,* 18.

26. Polybius knew of a tradition in which King Evander brought Arcadians to Italy and founded Rome. According to this same tradition, Pallas was Evander's grandson through his daughter Lavinia (Dionysius of Halicarnassus *Roman Antiquities* 1.31.1–2). Varro reported that Lavinium was the first Trojan settlement in Latium and the repository of the Trojan household gods (Varro *De lingua Latina* 5.144). Dionysius of Halicarnassus writes of the uniting of native and foreign stock by treaties and ties of marriage and of the adoption of the common name *Latinus,* but he does not know of a period of wandering that preceded the settlement in Italy (*Roman Antiquities* 1.60.2; 1.63.1). Livy records that Aeneas, driven from Troy but guided by Fate, went through a period of wandering (although the geographical details differ from those of Virgil) before landing in Italy. He also differs markedly from Virgil in the chronology of the settlement, marriage, and wars (Livy *Ab urbe condita* 1.1.4; 2.1.1). This particular synthesis of the pre-Virgilian traditions has been derived from Erich S. Gruen, *Culture and National Identity in Republican Rome* (Ithaca: Cornell Univ. Press, 1992), 6–51.

sea by power from on high, through cruel Juno's unrelenting wrath, and suffering many things in war also, until he should found a city and bring his
gods to Latium; whence came the Latin people, the Alban fathers, and the
walls of noble Rome.

Aeneid 1.1–7

Following the traditional epic convention established by Homer, the
Aeneid's proem sets forth the major themes of the narrative. Virgil's opening
lines are, however, unusually dense, containing not only the seeds of the major
conflicts and grand themes that will be developed during the course of the narrative but also the germ of the poem's essential structure, through which its
meaning will be mediated. The opening phrase, *Arma virumque cano,* is not
only a graceful acknowledgment of Virgil's debt to Homer's *Iliad* and *Odyssey,*
but it also sets forth, in reverse order, the basic thematic division of the poem.
Books 1 through 6, drawing heavily on the *Odyssey,* tell of Aeneas's exile and
wanderings; books 7 through 12, drawing equally on the *Iliad,* tell of wars that
ensue after his arrival in Italy. Furthermore, throughout both halves of the
story, it is Juno's wrath that is responsible for the protagonist's trials. This is also
foreshadowed in the grammatical structure of lines 3 to 5 of the proem, where
multum ille et terris iactatus et alto vi superum ("he, severely tossed about on land
and sea by power from on high"; books 1–6) and *multa quoque et bello passus*
("suffering many things in war also"; books 7–12) are linked by *saevae memo-
rem Iunonis ob iram* ("through cruel Juno's unrelenting wrath").[27]

The most important element in the first half of the proem, however, which
has no parallel in Homer, is the disclosure that it is the will of divine Fate[28] that
Aeneas should journey to Italy and found a new city for the Trojan gods, all
of which will lead ultimately to the rise of noble Rome (*alta Roma*). Thus,
already in the first seven lines of the proem, Virgil has introduced not only the
main protagonist and the types of calamity that he must undergo and overcome, but also the divine power behind the calamities and the higher power
that has ordained the lofty mission and that guarantees its ultimate success.[29]

At first glance, it may seem to be an artistic blunder that the central theme
and its teleological completion are placed in the middle, rather than at the end,

27. Pöschl, *Art of Virgil,* 24–25.

28. I use the singular and plural form of this word interchangeably in my analysis
because Virgil uses both forms interchangeably throughout the *Aeneid.*

29. "What is new [in the *Aeneid*], particularly in the tradition of heroic epic, is the
degree to which movement is initiated by the gods, not by assertive mortals who provoke a divine response" (Thomas van Nortwick, *Somewhere I Have Never Travelled: The
Second Self and the Hero's Journey in Ancient Epic* [New York: Oxford Univ. Press, 1992],
127).

of the proem. This, however, also anticipates the tripartite structure of the poem: books 1 through 4 centering on Aeneas's encounter with Dido, books 9 through 12 centering on his rivalry with Turnus, and books 5 through 8 centering on the grand themes of Aeneas's divine mission and its ultimate fulfillment in the restoration of the Golden Age inaugurated by the reign of Augustus.[30] It is the final section of the proem (lines 8–11), however, that introduces the poetic counterthemes of doubt and irony, casting evanescent shadows over the bright proclamations of future Roman power and glory.

> Musa, mihi causas memora, quo numine laeso
> quidve dolens regina deum tot volvere casus
> insignem pietate virum, tot adire labores
> impulerit. tantaene animis caelestibus irae?

> Recount to me, Muse, the reasons wherein thwarted in will and taking offense, the queen of the gods should have impelled a man exemplary in dutifulness to experience such adversity, to undergo so many hardships. Does fury so great exist in the hearts of the gods?

> *Aeneid* 1.8–11

The narrative proper begins by setting forth Juno's love of Carthage and her anger that Fate has ordained its future eclipse by a new city and people descended from the hated Trojans, over whom she thought she had triumphed after the destruction of their fabled city. The opening scene begins in the last year of the Trojans' seven-year exile, following their city's destruction. On Mount Olympus, Juno continues to rage against the plan of the Fates, which she acknowledges she cannot change (*quippe vetor fatis; Aeneid* 1.39). Nevertheless, she marshals the considerable heavenly forces at her disposal in order to postpone the hated outcome as long as possible. Ordering Aeolus to let loose the winds, she causes a violent storm, which scatters and threatens to destroy the Trojan fleet. Many ships and men are lost before Neptune finally intervenes and the weary survivors finally drift onto the shores of the Libyan coast (*Aeneid* 1.157–73). After they make camp, Aeneas speaks to his people. Hiding his own mounting despair, he feigns a hopeful expression (*spem voltu*

---

30. It is noteworthy that the dramatic structure of Luke-Acts is developed in a similar fashion, with the eschatologically weighted events of Jesus' crucifixion, resurrection, and ascension, together with the descent of the Spirit and the creation of the first Christian community forming the dramatic center of his work. This theological and literary keystone section is likewise preceded and succeeded by thematically balanced segments. It is preceded by Jesus' mission to Israel and succeeded by the disciples' mission to the world. For a more complete discussion and analysis, see chapter 5.

simulat) and, reminding them of their divine mission and of the prophetic assurances they have received in the past, he urges them to persevere.

The reference to Aeneas's face as a mask for his inner feelings (*Aeneid* 1.205–6) is the first of many such passages that reveal Virgil's indebtedness to the Alexandrian school, both in its use of significant detail and in its emphasis on private emotions. However, unlike the descriptions in Apollonius Rhodius's *Argonautica*, of which Virgil's description is clearly reminiscent, the private emotions of Virgil's characters are rarely allowed to dominate or diminish the loftier perspective of the narrative action. On the contrary, they are generally employed as a dramatic device to advance the central narrative theme: "so great was the struggle to establish the Roman people" (*Aeneid* 1.33). The degree to which the play of private emotions and personal fortunes influences the ultimate meaning of the poem and undermines its central religious theme, however, is a question that lies at the heart of recent critical inquiry. A detailed discussion of the most significant issues raised by such revisionist interpretations appears in appendix A.

In addition to the minor *Argonautica* allusions, the entire first scene of the narrative has been crafted with a considerable degree of correspondence to storm scenes in the *Odyssey*.[31] In the primary Homeric version, Poseidon's storm blows the wandering Odysseus farther off course and threatens to end his life, until Athena intervenes and he is blown safely to shore. There, subsequently, he will be befriended by a young princess and welcomed at a banquet held in the family palace. As commentators have long noted, Virgil intends for the reader to recognize the Homeric parallel and then to be struck by the nuanced disparities.[32] Even though Homer intends a wider and more profoundly communal significance to the story he relates, on the narrative level Odysseus's primary mission is, nonetheless, personal survival and a safe return home to Ithaca and to Penelope. Even his courageous leadership in *Odyssey* 12.208–59 is motivated primarily by these essentially private needs. Aeneas, on the other hand, must conceal his despair for the sake of his people and for the sake of their common mission, which they have been summoned by Fate to fulfill.

Pöschl has further argued that, on a dramatic level, the storm that begins the narrative in the *Aeneid* corresponds to the plague that opens the *Iliad*. It is this prelude to calamity that anticipates the problem of the entire poem and that can only find its resolution in the assurances of the Fates' decree. Furthermore, as the metaphor for the unleashing of demonic fury (*furor impius*), mediated

31. Particularly *Odyssey* 5.282–450, but also 12.208–59.

32. For example, R. D. Williams, "The Opening Scenes of the *Aeneid*," *Proceedings of the Virgilian Society* 5 (1965–66): 18.

through the forces of nature, it is more precisely the prelude for the first (Odyssean) half of the poem.[33]

After leaving Aeneas and his Trojan remnant camped on the Libyan shore on the outskirts of Carthage, the action again switches to Mount Olympus, where Venus seeks greater enlightenment and assurance regarding her beloved son's destiny. Jupiter assures her that the Fates remain unchanged (*manet immota . . . fata; Aeneid* 1.257). He then delivers one of the most important and dramatically illuminating prophecies of the entire poem, outlining in minimal but essential detail the long march of a generally glorious Roman history, from the upcoming wars in Italy and the first settlement in Latium, to Aeneas's early death and deification, to the establishment of the royal line at Alba Longa, to the birth of Romulus and Remus and the founding of Rome, to the military conquests of Julius Caesar, to his subsequent apotheosis awakening renewed hope for peace, and to this hope's eventual fulfillment as symbolized in Octavian's closing of the gates of war and his definitive containment of ungodly fury (*Aeneid* 1.257–96).[34] The empire that Rome is destined to rule is to be without limits, either temporal or spatial (*his ego nec metas rerum nec tempora pono; imperium sine fine dedi; Aeneid* 1.278–79).[35]

Another important aspect of Jupiter's speech is the relationship between the knowledge of prophecy and blessedness. Although it is somewhat elliptical, the language of line 262 (*longius et volvens fatorum;* "and further unrolling [the words] of the fates") implies that Jupiter is reading the prophecy directly from some sort of scroll, which he has to turn or wind. That Venus is allowed to

33. Pöschl, *Art of Virgil*, 12–14. The creation of a dramatic scene that functions within the story as a prelude to calamity is another element of Greco-Roman epic tradition that Luke-Acts has employed very effectively. See the discussion of Jesus' inaugural discourse (Luke 4:16-30) in chapter 4. With respect to the plague as prelude to calamity in the *Iliad*, see also, van Nortwick, *Somewhere I Have Never Travelled*, 41.

34. Numerous articles have been written discussing the identity of the Julius Caesar of lines 286–88 and the apparent incongruity between these lines and line 291 (*tum positis mitescent saecula bellis*). Williams, among others, assumes that the entire passage refers to Augustus (who was also entitled to the name Julius but was rarely, if ever, referred to as such). One of the most recent summaries of these arguments can be found in James J. O'Hara, *Death and the Optimistic Prophecy in Vergil's Aeneid* (Princeton: Princeton Univ. Press, 1990) 155–61. However, much of the ambiguity is eliminated if *tum* is interpreted as indicating succession of time, i.e., "afterwards" or "subsequently."

35. The dramatization of an inaugural prophecy to illuminate the ultimate goal to which the narrative points and to define the meaning of the hero's mission is yet another device that Luke appears to have borrowed from Greco-Roman epic. See the discussion of Luke 1:30-33 in chapter 5.

share so directly in these holy secrets indicates her privileged position (even among the gods) as a beloved daughter of Jupiter. Divine knowledge is imparted in varying degrees, depending on one's proximity to the highest heavenly power.[36] Such a pyramid of divine power is never clearly drawn in Homeric or Hellenistic epic,[37] but it is central to the meaning and importance of prophecy and divine guidance in the *Aeneid*.

Despite abuse from Juno and the hostility of all those who oppose Fate, either knowingly or unknowingly, Aeneas's preeminent status as beloved of the gods is continually and unambiguously reinforced by the constant stream of divinely inspired guidance attending him and his Trojan followers throughout the narrative. Thus, although divine guidance is crucial to the movement of the plot,[38] even more important is the halo of divine favor and illumination that this guidance confers on the Trojan remnant and, through them, on their Roman descendants. They alone are described as "blessed" (*felix*).[39]

Just as enlightenment is synonymous with divine favor, so also does lack of knowledge foreshadow disaster, despite present appearances to the contrary. This is the problem behind the tragedy of the Carthaginian queen Dido. Unlike Juno, who is deliberately and malevolently opposed to the decrees of the Fates, Dido is merely "unknowing" (*nescia*).[40] When Aeneas and his followers are finally guided into her city, she is presented as beautiful, queenly, and equally as virtuous as ever was *pius* Aeneas. He finds her surrounded by a host of admiring youths as she oversees the construction of a temple to Carthage's patron deity, Juno (*Aeneid* 1.494–97). The tragic irony of their meeting in Juno's temple is dramatically enhanced by the event that immediately pre-

---

36. That is, Jupiter. In the *Aeneid*, all lines of authority lead ultimately to him. The Fates work out the details for human history (sometimes tragically) in accordance with Jupiter's sense of cosmic order and justice, although not always with his full knowledge and consent. Similarly, Apollo's divine knowledge and guidance has been granted to him by his father. This view of an all-powerful Jupiter made popular by Virgil remained a popular conception even in the second century CE. See Aelius Aristides's *On Rome* and *Regarding Zeus*.

37. Homer's Zeus exerts much less authority. See, for example, Robert Coleman, "The Gods of the *Aeneid*," in *Virgil*, ed. Ian McAuslan and Peter Walcot, Greece and Rome Studies (Oxford: Oxford Univ. Press, 1990), 55–58; Pöschl, *Art of Virgil*, 14–17; R. O. A. M. Lyne, *Further Voices in Vergil's "Aeneid"* (Oxford: Oxford Univ. Press, 1987), 74.

38. Heinze, *Vergils epische Technik*, 331.

39. I prefer the translation "blessed" because "fortunate" does not convey the religious nuance that the use of *felix* and *infelix* appears to possess in Virgil's narrative.

40. Virgil *Aeneid* 1.299. See Karl Büchner, "P. Vergilius Maro," PW, 2d ser., 8.2 (1958):1345.

cedes it. As Aeneas waits outside the temple in expectation of an interview with Dido, he sees, painted on the temple's exterior, scenes from the battles of Troy. The paintings, which record what Juno clearly regarded as a celebratory triumph, cause Aeneas to weep.[41] He is particularly moved by the painted scene depicting Achilles' scornful violation of Hector's corpse amidst Priam's gestures of supplication (*Aeneid* 1.485–87). The inclusion of this pictorial description, with all of its attendant irony, is unquestionably intentional, as the entire narrative scene serves to anticipate the dramatic reversal that will take place in the final segment of the poem when Aeneas and the Trojan remnant are gradually transformed from vanquished to victors.

If Dido is presented as unknowing of Fate's plan, she appears also to be ignorant of her divine patroness's animosity toward the Trojans. Indeed, Dido welcomes Aeneas and his comrades with graciousness and friendship, as she explains with poignant irony: "not being ignorant of misfortune [myself], I am learning to succor the unfortunate" (*non ignara mali miseris succurrere disco; Aeneid* 1.630). Venus, however, mindful of Dido's dutiful reverence for Juno, resolves not to trust Aeneas's fortunes to Dido's good intentions. Rather, she persuades Cupid to pierce Dido to the core with an unholy passion (*Aeneid* 1.659–90) and to "beguile" her "with a strong potion," or "deceive" her "with poison" (*fallasque veneno; Aeneid* 1.688). Whichever translation one chooses, Venus's efforts are depicted by Virgil as just as malevolent in their effect as are the machinations of Juno. Henceforth, Dido is no longer merely *inscia* (unknowing), or *nescia*, she is above all *infelix*, with the connotation of "accursed" rather than simply "unhappy," as the remainder of the line makes clear.[42] Indeed, *infelix* becomes as characteristic of Dido as *pius* is of Aeneas.[43] Book 1 ends with a banquet scene in which the lovesick (or, perhaps, love-poisoned) Dido invites Aeneas to recount the final stages of the fall of Troy and his years of wandering prior to their meeting.

PROPHECY, JOURNEY, AND THE DIVINE MISSION

Although the artistic device of a banquet scene, in which the hero can extend the narrative's sense of time by relating important prenarrative action, is drawn directly from the *Odyssey,* the story of Aeneas and Dido and the overall structure of books 1 through 4 more strongly reflects Alexandrian influences. In terms of plot and description, Virgil has drawn heavily upon Apollonius

41. Coleman, "The Gods," 46.
42. *Pesti devota futurae,* "abandoned to impending ruin" (*Aeneid* 1.712).
43. *Aeneid* 1.712, 749; 4.68, 450, 529, 596; 6.456.

Rhodius's depiction of Medea. Indeed, Medea's betrayal of her father and kingdom was instigated by a fatally effective arrow shot by Eros, as a result of the connivance of Athena and Hera. Furthermore, although Apollonius's Medea is just a young princess and is not the beautiful and accomplished queen of Virgil's epic, her innocence and vulnerability only increase the reader's sympathy for her plight. Conversely, although Apollonius's description of the physical and psychological effects of Medea's wound is effective, it lacks the sinister quality that Virgil's description has suggested:

τοῖος ὑπὸ κραδίῃ εἰλυμένος αἴθετο λάθρῃ
οὖλος Ἔρως· ἁπαλὰς δὲ μετετρωπᾶτο παρειὰς
ἐς χλόον, ἄλλοτ' ἔρευθος, ἀκηδείῃσι νόοιο.

[S]o entwined round her heart, burned secretly cruel love; and, in her soul's distraction, the color of her soft cheeks changed back and forth, now pale, now flushed.

Argonautica 3.296–98

Unlike Apollonius's unscrupulous Jason, however, Virgil does not depict Aeneas as consciously taking advantage of Dido. Even the inevitable seduction scene is instigated and orchestrated by the temporary collusion of Venus and Juno. Yet, once this fatal course is set in motion by divine instigation, both characters are depicted in acts and attitudes of guilty complicity:

nec iam furtivum Dido meditatur amorem;
coniugium vocat; hoc praetexit nomine culpam.

No longer does Dido ponder love in secret;
she calls it marriage and disguises her guilt by this name.

Aeneid 4.171–72

By contrast, Aeneas's culpability is only hinted at indirectly. Yet, if anything, the indictment is harsher. Virgil suggests that Aeneas's surrender to luxury and vanity is the direct result of his guilty complicity in Dido's matrimonial delusion. When Mercury is sent to Carthage by Jupiter to remind Aeneas of his mission, the god finds him clothed in luxurious gifts from the queen.

[A]tque illi stellatus iaspide fulva
ensis erat, Tyrioque ardebat murice laena
demissa ex umeris, dives quae munera Dido
fecerat, et tenui telas discreverat auro.

[A]nd he had a sword glittering with yellow jasper,
a cloak hung from his shoulders and glowed with

Tyrian purple, gifts that wealthy Dido
had made and had edged with fine-spun gold.

Aeneid 4.261–64

It begins to appear that Virgil's Aeneas is not so different from Apollonius's Jason after all. Nor is the resemblance entirely superficial. When Mercury tells Aeneas of Jupiter's displeasure, the dutiful Aeneas is quick to respond to the divine directive. In his considered calculations of how best to handle the passionate queen, however, Aeneas's resemblance to the calculating and opportunistic Jason appears to be more than skin-deep (*Aeneid* 4.279–95).[44] The tragedy that ensues is inevitable. In order to fulfill the plan of Fate, which involves not only his own future but also that of the Trojan people and their descendants, Aeneas must extricate himself from his mistaken alliance with Dido. From her perspective, however, which Virgil clearly intends the reader to share, this is seen as ruthless betrayal and cruel abandonment. As she prepares to die by her own hand, she utters a curse, not only against Aeneas but also against his Roman descendants. The Carthaginians will henceforth violently oppose everyone remotely connected with the now hated Aeneas. "Let them wage war, they and their children's children" (*pugnent ipsique nepotesque; Aeneid* 4.629).

By ending the first segment of the poem with this curse and all of its attendant historical implications, Virgil rescues the narrative from sinking irretrievably into a diminished Alexandrian perspective. To a degree that Apollonius Rhodius neither could have nor would have, Virgil successfully holds in creative tension an interest in greatness of spirit and grandeur of scale reminiscent of Homeric epic, an emphasis on historical and moral concerns traditional for Roman epic, and the infinitely more subtle and complex artistic requirements of Alexandrian epic.

Not only does Virgil make considerable use of Alexandrian techniques of characterization, but his work is greatly influenced by Alexandrian refinements in literary form and structure as well. A concern with structural unity, with principles of contrast and balance, with parallelisms and a careful selectivity of detail, and, above all, with an intricacy of construction—all of these elements are synthesized and brought to perfection in the *Aeneid*. As has already been mentioned, in addition to its introduction of the poem's major

---

44. This observation has been nicely developed by Wendell Clausen, *Virgil's Aeneid and the Tradition of Hellenistic Poetry* (Berkeley: Univ. of California Press, 1987), 45–46. On the mutability of Aeneas's identity, see also van Nortwick, *Somewhere I Have Never Travelled*, 134.

themes, the proem also anticipates the epic's basic structural divisions: (1) the
bipartite division composed of Odyssean wanderings (books 1 through 6) and
Iliadic wars (books 7 through 12); and (2) a tripartite division in which the central section, featuring Aeneas's full recognition of the importance of his mission (books 5 through 8), is supported on either side by the mini tragedies
involving Dido (books 1 through 4) and Turnus (books 9 through 12).

Toward this end of providing the thematic link between these early events
and what is to follow, several passages are worthy of mention. In Aeneas's narration of the fall of Troy, the reader learns that Hector appeared to him in a
dream vision, foretelling the city's doom and directing him to take the city's
sacred fire and protecting gods (the Penates) before embarking on a journey
of unknown duration until he should reach an unspecified destination, at
which point he should establish a new city (*Aeneid* 2.293–97). This enigmatic
disclosure is Aeneas's first intimation of his mission. It is noteworthy, therefore,
that from the beginning his task is imbued with sacred meaning. Nevertheless,
since it means forsaking Troy while others continue to fight in its defense,
Aeneas is reluctant to comply. Only after the intervention of Venus and a dramatic omen from Jupiter himself does Aeneas gather his family and the sacred
objects of Troy and prepare to flee the city. Virgil marks this resolute turning
away from Troy and embarking upon an unknown course in obedience to the
will of the gods with the description of Aeneas lifting his aged father, Anchises,
onto his shoulders. Although this image of the dutiful Aeneas carrying his
father from the ruins of Troy was already part of the legendary cycle the poet
had inherited,[45] Virgil employs it to symbolize Aeneas's willingness to bear the
burdens that the Fates will impose.

Even as Virgil emphasizes Aeneas's willingness, however, he causes the reader
to question the hero's readiness. Aeneas's carelessness with women receives its
starting point in Troy when his wife, Creüsa, who has been following "at a distance" (*longe*), becomes separated from the male family members and is never
seen alive again. When Aeneas discovers that she is missing, he frantically begins
to search for her. Shortly thereafter, she appears to him in a vision with the
consoling words that her loss was willed by heaven and could not have been
prevented. She then adds to these words the comforting prophecy that he

---

45. The Tabula Iliaca Capitolina, a relief dating to the Augustan period, combines
scenes from the *Iliad* with scenes from later poems of the same cycle, written by the
sixth-century Sicilian poet Stesichorus. The central panel of the tabula includes a representation of Aeneas leading his son Ascanius by the hand and carrying his father,
Anchises, who holds in his arms the household gods. See Gruen, *Culture and National
Identity,* 13.

must now focus on the future, which will include joyous times, kingship, and a royal wife (*Aeneid* 2.779–84). Although Creüsa's prophecy provides enough geographical detail to preclude ambiguity, it is nonetheless sufficiently sugges-tive to allow Aeneas to persuade himself, at least for a brief time, that Dido might be the royal wife with whom happy times are foretold. Despite certain ambiguities in his personality, however, Virgil's hero is unambiguously charac-terized as brave and dutiful. Therefore, amidst the palpable threat of danger and uncertainty, Aeneas sets sail "uncertain in what manner the fates may lead or where it may be granted to settle" (*quo fata ferant, ubi sistere detur; Aeneid* 3.7). The long period of wanderings begins with Aeneas pictured at the head of a small fleet of ships, setting sail together with his father, son, comrades, and the great gods of the Penates.

From a thematic perspective, books 5 through 8 form the central section, or in George Duckworth's words, the "keystone section," of the epic,[46] the sec-tion that most dramatically and consistently points to the future and to Rome. Although book 5, which is devoted almost entirely to funeral games and is modeled on *Iliad* 23, is frequently dismissed as a dramatic interlude, it actually serves an important transitional function. As Michael Putnam has shown, the death of the helmsman Palinurus at the end of book 5 provides a fitting *inclu-sio* (enclosure) for the Odyssean wanderings of Aeneas and his followers, inas-much as a helmsman is also swept overboard at the outset of the narrative, dur-ing the storm of book 1.[47] At the same time, the funeral games serve as a symbolic prelude to the later books in two respects. On a dramatic level, the games anticipate the wars that will ensue once the Trojans reach Italy.[48] On a thematic level, the agonistic play of Trojan heroes serves as prelude to Virgil's presentation of the triumphs and tragedies of Roman history, particularly as they are depicted in the important prophetic tableaux of books 6 and 8.

Aeneas's trip to the Underworld—which comprises all of book 6 and the details of which were inspired by a number of sources, both Greek and Latin[49]—is nonetheless unique in its narrative purpose. In the first section, the

46. George E. Duckworth, *Structural Patterns and Proportions in Vergil's* Aeneid (Ann Arbor: Univ. of Michigan Press, 1962), 11.

47. Michael C. J. Putnam, *The Poetry of the* Aeneid (Ithaca: Cornell Univ. Press, 1965), 67–77.

48. Ibid., 66.

49. Orphic poems describing a descent into the Underworld date from the early fifth or even the sixth century BCE. Depictions of Elysium as the penultimate paradise can be traced back at least as far as Plato (*Phaedo* 114 B–C). Ennius's reference to the trans-migration of souls (*Annals* 15.5) indicates that Orphic and Pythagorean motifs had pen-etrated Latin literature long before Virgil's time.

journey (*katabasis*) through the various netherworld territories, Aeneas is confronted with the shades of people he has loved and who have suffered violent or tragic deaths during the siege of Troy and the early stages of the mission.

The more important second section takes place in and around Elysium. Passing through its blissful groves, Aeneas finally reaches the object of his journey: the meeting with his father, who has been empowered to impart to his son the divine revelation of a glorious Roman future. Anchises leads him to the river Lethe, where a huge crowd of worthy souls who have been cleansed of sin are waiting to drink the waters of forgetfulness and be reborn. They are to become the heroes and famous leaders of Roman history, and the guarantee of their future existence is the mission that Aeneas has been called by Fate to accomplish.

Mirroring the structure of the poem as a whole, the high point of this pageant of Roman heroes comes not at the end but in the middle. The pageant begins with the earliest kings of Alba Longa and reaches its climax with the birth of Romulus, the legendary founder of Rome. Immediately following him, interrupting the chronology, is Augustus Caesar, described as son of a god and the second founder of Rome, the leader destined to bring the return of the Golden Age and fated to extend his empire beyond the boundaries of the known world (*Aeneid* 6.792–96).

At this point the pageant resumes its chronological progression, listing other early Roman kings, who are followed by Brutus, the founder of the Republic. The progression again slips out of chronological order with an allusion to Caesar and Pompey, opposing leaders in the recent civil war. Finally, Virgil ends with a review of military leaders of the Republican era who won important victories for Rome in Greece and Africa. The pageant is concluded by one of the most famous passages of the poem:

[E]xcudent alii spirantia mollius aera,
(credo equidem), vivos ducent de marmore voltus,
orabunt causas melius, caelique meatus
describent radio et surgentia sidera dicent:
tu regere imperio populos, Romane, momento
(hae tibi erunt artes) pacisque imponere morem,
parcere subiectis et debellare superbos.

More pleasingly (I readily grant) will others hammer out vibrant bronze, will they draw lifelike features from marble; they will plead cases more eloquently; measuring with the rod the pathways of heaven and reporting the rising of stars: Be sure, Roman, that you guide the people with your power (for these will be your arts), to establish peace and order, to show mercy to the humbled and to subdue the proud.

Aeneid 6.847–53

Rather than just proclaim the coming power of Rome, Virgil has Anchises define how that power is to be exercised. It is to be exercised wisely, with restraint and compassion, thereby enabling Rome's subject peoples to contribute to, as well as to share in, the adornments of a common civilization. It is an idealistic vision of world reconciliation befitting the attendant eschatological claims of the return of the Golden Age. Moreover, although articulated in authoritarian terms, it is nevertheless a rather modest and humane statement of mission for a city and a people who are "blessed" (*Aeneid* 6.784), who are descended from gods (*Aeneid* 6.834), and who, at the time of Virgil's writing, were in fact on the verge of holding undisputed world power. Book 6 not only represents the high point of the divine prophecies pertaining to Rome, its glorious future dominion, and its stewardship of a restored Golden Age, but it also marks the close of the Odyssean half of the epic narrative. Aeneas's final resolve to obey the divine imperative, which has at last been clarified for him in the most wondrous and compelling terms, marks his definitive separation from the private concerns of an Odyssean world.

Book 7 begins with the momentary promise of the fulfillment of Creüsa's prophecy when, in response to an oracle, King Latinus welcomes Aeneas and promises him marriage to his daughter. The hope for the peaceful achievement of the mission is quickly dashed, however, when a still unreconciled Juno, aided by her hellish minion Allecto, inflames the Latin peoples with the mad desire for war. Amidst continued preparations for the unavoidable fighting that lies ahead, book 8 nonetheless brings to a triumphant resolution the poem's depiction of the ultimately glorious rise of Rome and the successful fulfillment of its central role in the divine plan of peace and reconciliation.

On advice from the river god Tiberinus, Aeneas searches for King Evander, who presides over an idyllic settlement of Arcadians on land that is to become the future site of the city of Rome. Virgil's depiction of Arcadia in its rustic poverty and simple piety is an intentional idealization of the values and traditions on which Rome was founded and which the nation should continue to revere and to emulate.[50] When Aeneas eventually finds King Evander, the latter is offering sacrifice to Hercules. Evander's explanation of this veneration is

---

50. Virgil's selection of Arcadia, the legendary refuge of the Achaeans of the heroic Mycenaean age, as the kingdom that forms the closest alliance with Aeneas is another element in his skillful appropriation of the Greek mythical past.

that Hercules had once saved his people from Cacus, a monster in semihuman form and the embodiment of evil that his Greek name (*Kakos*) implies. Virgil's point in narrating this etiological digression is that, although in primordial times Hercules had been able to rid Italy of this legendary monster, the evil that it embodied has now returned. The vicious cycle of wars that Juno has symbolically unleashed will continue more or less unabated until Augustus, as the new Hercules, brings the promise of lasting peace to the entire world through his victory at the battle of Actium.

It is not surprising, therefore, that a richly and dramatically evocative depiction of this battle occupies the center of the divinely crafted shield that Venus triumphantly presents to Aeneas at the close of this central section of the poem. The shield, with its series of symbolic tableaux, is Virgil's final synthesis of prophecy and history before the epic proceeds to its increasingly violent and somewhat disturbing conclusion. As with the prophetic pageant of heroes in book 6, the shield depicts a number of scenes chronicling Rome's early history. But the description of the battle of Actium dominates the shield to a far greater degree than the references to Augustus and his deeds received in the pageant prophecy. Indeed, the description of this one scene is longer than the descriptions of all the other shield scenes combined. It is clear that Virgil has taken great care to make it the unifying fulfillment of all the hopes and promised deliverances that have gone before.

At the shield's center, Virgil depicts Augustus Caesar in the stern of a ship, leading the fathers and people into battle. With him are the great gods of the Penates, and the scene is drawn in deliberate parallelism to the opening scene of book 3. Thus, the victory of Actium becomes the symbolic fulfillment of the quest begun with Aeneas's exile from Troy.[51]

Juxtaposed with this depiction of Augustus and the Roman people, Virgil places Mark Antony, accompanied by Cleopatra and all the impious and barbarous forces of the East (*Aeneid* 8.685–88). The scene is one of intense action and fierce fighting, in which the monstrous half-animal, half-human Egyptian god Anubis lashes out against the Olympian triad of Neptune, Venus, and Minerva (*Aeneid* 8.678–700), making the battle truly cosmic. The inclusion of the Furies and the exultation of Discordia, the fearsome goddess of civil strife, complete Virgil's pictorial description of total evil and of what, therefore, is at stake in Augustus's glorious triumph. By allusion and analogy, Augustus becomes the new Hercules, who, through his valor, has saved the world from the monstrous evil that threatened to destroy it.

---

51. Clausen, *Tradition of Hellenistic Poetry*, 83.

Finally, the shield depicts Augustus as dutiful to the gods in victory, dedicating three hundred shrines throughout Rome to their honor (*Aeneid* 8.716), even as he reviews the parade of conquered peoples who lay down their arms before him. With this *ex eventu* (after the fact) prophetic vision of eschatological fulfillment, the central section of the poem ends.[52] The burden of the defeats of the past, symbolized by Aeneas's lifting of Anchises onto his shoulders after the defeat of Troy (*Aeneid* 2. 707–8), is about to be replaced by the burden of the victories of the future, symbolized by Aeneas's lifting of the divine shield onto his shoulders. Memory is thereby transformed into hope, and this final scene of book 8 is the dramatization of the two in equipoise.[53]

WAR AND REVERSAL

Like a bomb left quietly ticking, Virgil sets all the elements of war and suffering in place in book 7, woven into the very core of the prophecies of Rome's future power and glory. Juno's wrath takes a more sinister turn when she summons the fury Allecto (*Aeneid* 7.323–39) to stir up the flames of war and madness. Like the demonic incendiary that she is, Allecto sets strategic brushfires among the Latin rulers and people. First, she sends her poisoning madness into the very bones of King Latinus's wife, Queen Amata, so that she will oppose the marriage of her daughter Lavinia to the Trojan intruder. Like Dido, Amata becomes a helpless pawn in Juno's schemes, and, like Dido, she is referred to as "accursed" (*infelix; Aeneid* 7.376).

Next, Allecto applies her poison to Turnus, the Rutilian king who had expected to marry Lavinia. Turnus then spreads the madness of war to the soldiers under his command. Allecto's work, however, is still not complete. Her final act is to stir up the hounds of Aeneas's young son Ascanius/Iulus, who has been out hunting with his friends. The hounds then lead the Trojan youths to the prize deer of the Tyrrhenians. When the deer is killed, fighting breaks out between another generation of Trojans and Latins. It remains only for Juno herself to burst open the gates of war (*Aeneid* 7.620–22).

The Iliadic half of the narrative has already been anticipated in the Sibyl's prophecy delivered at the beginning of book 6, just before she accompanied Aeneas to the Underworld:

---

52. Here the reader may note a certain degree of similarity between Virgil's description of the parade of conquered poeples laying down their arms before Augustus and the catalogue of nations who are depicted by Luke as being proselytized by the early church (Acts 2:9-10). For a detailed discussion, see chapter 4.

53. Pöschl, *Art of Virgil*, 36–38.

[B]ella, horrida bella . . . cerno. . .
allius Latio iam partus Achilles,
natus et ipse dea . . .
causa mali tanti coniunx iterum hospita Teucris
externique iterum thalami.

Wars, horrible wars . . . I see . . .
Even now another Achilles has been spawned in Latium, he, too, goddess-
born . . .
The cause of all this Trojan misfortune is again a foreign bride, again a foreign marriage.

Aeneid 6.86–94

Although this is arguably the most important of the ambiguous prophecies, it was not until the brief but incisive study of William S. Anderson that attention was drawn to its underlying significance. According to Anderson, Virgil presents as a dramatic reversal in fortune the battles that ensued as a result of Aeneas's efforts to found a city in Latium. They symbolize a new Trojan War in which those who were formerly beaten and humiliated are now transformed into the victorious conquerors. In the divine support for the establishment of the new city in Italy, the judgment of the gods that doomed Troy and threatened her race with oblivion has now been dramatically reversed.[54] The Iliadic allusions intensify, beginning in book 9. Building upon the ambiguity of the Sibyl's prophecy, it is Turnus who is initially identified with Achilles (*Aeneid* 9.742). Or, as Anderson points out, it is Turnus who sees *himself* as the new Achilles.[55]

In reality, however, Aeneas, not Turnus, will ultimately become the new Achilles, the one who (like Achilles) is goddess born, the one for whom (like Achilles) a divine shield has been made. Not until an exultant Turnus kills Pallas (son of the Arcadian king Evander and beloved ally of Aeneas) in a manner that closely parallels Hector's killing of Patroclus, however, does Aeneas begin to resemble the fierce warrior of Homer's *Iliad*.[56] When the true Achilles of Virgil's *Iliad* returns to battle, Turnus recognizes the ironic reversal and its tragic consequences for his own hopes. Like Hector, Turnus bravely and defiantly faces

---

54. William S. Anderson, "Virgil's Second *Iliad*," in *Oxford Readings in Virgil's* Aeneid, ed. S. J. Harrison (Oxford/New York: Oxford Univ. Press, 1990), 241.

55 Ibid., 246.

56. Clausen (*Tradition of Hellenistic Poetry,* 90) marks the change in Aeneas as having occurred somewhat earlier.

Aeneas in single combat, knowing already that the gods have abandoned him to his fate.

Prior to the final battle between Turnus and Aeneas, however, the sealing of Turnus's fate is ratified on Mount Olympus as part of the price of cosmic reconciliation, dramatized in the final dialogue between Jupiter and Juno (*Aeneid* 12.791–842). Jupiter confronts Juno and attempts to coerce her into giving up her spiteful resistance to what Fate has rendered inevitable. Although Juno reluctantly acquiesces, she extracts one last condition. When the Latin and Trojan peoples finally merge in peaceful union, the Trojan identity will be completely and irrevocably dissolved. Henceforth, the new people will bear the name, language, and customs of their common Latin land.

THE *AENEID* AS A PARADIGM AND INSPIRATION FOR LUKE-ACTS

At the conclusion of this résumé of Virgil's epic, one may note a number of literary motifs as well as stylistic and dramatic techniques that are employed in an analogous manner by the author of Luke-Acts, a correspondence lending credence to the contention that it may be more hermeneutically fruitful to treat this early Christian narrative as prose epic than as historiography. To begin with, there is the theme of divine mission in the form of a journey that will lead to the formation of a new people. In the *Aeneid* and, as will be shown, also in Luke-Acts, this theme is the central narrative thread around which the entire composition is organized. Other elements that define the unity of Virgil's composition and that will be shown subsequently to have corresponding functions in Luke's narrative are the basic structural divisions by which the work is divided into halves from a thematic perspective as well as segmented into thirds from a dramatic perspective.

In addition to these essential elements of composition, Virgil employs a number of literary and stylistic devices that also appear to have some relevance for the analysis of Luke-Acts. Among these is the creation of an opening scene that serves as a harbinger of the major obstacles of the narrative plot that the hero must meet and overcome (prelude to calamity). Also noteworthy is Virgil's skillful application of the stylistic device of divided action and interlacement. In addition to stylistic elements such as these, Virgil's strategic placement of divine guidance in the form of prophecy, vision, and oracle (elements of the supernatural that serve to enhance the suspenseful unfolding of the plot), and his ubiquitous use of divine messengers to aid or impede the progress of the human characters bear mentioning.

In the final segment of Virgil's epic, one additional dramatic device characteristic of Greco-Roman epic in general, used to perfection in the *Aeneid*, and extremely relevant to the composition of Luke-Acts becomes prominent. This is the skillful use of ambiguous prophecy as a means of imposing dramatic reversals to the anticipated fates of the major human participants. All of these components of Greco-Roman epic style that have emerged from the preceding analysis of the *Aeneid* will be discussed in further detail in chapters 4 and 5, which examine the structure and composition of Luke-Acts.

Thematically as well as stylistically, the above exposition points to a number of ways in which the *Aeneid* qualifies as a paradigm for Luke-Acts. At its core, Virgil's epic is suffused with religious meaning. It is the story of a defeated remnant called by Fate to journey to a new land, there to reconstitute its community with former enemies of foreign stock. Indeed, the Fates decreed the creation of a new people with a new name, whose role it would be to preside over the restoration of an eschatological Golden Age. The central theme of the poem is the divinely willed birth of Rome, whose future greatness is guaranteed by prophecy even before Aeneas has set out from Troy. And because Rome's rise has divine sanction and assurance, it may be checked temporarily (as Turnus and Dido wittingly or unwittingly try to do), but it cannot be stopped by mere human opposition.[57]

Although this theme of the divinely ordained growth of Roman *imperium* (dominion) was widespread in the literature of Augustus's reign, in no other work is it expressed with such artistic power, clarity, and religious overtones as it is in the *Aeneid*.[58] That Virgil continued to be the spokesman and prophet par excellence for this message is confirmed by the late-fourth- and early-fifth-century church father Augustine, who, in a sermon delivered after the fall of Rome in 410 CE, quoted Virgil dismissively, taunting his pagan descendants with their own failed prophecy.[59] Apparently, even in late antiquity, Christianity remained mindful of the once-great power of this rival gospel.

Although explaining Rome's rise in human history and its role in the cosmic order was the underlying purpose of the *Aeneid*, it was certainly not the

57. Williams, "The *Aeneid*," 76.

58. For example, Cicero, Livy, and Dionysius of Halicarnassus also make use of the theme, but they are just as likely to attribute it to natural or historical processes as they are to superhuman causes. Cicero *De re publica* 1.17.26–27; 2.5.10–6.11; 5.1.1. Livy *Ab urbe condita* 1.9.9; 1.30.1, passim; but see also, 1.16.6–7, passim; Dionysius of Halicarnassus *Roman Antiquities* 3.11.5–8.

59. Augustine *Sermon* 105.10, cited in N. M. Horsfall, "Virgil, History and the Roman Tradition," *Prudentia* 8.2 (1976): 74.

only one. The vatic task, which Virgil seems to have taken with utmost seriousness, was not only to define the nation's religious values, but also to provide a renewed moral vision for its citizens to emulate. The *Aeneid* contains numerous illustrations of Virgil's insinuation of morality tales into his narrative of the heroic prehistory of Rome. One notable example is his idyllic depiction of King Evander's primitive Arcadian realm (*Aeneid* 8.359–69). Here, the values of poverty, piety, simplicity, hospitality, and generosity are embodied in the good king, who befriends Aeneas and, through his son Pallas, joins in the Trojan cause.

Conversely, the qualities of greed and arrogance are singled out for opprobrium in the tales of the two valiant Trojans Nisus and Euryalus, the Latin warrior maid Camilla and, of course, Turnus and his killing of Pallas. Although all of these characters are portrayed as brave and indeed heroic, both Euryalus and Camilla become victims of their own greed, and they are killed when their judgment becomes clouded by an uncontrolled desire for spoils (*Aeneid* 9.359–62, 390–450; 11.778–835). Turnus does not die as an immediate consequence of his greed and arrogance, but the narrative voice assures the reader that death will ultimately come as a result of this reprehensible act (*Aeneid* 10.503–6). Virgil portrays the bitter fruits of impiety in a similar manner. The Latin chieftain Mezentius, who is characterized as "a scorner of the gods" (*contemptor deum; Aeneid* 7.647–48; 8.7), is overthrown by his people and subsequently killed by Aeneas (*Aeneid* 10.907–8).

Another purpose at work in the *Aeneid* is apologetic. Virgil has an interest in rehabilitating the Trojans and transforming them from victims into victors. Whereas in the *Iliad* the Trojans became a defeated people whose leader was killed by consent of the gods, in the latter books of the *Aeneid* there is a dramatic reversal. The surrogate Hector, with the help of the gods, manages to reverse the previous verdict of history; the once defeated Trojans, by merging into a new identity and a new people, are ultimately promised victory.

Yet, even though the subject was historical, Virgil's epic differed markedly from contemporary historiography, not only in its poetic form, but more importantly also in the selection and arrangement of its content, which was governed not by the historian's criteria of sources and traditions but by the artist's concern for cosmic universality as it is revealed in human particularity. In addition to the selection and arrangement of its thematic content, it is Virgil's skillful handling of narrative structures and his adherence to artistic principles of form, balance, and unity that most clearly demonstrate the *Aeneid*'s subordination of historical concerns to literary control.

As previous discussion in this chapter has illustrated, principles of balance, symmetry, and unity of form are carefully and subtly integrated in the *Aeneid's* narrative structure. One order of that structure is bipartite. In terms of the narrative plot, books 1 through 6 relate Aeneas's journey to the shores of Italy, relying on the narrative scheme of the *Odyssey* as their paradigm; following rather closely the model of the *Iliad*, books 7 through 12 relate the battles and other trials to be overcome after their arrival in Italy. Moreover, it is not merely the *content* (journeys versus trials) that suggests a bipartite scheme. Rather, specific features of the narrative structure suggest the author's careful and consistent use of parallelism and symmetry. For example, the journey of Aeneas from Troy to Latium is announced in the beginning of the poem (*Aeneid* 1.1–4), just as Aeneas's trials and victories after his arrival are alluded to in the following section (*Aeneid* 1.5–7). The bipartite division is also emphasized structurally by the invocation at the beginning of book 7 (lines 37–44) and by the parallel Juno speeches (*Aeneid* 1.37–49; 7.292–322).[60]

Into this basic bipartite division, however, Virgil has also woven a tripartite structure. In terms of the development of the poem's central themes, the climax comes in the middle rather than at the end. This tripartite division of the epic has as its keystone section books 5 through 8, the books featuring Rome and Augustus. Books 1 through 4 and 9 through 12, which depict Aeneas's struggles with Dido and Turnus respectively, emphasize the obstacles that must be met and overcome in order for the mission to reach its ultimately successful conclusion.

This tripartite scheme also receives support from the way in which the narrative has been structured. There are four major passages that refer to events far ahead of the story line, and they are distributed symmetrically according to the tripartite scheme (*Aeneid* 1.257–96; 6.756–866; 8.626–728; 12.791–842). Furthermore, the opening section of book 1, which anticipates the dominant themes of the two halves, also alludes to the tripartite construction in the following ways. First, the mention of Carthage (*Aeneid* 1.13–22) prefigures the tragedy of Dido and the later hostility between the two nations. Thus, the theme of Rome and Carthage stands both at the beginning and at the end of the first segment of the poem. Second, the prophecy of Jupiter (*Aeneid* 1.257–96) anticipates the central segment, in that Jupiter alludes to Rome's destiny and to Augustus as the initiator of a new age of peace. With respect to the third and final segment, Jupiter's mention of the enchainment of *furor impius* (godless fury; *Aeneid* 1.294–96) anticipates Aeneas's victory over

60. Duckworth, *Structural Patterns*, 11.

Mezentius (*Aeneid* 10.896–908) and his final victory over Turnus (*Aeneid* 12.887–952).[61]

Finally, although the narrative focuses on the remote prehistory of Rome's mythical past, the *Aeneid* nevertheless achieves, in N. M. Horsfall's words, "a coherent interpretation of the whole course of Roman history, an interpretation that constitutes, in large measure, the poem's very meaning and purpose."[62] Although some modern critics believe that Virgil's historical judgment is ultimately negative, even they do not question that his aim was to use artistic technique and the power of epic drama to interpret Rome's history uniquely and definitively. In the judgment of Wendell Clausen, for example, "it is Virgil's perception of Roman history as a long Pyrrhic victory of the human spirit" that makes him Rome's truest historian.[63] Despite its pessimistic evaluation of the poet's message, Clausen's affirmation of Virgil as Rome's most authentic and profound historian forms a fitting conclusion to this brief survey of Virgil's epic and its potential significance as a paradigm for Luke-Acts.

61. Ibid., 11.
62. Horsfall, "Virgil, History and the Roman Tradition," 74.
63. Wendell Clausen, "An Interpretation of the *Aeneid*," *HSCP* 68 (1964): 143, 146.

3

FIRST-CENTURY ADAPTATIONS OF VIRGILIAN EPIC

PROMULGATING THE MYTH AND MESSAGE OF THE *AENEID*

Even during his lifetime, Virgil was regarded as Rome's greatest living poet, not only by other writers but also by the general public.[1] Very early he became a model author for grammarians and rhetors, and throughout antiquity his poems comprised one of the most widely used school texts.[2] In the first century CE, Virgil remained the premier Latin author,[3] as witnessed by the flood of minor poetic imitations of his style written during this period.[4] Furthermore, evidence that the *Aeneid* had penetrated deeply into popular culture is to be found on the walls of excavated Pompeii, where some of its verses can still be seen, etched on the surfaces. Indeed, in that city alone there remain some twenty examples of the popular quotation of Virgilian phrases.[5] As William Harris has observed, "the *Aeneid* shows every sign of having been genuinely famous."[6]

---

1. Suetonius *Vita Vergili* 3 records the charming tale of Virgil's mother's dream that she gave birth to a laurel branch which, once it touched earth, took root and grew instantly (*ilico*) into a full-grown tree, covered with fruits and flowers of various kinds.

2. For the early use of Virgil by grammarians, see Clifford H. Moore, "Latin Exercises from a Greek Schoolroom," *CP* 19 (1924): 325, nn. 4–6. For the continuing use of Virgil as a teaching aid, see Bruno Rochette, "Les traductions grecques de l'Énéide sur papyrus," *LEC* 58 (1990): 333–46.

3. Despite the preference of Seneca and his circle for Ovid.

4. See, for example, Wendell V. Clausen, ed., *Appendix Vergiliana,* Scriptorum classicorum bibliotheca oxoniensis (Oxford: Clarendon, 1966).

5. Marcello Gigante, *Civiltà delle forme letterarie nell'antica Pompei* (Naples: Bibliopolis, 1979), cited in William V. Harris, *Ancient Literacy* (Cambridge, Mass.: Harvard Univ. Press, 1989), 261.

6. Harris, *Ancient Literacy,* 261.

Virgil's fame rested on far more than the refinement of his grammar or the artistic purity of his style. At Augustus's behest, the poet had created a powerful and appealing foundational myth for the new Principate, Rome's first, greatest, and only lasting salvation history.[7] The *Aeneid* incorporated earlier myths of Venus, the fall of Troy, and the wanderings of Aeneas into a profoundly new epic of national origins and eschatological promise in which not only the future rule of the Julian house but the whole history of Rome was portrayed as one of heroic struggle, culminating in predestined triumph and universal salvation. According to Paul Zanker, Virgil's immediate and widespread fame attests to the profound degree to which Romans identified with the foundational story that he created.[8]

Moreover, throughout his reign Augustus astutely exploited this popular identification by seeing that the *Aeneid's* prophetic message and imagery were echoed in imperial architecture and iconography. The monument that most fully expresses Augustus's continued promotion of Rome's national myth is the *forum Augusti*. In the temple dedicated to Mars Ultor, which is located in the center of the eastern end of the forum, a variety of related deities and divinized heroes were also honored. In the *cella* (inner room of the temple), Mars was flanked by the goddess Venus and the divinized Julius Caesar. Statues of Romulus, Fortuna, and Roma joined Venus and Mars in the *pronaos* (vestibule, antechamber). A representation of Aeneas, depicted fleeing from Troy with his father, son, and the Penates, was flanked by representations of the kings of Alba Longa and by the *gens Iulii* (members of the Julian house) in wall tableaux which lined the north exedra of the forum. In the south exedra, Romulus, the son of Mars, depicted as a *triumphator,* was flanked by representations honoring the *summi viri*, the military heroes of Rome's early history.[9]

The juxtaposition of Aeneas and Romulus in the north and south exedrae of the *forum Augusti* is also repeated in the reliefs on the front side of another major monument of Augustan Rome, the *ara pacis* (Altar of Peace). But whereas the surviving reliefs and wall paintings from the *forum Augusti* indicate that there the emphasis was on the exemplary deeds of the founding heroes, in the *ara pacis* reliefs, Aeneas and Romulus are depicted in scenes celebrating the guid-

---

7. Inasmuch as it is "a history of God and his activity directed toward the salvation of his chosen people." This definition is taken from Dennis C. Duling and Norman Perrin, *The New Testament: Proclamation and Parenesis, Myth and History,* 3rd ed. (New York: Harcourt Brace, 1994), 358.

8. Paul Zanker, *The Power of Images in the Age of Augustus,* Jerome Lectures 16 (1988; reprint, Ann Arbor: Univ. of Michigan Press, 1990), 192–94.

9. Ibid., 194, 201, 210. The inspiration for the parade of *summi viri* (military heroes of Rome's early history) was *Aeneid* 6.756–885.

ance of divine providence. In the case of Romulus, the altar depicts the traditional scene of the infant twins being suckled by the she-wolf. As for Aeneas, the altar depicts his arrival in Latium. The guidance of providence is emphasized in that Aeneas is shown beneath an oak tree, with a sow and her piglets, as had been prophesied in Virgil's epic.[10] Another aspect of Augustus's exploitation of the symbols and images of the newly elaborated national myth was his lavish attention to the cult of Vesta. After he became Pontifex Maximus in 12 BCE, he built a sanctuary to the goddess. Thereafter, when Augustus, the descendant of Aeneas, conducted a sacrifice in front of the *templum Vestae* (Temple of Vesta), wherein the Palladium was appropriately honored, it became a symbolic reenactment of Aeneas's rescuing of the Penates and the Palladium. Indeed, as Zanker remarks, "Augustus *had* in fact rescued the images of the gods—from neglect and oblivion."[11]

Augustus's careful orchestration of the symbols of the ideals and achievements of his reign was primarily designed to silence any lingering opposition to his rule and to enhance the spiritual and cultural cohesion of the Italian provinces. Nevertheless, it is probable, if not inevitable, that echoes of the new mythology also resounded in cities far distant from Rome's center. It is well known, for example, that even in republican times statute law and even senatorial decrees were frequently publicized in bilingual translation throughout the major cities under Roman hegemony. After the establishment of the Principate, imperial edicts, letters, and decrees were also frequently placed in public view.[12] Moreover, the politically astute Augustus was quick to implement these publicity techniques for purposes of propaganda and public relations. Thus, he stipulated that after his death, the complete text of his *Res Gestae* be reproduced in bilingual translation on bronze tablets and placed in public view throughout the major cities of the empire. Although this sort of publication was an exceptional gesture, coins were an everyday means by which words and images celebrating various aspects of imperial rule were promoted throughout the provinces.

It is against this social and cultural background that one should consider the probability of the promulgation of the myth and message of Virgil's *Aeneid*. That first-century Roman authors were known and read throughout the empire is a virtual certainty. Poets from Horace to Martial exult in the knowledge that their works are being read in the farthest reaches of the civilized world.[13] Indeed,

---

10. Ibid., 203; cf. *Aeneid* 3.390; 8.84.
11. Zanker, *Power of Images,* 207.
12. Harris, *Ancient Literacy,* 206–7.
13. Horace *Carmina* 2.20.13–20; Martial *Epigrammata* 7.88; 11.3.

in Rome, and probably also in the major provincial cities, public readings of the more famous or popular works were a common form of cultural entertainment.[14] Furthermore, there is little doubt that among even those moderately cultivated inhabitants of the empire who considered themselves "Roman," the *Aeneid* was known virtually by heart.[15]

Nevertheless, it must be acknowledged that although most educated Romans read Greek, far fewer educated Greeks knew Latin. Plutarch's professed lack of proficiency, although probably an exaggeration, is generally cited as typical of upper-class Greek attitudes toward the relative unimportance of Roman culture.[16] Rome, for its part, never compelled its Greek subjects to learn Latin.[17] Indeed, it readily accommodated Greek sentiment by promulgating its administrative and public relations gestures in the Greek language, as well as in the Greek cultural idiom.

Although the most striking example of this accommodation to the autonomy of Greek language and culture is the Greek imperial coinage, bilingual imperial correspondence offers another important example. Imperial secretaries, who were frequently Greek slaves or freedmen in the emperor's household, were responsible for translating the emperor's correspondence to cities or private individuals in the Greek-speaking areas of the empire. Indeed, it was in his capacity as correspondence secretary for the mid-first-century emperor Claudius that the powerful and influential freedman C. Iulius Polybius composed a Greek translation of Virgil's poetry in Greek prose.[18]

How widespread the publication of such a translation may have been is uncertain, but it is likely that it was intended primarily for use in the major cities of the empire—cosmopolitan cities such as Corinth, Ephesus, Antioch, and Alexandria.[19] Moreover, indirect knowledge of the major themes and story

14. See, for example, Plutarch *Moralia* 711a–713f; Pliny *Epistulae* 1.15.2; cited in Harris, *Ancient Literacy*, 226.

15. Tacitus *Dialogus* 13.2. "This is vouched for by the letters of Augustus, and by the behavior of the citizens themselves; for on hearing a quotation from Virgil in the course of a theatrical performance, they rose to their feet *en masse* and paid homage to Virgil, who was there watching, just as they would have [paid homage to] Augustus."

16. Plutarch *Life of Demosthenes* 2.2–3.

17. Although Greeks who wished to become Roman citizens were expected to speak and read Latin, it is doubtful that this requirement was rigorously enforced, especially by the end of the first century CE.

18. In addition to the Seneca citations noted in chapter 1, see Johannes Irmscher, "Vergil in der griechischen Antike," *Klio* 67 (1985): 281–82.

19. Harris (*Ancient Literacy*, 274) cites the more than five thousand known inscriptions from Ephesus as evidence of that city's high degree of literacy and cultivation.

of the *Aeneid* would have been considerably more well known, inasmuch as the promise of eschatological fulfillment during the reign of Augustus coincided with the vision of peaceful empire.

FROM AUGUSTUS TO VESPASIAN: LUCAN'S *DE BELLO CIVILI*

Not all of the later Latin epics sought to celebrate the political and religious claims made for Rome in the *Aeneid*. On the contrary, some imitated Virgil in order to refute the equation of Augustan imperial rule with the will of heaven, an equation made famous by Virgil's epic. Nevertheless, this promise of the imminent return of the Golden Age had seemed on the verge of fulfillment in the earliest years of the Principate. The reign of Augustus was long, generally peaceful, and spectacularly successful. Although some historians and literary critics demur, most would agree with David Stockton that the vast majority of inhabitants, both Romans and provincials, "welcomed the peace and stability, material prosperity, and increased administrative efficiency which came with the [Augustan] Principate."[20]

Furthermore, Augustus's personal style was immensely popular, particularly in Rome and throughout Italy. Although he had incorporated into the new imperial culture the sophistication and refinement of Greek artistic and aesthetic standards, his reign was characterized predominantly by the return, at least on a symbolic level, to revered Roman ancestral values. The skeptic's suspicion that these values actually reflected pious memory or even poetic fiction is essentially irrelevant. What matters is that the Augustan program of "regeneration and progress"[21] made the promotion of these values a central concern of the Roman state. Indeed, *pietas* was both the hallmark of Augustan propaganda and the focus of Augustan achievement, because it was only through faithful acts of *pietas* (devotion to the gods and to country) that the continued favor of the gods would be ensured. This favor meant, above all else, the blessings of a lasting peace.

That Augustus was greatly successful in personifying for the nation the values of courage, duty, modesty, simplicity, and *pietas* is attested abundantly by

20. David Stockton, "The Founding of the Empire," in *The Roman World,* ed. J. Boardman, J. Griffen, and O. Murray, Oxford History of the Classical World (Oxford: Oxford Univ. Press, 1988), 129.

21. Ibid., 137.

Suetonius's depiction of his reign.[22] Indeed, it is a tribute to Augustus's superb tact and keen political insight that he was able to maintain a firm but subtle distinction, identifying the role of *princeps* (first citizen, leader; in effect, emperor) with the embodiment of these archaic virtues, while at the same time insisting on, and in every way advancing, the power, majesty, and dominion of the Roman state. This delicate balance between personal modesty and imperial majesty is perhaps best exemplified in the studied contrast between the relative simplicity of Augustus's private residence on the Palatine and the magnificence of the public buildings that he erected and restored, chiefly in Rome but also throughout the empire.

Despite his revival of archaic and perhaps mythical republican virtues, however, Augustus did not, and probably could not, restore republican liberty. Indeed, the very essence of his political achievement lay in his successful elimination of all plausible avenues of opposition. The negative implications of this tactical success were already visible in the last years of his reign, with, for example, his exercise of harsh censorship measures against what he deemed to be undesirable literature.[23] Although it would not become apparent until some years later, Ronald Syme is no doubt correct in suggesting that the seeds of the fall of the Julio-Claudian dynasty were laid by Augustus himself.[24]

The reigns of Tiberius, Gaius, and Claudius each have their own distinct character, Claudius's being the most successful and popular of the three and Gaius's being by far the most disastrous. Nevertheless, what they all share is a complete turning away from the Augustan ideal of the *princeps* as exemplary citizen and virtual embodiment of the values and aspirations of the Roman people. It was, however, the reign of Nero that threatened to reduce the legacy of Augustus to ashes. After a brief period of stable rule supervised by the wise counsel of Seneca and Burrus, Nero plunged the capital into a reign of murder, intrigue, ruinous extravagance, corruption, and decadence. The most dramatic symbol of Nero's complete inversion of the Augustan model of the role of the *princeps* was his conversion to his own private use of some four hundred acres of centrally located city land, formerly occupied by temples, public buildings, and densely populated private dwellings recently destroyed by fire. Rather than restoring this valuable land to public use, Nero claimed the space for an

---

22. Suetonius *Divus Augustus* 17.2–3; 20 (courage); 33.1–3; 98.5; 101 (duty); 51.1; 86.1 (modesty); 79.1; 86.2 (simplicity); 23.2; 29.1–5; 31; 52; 93 (*pietas* [devotion to the gods and to country]).

23. Ronald Syme, *The Roman Revolution* (1939; reprint, Oxford: Oxford Univ. Press, 1992), 487–88.

24. Ibid., 507.

immense and extravagantly appointed private palace, the so-called golden house.

It was during Nero's decadent and demoralizing reign that the first post-Virgilian epic was written. The wealthy scion of a senatorial family and only twenty-six years old when he died an enemy of the state, M. Annaeus Lucanus had begun his literary career just a few years before as one of Nero's most promising protégés.[25] Owing to the tragic circumstances of the poet's forced suicide, the *De bello civili* was never completed. Even in its unfinished state, however, the epic is a bitter indictment of the Julio-Claudian legacy as perceived by the poet, namely, an insatiable and willfully destructive lust for power. The opening lines of the poem reveal that Lucan intends his work as almost a mirror reversal of Virgil's inspiring tale of *virtus* (courage) and *pietas*:

Bella . . . plus quam civilia
. . . iusque datum sceleri . . .

Wars . . . more [horrible] than civil
. . . and legality granted to crime . . .
De bello civili 1.1–2

As has frequently been observed, Lucan's *De bello civili*, like Virgil's *Aeneid*, is structured around a series of prophecies. But whereas the *Aeneid's* prophecies reveal Rome's divinely ordained dominion, the prophecies of the *De bello civili* foretell only impending ruin.[26] Moreover, Virgil's emphasis on the guiding role of divine *fatum* (Fate) is completely denied in Lucan's epic tale of social, political, and spiritual disintegration.

Lucan's *De bello civili,* which eschews mythology, selects for its subject the civil war of the mid–first century BCE, in which Julius Caesar and his former son-in-law Pompey are contending for the right to rule Rome. Since Caesar is this anti-Virgilian poem's antihero, the personification of unrestrained fury, his ultimate victory symbolizes "the triumph of those irrational forces that in the *Aeneid* had been curbed and defeated."[27] In his powerful, if technically flawed, poem, Lucan transfers to the founder of the Julio-Claudian dynasty—

---

25. Indeed, *De bello civili* contains a panegyric to the emperor (1.33–66) in which the last four lines implicitly set forth Nero's role as patron. Lucan's praise of Nero as the guarantor of the *pax Augusta* (lines 33–45) takes on a decidedly ironic cast, however, when placed within the context of the epic's castigation of the Julio-Claudian's role in Roman history. See Mark Morford, "Nero's Patronage and Participation in Literature and the Arts," *ANRW* 2.32.3 (1985): 2010–14.

26. Gian Biagio Conte, *Latin Literature: A History* (Baltimore: Johns Hopkins Univ. Press, 1994), 446.

27. Ibid., 447.

Julius Caesar himself—his bitterness and disillusionment with the dynasty's last representative, the ruthless and devious emperor Nero. By implication, therefore, the dynastic succession of Augustus and all of the Julio-Claudians who were heirs to his power becomes a kind of negative salvation history in which the Roman people move ever closer to disintegration and ruin, under the malevolent guidance of a hostile Fortune.

Although Lucan did not live to see it, he probably would not have been surprised to learn that the exalted Julio-Claudian house, born in violence, also ended in violence, inasmuch as Nero was forced to commit suicide and Rome was once again immersed in a period of lawlessness and civil war. The rebellion against Nero's rule was initiated and concluded within the top ranks of his own governing circle.[28] The struggle for supreme power that took place in 68–69 CE,[29] therefore, bore certain similarities to the struggle for power that had occurred in the wake of Julius Caesar's death just over a century before. Although Vespasian was a more able and accomplished general than the young Octavian had been, like Octavian, Vespasian ultimately prevailed over his rivals because of his adroit mastery of the crucial levers of power and his extremely skillful manipulation of public opinion. In December of 69, Vespasian was formally declared emperor by the Roman senate. "Finally, the Flavian family took over and secured the imperium, which, with the usurpation and fall of three emperors, for a long time had been irresolute and almost without direction" (Rebellione trium principum et caede incertum diu et quasi vagum imperium suscepit firmavitque tandem gens Flavia).[30]

With these words, which begin his biography of Vespasian, Suetonius attests to the similarity of circumstances between Vespasian's assumption of power and that of Octavian nearly a century before. Although the period of civil wars from which the latter had emerged victorious was much longer, it was in some respects no more traumatic. Indeed, it is probably no exaggeration to suggest that in the years 68–69 CE, "the Principate had come close to disintegra-

28. Vindex and Galba were both governors and commanders of Roman legions in Gaul and Spain respectively. Otho had been appointed by Nero as military governor of Lusitania (Portugal) in 58. Vitellius was appointed military governor of Lower Germany by Galba in 68; Vespasian, as is generally known, was appointed military governor of Judaea earlier in 68, while Nero was still emperor. Some sources assert that Vespasian was appointed governor of Judaea in 67. See Stockton, "Founding of the Empire," 147.

29. The year 69 CE is known as "the year of the four emperors" because Galba, Otho, Vitellius, and Vespasian, each in succession, wore the purple during that one turbulent year.

30. Suetonius *Divus Vespasianus* 1.1.

tion at its very core."[31] Thus Vespasian, as Augustus before him, was welcomed by a populace longing for the restoration of peace, order, and some measure of security. Vespasian, for his part, encouraged and, through many elements of his propaganda, actively fostered identification of his reign with that of his illustrious predecessor.

LITERATURE AND IDEOLOGY UNDER VESPASIAN, TITUS, AND DOMITIAN

Without doubt the restoration of peace became a cornerstone of Vespasian's propaganda, just as it had been for Augustus. Not only did he erect the *templum pacis* as the Flavian counterpart to the *forum Augusti*, but he even concerned himself with small symbolic gestures, such as his reclosing of the doors of the Janus temple.[32] Moreover, Vespasian deliberately fostered the perception of close identity with the early Principate by reproducing Augustan coin types featuring the battle of Actium, the Augustan annexation of Egypt, and the restoration of the Republic of 27 BCE.[33]

Another key element of Augustan propaganda had been its cultivation of the prestige of the Julio-Claudian family. Toward that end, Augustus had promoted the divinization of his adoptive father, Julius Caesar, and the glorification of his ancestors, whose origins were traced back to the mythical founding hero Aeneas and, through him, to the goddess Venus. In the *Aeneid*, divine *fatum* is depicted as guiding the continuity and glory of Roman history, from its inauspicious origins out of the ashes of Troy all the way to its culmination in the reign of Augustus. Augustus's reign, therefore, had been depicted as the end and goal of Fate's plan, the beginning of the restoration of the primeval Golden Age, a new paradisial era that would continue into the indefinite future, *imperium sine fine* (*Aeneid* 1.279).

Because of the disastrous reigns of the later Julio-Claudians, however, it would not have been prudent for Vespasian to emphasize the arrival of the *aureum saeculum* (Golden Age) under Augustus, much less imply its continuation under his unworthy successors.[34] Early Flavian propaganda, therefore,

---

31. Brian W. Jones, *The Emperor Titus* (New York: St. Martin's, 1984), 77.

32. Tacitus *Fragmenta historiarum* 4–5; Kenneth Scott, *The Imperial Cult under the Flavians* (1936; reprint, New York: Arno, 1975), 25.

33. Niels Hannestad, *Roman Art and Imperial Policy* (Aarhus: Aarhus Univ. Press, 1988), 121.

34. The theme of the *aureum saeculum* had been further sullied by Nero's clumsy appropriation of it in his own propaganda efforts.

attempted to strike a delicate balance between emulating Augustus but disavowing the finality of his achievements. Indeed, in later Flavian epic, the
national hope of eternal peace and blessedness, which in the *Aeneid* had been
prophesied for the Augustan present, has receded into the undisclosed future.
Vespasian's substitution of the theme of *Roma resurgens* (Rome rising),[35] however, marks his renewed emphasis on the promotion of Augustan social values,
particularly *virtus* and *pietas*. Indeed, although peace and prosperity were important symbols of Flavian rule, as they had once been hallmarks of Augustan rule,
Flavian propaganda also emphasized the heroic deeds of the new dynasty.
These achievements, rather than noble birth, were the bases of its claim to
legitimacy.

Although it appears that with respect to the arts and literature—as with
nearly everything else—Vespasian sought to emulate Augustan policies of modesty and restraint,[36] Vespasian's elder son and successor, Titus, gives every indication of at least having tolerated, if not actually having encouraged, the obse-
quious flattery of those seeking literary fame.[37] Nevertheless, it is Vespasian's
younger son Domitian who is most identified with actively promoting this sort
of court flattery. Even in the case of Domitian, however, it was not merely a
desire for flattery. As will become apparent in the discussion that follows, the
literature of Domitian's reign was produced either directly or indirectly in
response to the emperor's well-orchestrated public relations campaign, a campaign designed to promote his claim to replace Augustus as Aeneas's true heir,
the Roman leader designated by the gods to usher in the long-awaited return
of the Golden Age. One of the literary works produced either during or
immediately following Domitian's reign was, of course, the early Christian
narrative known as Luke-Acts.

The favorable climate for a renewal of significant literary production, which
Vespasian had initiated by a variety of grants and administrative measures
designed to bring intellectual pursuits under the aegis of the imperial estab-

35. Silvie Franchet d'Espérey, "Vespasien, Titus et la littérature," *ANRW* 2.32.5 (1986):
3054.

36. Yet, prior to attaining the *imperium* (supreme power), Vespasian seems to have
been most cunning and resourceful in promoting a variety of blatantly self-serving propaganda initiatives. The extensive accounts of divine healing miracles, prophecies, and
omens reported in Josephus and Suetonius are derived from earlier sources that give
every indication of having originated within Vespasian's own inner circle. See d'Espèrey,
"Vespasien, Titus et la littérature," 3068–69. See also Scott, *Imperial Cult under the
Flavians*, 16.

37. See, for example Martial *Epigrammata* (book 1, *De spectaculis*) 20 (17); 34 (30); compare Pliny the Elder *Naturalis historia* praefatio 11.

lishment,[38] began bearing political fruit during the brief reign of Titus, when a hitherto unknown poet published the first of what were to be many books of epigrams. Martial's first collection of epigrams was entitled *De spectaculis* because it was published in 80 CE, in celebration of the opening of the recently completed Flavian amphitheater. These witty epigrams were apparently the proper mixture of the profound and the profane, thus establishing their immediate and widespread popularity. This fact, in addition to Martial's inclusion of scattered praise for the Flavian dynasty and some gratuitous flattery for the reigning emperor, prompted Titus to reward the parvenu poet by granting him equestrian status. It also assured Martial a valued place in the Flavian *clientelia*.[39]

It was, however, under Titus's brother Domitian that Martial wrote the majority of the remaining thirteen books of his epigrams, and it was for this last Flavian emperor that Martial became a primary literary spokesman. That Domitian both read Martial's epigrams and had them recited at court functions is immodestly acknowledged by the poet himself (*Epigrammata* 6.64.15; 7.99.4). These mutually reciprocal favors of allegiance and flattery on the part of the client and promotion and protection on the part of the patron had a long and honored history across the broad spectrum of literary patronage, pertaining equally to the relationship between the wealthy and influential private patrons and their talented literary clients or "friends."[40] In the relationship between the emperor and his court poets, however, much more was at stake. These poets were not engaged simply, or even primarily, in idle flattery. Rather, they were expected to promote in the public imagination the important ideals and images of the emperor's reign, as the emperor himself clearly defined or inchoately expressed them. In this sense, their literary products were as integral a segment of the emperor's public relations effort as were the coin types and architectural adornment that he commissioned and funded.

For his part, Martial clearly viewed his labors on behalf of the emperor as extensive and valuable—indeed, as glittering accomplishments for which he should have been generously rewarded—even as he perceived Virgil to have been rewarded by Maecenas (*Epigrammata* 8.55[56]). Although Martial's literary self-promotion seems rather impudent and audacious to the modern

38. D'Espérey, "Vespasien, Titus et la littérature," 3052–56.

39. J. P. Sullivan, *Martial: The Unexpected Classic* (Cambridge: Cambridge Univ. Press, 1991), 130.

40. See Peter White, "Amicitia and the Profession of Poetry in Early Imperial Rome," *JRomS* 68 (1978): 74–92.

reader, a perusal of his writings amply illustrates the multiple facets of Domitian's propaganda that the poet carefully integrated and scattered throughout the many books of his popular writings.[41]

In addition to literary praises for Domitian's benefactions, as well as for his legislative, administrative, and military accomplishments, Martial and Statius (an equally important poet in Domitian's service)[42] labored to create the image of the emperor as especially beloved of the gods, as Hercules incarnate, indeed as Jupiter's chosen representative on earth.[43] Although by the late first century pious assertions that a given emperor was specially favored by the gods was a well-worn theme in Roman imperial literature, it is one that Domitian endeavored to exploit fully. Minerva is depicted as Domitian's patron deity and special confidante (*Epigrammata* 5.2.6–8; 6.10.9–12; 9.3.10); Apollo speaks to him directly (Statius, *Silvae* 5.1.14); and he is beloved by the gods (Statius, *Silvae* 1.4.4).

Martial's younger contemporary Statius had begun to achieve fame and recognition even prior to his incorporation into court life. Apparently, it was his public recitation of portions of his first epic poem, the *Thebaid*, that brought his talent to the attention of the emperor.[44] Probably even before this poem's completion, however, Statius became closely involved with the interests of the emperor and his governing circle. It was in this later situation, between 92 and 95 CE, that he completed and edited for publication the first four of five books

---

41. Domitian is praised as a great warrior and commander of his troops (*Epigrammata* 7.1; 7.2; 7.5; 7.6; 7.8; 8.65); his patron deities are promoted and their special relationship to the emperor duly noted (*Epigrammata* 8.1; 8.39); his legislative programs and moral reforms are heralded (*Epigrammata* 6.2; 6.4; 9.5[6]; 9.7); and the emperor's generosity and *pietas* are emphasized in the scattered references to his completion and restoration of numerous temples and other public buildings (*Epigrammata* 5.7; 5.19; 6.4). Although in all of these instances Martial has clearly exaggerated the importance of Domitian's personal role, and often the merit of the achievement, most of these subjects of praise do correspond to actual accomplishments of Domitian's reign. And, at least with respect to Domitian's building achievements, effusive praise may have been justified, inasmuch as Domitian is generally recognized as Rome's most important benefactor since Augustus. See Sullivan, *Martial*, 149; *Martial: Epigrammata*, LCL, vol. 2, ed. D. R. Shackleton Bailey (Cambridge, Mass.: Harvard Univ. Press, 1993), 237, n. f; see also, Scott, *Imperial Cult under the Flavians*, 90.

42. Brian W. Jones, *The Emperor Domitian* (London: Routledge, 1992), 24–28.

43. Long ago Franz Sauter (*Der römische Kaiserkult bei Martial und Statius* [Stuttgart, Ger.: Kohlhammer, 1935], esp. 19–31) collected an extensive list of references in Martial and Statius that either imply or explicitly state these and a variety of other imperial claims.

44. Statius *Thebaid* 12.814.

of occasional poems, the *Silvae*. Although these books contain some older material, taken as a unity this collection clearly reflects Statius's new position as court poet.

Perhaps the most important complex of themes developed in this group of poems devoted to the emperor and published within what was to be the last full year of his reign was the portrayal of Domitian not merely as one greater than Augustus but, indeed, as the definitive successor and heir to Aeneas himself. As such, Domitian becomes the true harbinger of the earnestly desired but thus far illusory *aureum saeculum*. In his brief but audacious emendation of Virgil's prophecy regarding Augustus (*Aeneid* 6.792–93), Statius deliberately evokes the mythical and metaphorical language of his Augustan model (*Silvae* 4.1.5–8; 4.2.1–2; 4.3.114–17). Against this backdrop he sets forth some of Domitian's significant accomplishments.[45]

All of this, however, is mere prelude to the poet's central concern, which is set forth at length in the last of this series of Domitianic poems placed at the beginning of book 4 of the *Silvae*. This particular poem was written to mark the completion of the *Via Domitiana*, a new highway built in 95 CE in order to improve travel between Sinuessa and Naples. The poet uses this occasion to make a very significant claim for the emperor, a claim that Statius places—as had Virgil before him—in the mouth of the Sibyl of Cumae.

> . . . hic est deus, hunc iubet beatis
> pro se Iuppiter imperare terris;
> quo non dignior has subit habenas,
> ex quo me duce praescios Averni
> Aeneas avide futura quaerens
> lucos et penetravit et reliquit.

> Before you is a god, at Jupiter's command
> he rules the blessed world for him;
> None worthier than he has taken up these reigns
> since, with my guidance,
> Aeneas, eagerly inquiring into the future,

---

45. Statius presents Domitian's record seventeen-year dominance of the office of consul as a major triumph, contrasting it favorably with the mere thirteen years in which Augustus permitted himself to hold this office (*Silvae* 4.1.31–32). Moreover, the poet claims that Domitian has surpassed Augustus in providing the people with competent and comprehensive administration of justice, in restoring the abundance of the land long denied, in reforming public moral standards, and in erecting and restoring temples for the gods (*Silvae* 4.3.9–19).

penetrated Avernus' prescient groves
and [then] went forth.

Silvae 4.3.128–33

Here again the omission of Augustus is deliberate, emphasizing Domitian's desire to replace his revered predecessor as the worthiest and most divinely favored descendant of Aeneas. In an effort to further emphasize the complete replacement of Augustus by Domitian as the favorite of the gods, Statius has the Sibyl observe that whereas Augustus had been accorded access to the divine oracles only indirectly,[46] she had been authorized to impart her knowledge to Domitian face-to-face (*Silvae* 4.3.139–44).

Within the opening segment of the last book of Statius's poetry published during his lifetime, the poet presents the current emperor not merely as the worthy successor to the widely revered Augustus, as had been the goal of earlier Flavian propaganda, but as the worthy successor of Aeneas himself and, therefore, as the living symbol of Rome's divine election and the guarantor of its destiny. Thus, it would appear that the poetic efforts to portray Domitian as Hercules incarnate and as Jupiter's representative on earth were not merely the excessive pretensions of the emperor's overinflated ego, as is frequently supposed, but indeed were disparate elements of a well-orchestrated imperial campaign directed toward one fundamental propaganda goal: reviving and redirecting the powerful coalescence of myth and history, which had been dramatically formulated by Virgil and subsequently promoted by Augustus.[47] Whereas the earlier Flavian emperors had been content with evoking the memory of Augustus's popular and successful reign, the extremely ambitious Domitian sought to acquire for himself the mystique and the glory of having inaugurated a unique eschatological moment of Roman history, a moment that hitherto had been unequivocally identified with the triumphal reign of Augustus.

STATIUS'S *THEBAID:*
PESSIMISTIC REJOINDER TO VIRGILIAN PROPHECY

That the re-creation and appropriation of Virgilian salvation history was indeed a central focus of Domitianic propaganda is also suggested by the corresponding flood of new epics begun just before or during his reign, each of which in different ways and to varying degrees responds to Virgilian themes and chal-

---

46. That is, under the auspices of Apollo and through the mediation of his priests, in whose temple the *Sibylline Oracles* had been placed.

47. See Zanker, *Power of Images*, 193–95, passim.

lenges Virgilian solutions. The enduring popularity and, indeed, the reverence in which the great epic of the Augustan period was held probably made it inevitable that when the historical circumstances of the Flavian era produced a somewhat analogous political milieu, epic poetry would again appear perforce.

Written by authors of disparate ages and circumstances, two epics were completed during the reign of Domitian. The third, although possibly begun just prior to the emperor's accession, remained incomplete at the time of the author's death, late in Domitian's reign.[48] None of these authors succeeded in capturing, and in some cases did not even desire to capture, the spirit or the style of the *Aeneid;* nevertheless, each has written a work that in some respect presents an overt and intentional response to Virgil's seminal epic narrative. Moreover, although only one[49] was historical with respect to its subject, all three comprised subtle commentaries on recent historical events and on the ideological claims of the Flavian emperors.

Of the three epic poets of this later Flavian period, Statius is generally considered to have been the most talented and, therefore, the most important. The *Thebaid* was published in the early nineties,[50] before Statius, as established court poet, began editing and publishing his occasional poems. Begun perhaps as early as the final years of Vespasian's reign,[51] the *Thebaid*, which took some twelve years to complete, drew its narrative inspiration from an ancient tale of Greek mythology. In order to write his reflection on the evils of the Julio-Claudian house and the ensuing wars from which Vespasian had ultimately emerged, Statius chose for his epic's story line the ancient Theban legend recounting the fall of a doomed dynasty—the house of Oedipus—and the destruction and devastation that are inevitably unleashed in its wake.

---

48. A fourth epic, Statius's *Achilleid*, begun late in Domitian's reign, will not be discussed because what has come down to us is too preliminary and incomplete to provide a sound basis for analysis.

49. Silius Italicus's *Punica*.

50. According to D. W. T. Vessey ("Flavian Epic," in *Latin Literature*, vol. 2 of *Cambridge History of Classical Literature*, ed. E. J. Kenney and W. V. Clausen [Cambridge: Cambridge Univ. Press, 1982], 561), the epic was published in 90–91 CE; according to Conte (*Latin Literature*, 481), the year of publication was probably 92.

51. In these early years, Statius spent much of his time in and around Naples, an area where Greek culture still mingled closely with Latin. Moreover, Virgil was buried near Naples, and Statius writes of visiting Virgil's tomb for solace and inspiration (*Silvae* 4.4.53–55). Statius, however, did not wish to imitate Virgil slavishly, but rather to be a new Virgil for his own particular time and place (*Thebaid* 1.1–3; 12.816–17). And, indeed, most critics agree that intellectually and stylistically his work is more reminiscent of Lucan or Ovid than it is of Virgil. On this last point, see D. W. T. Vessey, *Statius and the* Thebaid (Cambridge: Cambridge Univ. Press, 1973), 11.

The salient elements of Statius's version of this ancient tale may be summarized briefly as follows. The aged Oedipus summons the Furies of the Underworld to persecute the royal house of Thebes. Oedipus's two sons, Eteocles and Polyneices, are to be given alternate turns governing the kingdom, an arrangement, as becomes readily apparent, that is utterly impossible to fulfill. Eteocles assumes power, and Polyneices is driven from the kingdom. Polyneices goes to Argos and is recognized by the aged Argive king, Adrastus, as the stranger destined to marry one of his two daughters, whereupon Adrastus's other son-in-law, Tydeus, is sent to Thebes in order to claim the throne on behalf of his new brother-in-law, Polyneices. When Eteocles refuses to yield to reason, Argos wages war against Thebes, and seven heroes (Adrastus, Polyneices, Tydeus, Campaneus, Parthenopaeus, Hippomedon, and Amphiaraius) march on the city with their troops.

The ensuing battle produces untold carnage on both sides, which is finally brought to an end when the two rival brothers kill each other in a duel. The severely decimated Argive army withdraws, with King Adrastus as the only survivor of the original seven heroes. Creon becomes the new king of Thebes and is quickly revealed to be as evil a tyrant as Eteocles had been, even forbidding burial of the enemy corpses. Finally, however, after the Argive and Theban women travel to the sacred altar of Clementia in Athens, Theseus, king of Athens, intervenes and restores justice and piety to Thebes.

Structurally, as Gian Biagio Conte observes, the *Thebaid* is closely imitative of the *Aeneid*.[52] It is composed of twelve books, divided into two equal halves. The second half of the *Thebaid*, like the second half of the *Aeneid*, is an Iliadic story of war. The first half, which, like the first half of the *Aeneid*, features Odyssean wanderings, also contains a catalogue of armies, scenes from the Underworld, and a lengthy description of funeral games. Moreover, like Virgil, Statius uses myth to suggest by analogy an interpretation of recent Roman history that is particularly compatible with contemporary imperial propaganda. The fall of the once distinguished but now corrupt house of Thebes, and the attendant devastation and civil war visited upon the city, could not help but evoke in its Roman audiences memories of the recent extinction of the Julio-Claudian line as a result of the excesses of Caligula and, most recently, Nero. It was the violent death of this last Julio-Claudian emperor that brought in its wake the civil wars of 68–69 CE. Indeed, Theseus, the outsider who restores peace and justice to Thebes and who is depicted by Statius as a Roman gen-

52. Conte, *Latin Literature*, 485.

eral in triumphal parade accompanied by his Amazon captives,[53] is clearly drawn so as to complement a centerpiece of Flavian propaganda: the Jerusalem triumph and Vespasian's subsequent restoration of peace and prosperity to a war-weary capital.

Yet, for all of these superficial similarities between the *Aeneid* and the *Thebaid*, it is fundamentally true that Statius, like Lucan, is not merely post-Virgilian but is indeed anti-Virgilian.[54] Not simply is his artistic sensibility less restrained and less classical than Virgil's,[55] but, more importantly, the historical issues of legitimacy and power had been so very different for Augustus than they had become for Vespasian and his heirs. In order to remove the image of himself as a usurper of power, Augustus had been pleased to accept the pious fiction of the Julian family as descended from Venus, whose association with Rome through the Trojan hero Aeneas predated the city's founding by Romulus.[56]

It was Virgil's genius to incorporate this foundational myth within a cosmic drama in which the establishment of Rome in the legendary past and the restoration of the idealized Golden Age in the poetic future are inextricably linked by the grand design of divine Fate. The eschatological fulfillment of Fate's providential plan, as proclaimed in the *Aeneid's ex eventu* prophecy (prophecy after the fact), is designated as unfolding in the historic present of Augustus's reign. Thus, in Virgil, Jupiter (the master of *fatum*) is the stern but ultimately benign ruler of a universe in which the Roman people and their history are the instruments of his divine restoration of lasting cosmic justice and order.

The historical situation of the Flavians was quite different, and its political and philosophical difficulties are subtly reflected in Statius's development of his legendary material. Just as the *Aeneid* had served to create the halo of divine sanction for the Julian house, the *Thebaid*, by analogy, appears to destroy it or, at the very least, to curtail it seriously, thereby giving justification to its supplanting by the *gens Flavia*. In the *Thebaid*, the ruling house of Oedipus has become so riddled with sin and corruption that Jupiter decides it must be destroyed root and branch, so that divine order and justice can be restored (*Thebaid* 1.214–47).

53. Frederick M. Ahl, "Statius' 'Thebaid': A Reconsideration," *ANRW* 2.32.5 (1986): 2893. See also, Vessey, *Statius and the* Thebaid, 312.

54. Vessey, *Statius and the* Thebaid, 11.

55. H. Bardon, "Le goût à l'époque des Flaviens," *Latomus* 21 (1962): 741.

56. Frederick Ahl, "The Rider and the Horse: Politics and Power in Roman Poetry from Horace to Statius," *ANRW* 2.32.1 (1984): 47.

Moreover, in the *Thebaid,* as was the case in Lucan's *De bello civili,* Fate is essentially a malevolent force. In a mirror reversal of Virgilian logic, the fulfillment of prophecy begins with hope but ultimately ends with destruction and doom.[57] Indeed, with respect to the *Thebaid,* it might be said that "Augustan propaganda is turned against itself."[58] The house of Oedipus is a dark parallel to the Julio-Claudian imperial house. Again by analogical comparison, the dawn of the fabled Golden Age, which is the hope and the promise of the *Aeneid,* is transformed retrospectively in the *Thebaid* into the dawn of an era of venality and corruption. Even though the epic ends on the positive note of Theseus's restoration, the themes and images pervasive throughout most of the poem are unrelentingly dark and destructive. Even in the epic's optimistic denouement, there is no renewed promise of a Golden Age, only the assurance of peace and clemency. Evidently, the early Statius limited his poetic hopes to the more restrained viewpoint of early Flavian propaganda.

In a curious epilogue, the poet prays that his work will receive lasting fame and honor, not as a rival to the divine *Aeneid,* but as a worthy sequel (*Thebaid* 12.816–17). Inasmuch, however, as the *Thebaid* presents a rival and largely negative view of the meaning of Roman history in the grand design of Fate, Statius failed to achieve his stated objective. The task of providing a Flavian sequel to the eschatological promise of the *Aeneid* fell, unfortunately, to lesser poets.

VALERIUS FLACCUS'S *ARGONAUTICA:* REVISING AUGUSTAN ESCHATOLOGY

Although Valerius Flaccus died in the early nineties[59] before completing his epic,[60] was generally ignored by subsequent generations, and is frequently disparaged by modern critics,[61] the *Argonautica*—written from a late-first-century

---

57. For example, King Adrastus's welcoming of the stranger Polyneices, in pious recognition of prophecy, begins well enough with an uncontested marriage, but nevertheless leads ultimately to disaster, not only for his realm, but also for Thebes. In the *Aeneid,* on the other hand, King Latinus's welcoming of Aeneas begins with a contested marriage and war but ultimately leads to the formation of a new people.

58. Ahl ("Rider and the Horse," 63), however, said this with respect to Ovid.

59. From Quintilian *Institutio oratoria* 10.1.90, it can be inferred that Valerius Flaccus died shortly before 92 CE.

60. Nearly eight books are completed of what appears to have been a twelve-book structural scheme.

61. Vessey's remark ("Flavian Epic," 585) that Valerius is "a Virgil without *ingenium* [genius]" is fairly representative of the poet's reputation among modern literary critics.

perspective—is nonetheless of considerable importance as a literary parallel to the *Aeneid*. With the exception of the date of his death, however, virtually nothing is known about Valerius, beyond the possible clues that his unfinished work, the *Argonautica*, supplies.[62]

Even if the precise date of the beginning of the *Argonautica* is in doubt, however, the temporal perspective of the poet's opening address would still seem to indicate that Valerius was writing during the early period of Domitian's reign. In the eight books that have been preserved, Valarius narrates the circumstances that impel Jason to undertake his quest in search of the Golden Fleece, the *Argo*'s adventure-filled journey to Colchis, the intrigues and hostilities encountered at the court of King Aeetes, and the love that is kindled for Jason in the heart of the king's younger daughter, Medea. Although, therefore, Valerius does follow the essential outline of the ancient legend previously poeticized in the Hellenistic epic of Apollonius Rhodius, he has completely transformed the sophisticated skepticism of his Callimachean predecessor into an edifying encomium on the struggles and rewards of heroic *virtus*. Jason and his companions are consistently portrayed as demigods and heroes, whose adventures and struggles appear to have been deliberately expanded by the author in order that these mythological and heroic Roman prototypes might exhibit their courage and superior merit to the fullest.

This Flavian poet's interest, however, goes well beyond merely presenting an edifying moral tale. Indeed, he has given the poem's legendary theme a contemporary political relevance by incorporating into the proem praise for the now deified Vespasian, who is celebrated as the one who opened up the Caledonian Ocean,[63] thereby inviting a flattering comparison of the achieve-

---

However, there appears to be an effort on the part of some recent studies to credit Valerius Flaccus with a hitherto unobserved subtlety and cynicism reminiscent of the Callimachean disciple Apollonius Rhodius. See, for example, Martha M. Malamud and Donald T. McGuire Jr., "Flavian Variant: Myth. Valerius' *Argonautica*," in *Roman Epic*, ed. A. J. Boyle (London: Routledge, 1993), 192–217.

62. On the basis of the poet's opening invocation to the Sibyl of Cumae and a subsequent allusion to the bath of Cybele (*Argonautica* 8.239–41), it has been argued that Valerius may have been a member of an exclusive college of priests, the *Quindecemviri sacris faciundis,* which, if true, would necessitate his having held at least equestrian rank. The only other biographical clues provided by the text occur in the proem and concern the question of when and under what circumstances Valerius undertook the writing of his epic. Unfortunately, scholars continue to differ widely as to precisely what these clues imply. For further discussion of this issue, see appendix B.

63. A claim that refers to Vespasian's successful role in command of a legion in the invasion of Britain during the reign of Claudius. For the collection of citations indi-

ments of the legendary Jason and his heroic companions with those of the late emperor and his progeny.[64] Furthermore, as in the opening poems of the fourth book of Statius's *Silvae*, in which Domitian is portrayed as one greater than Augustus and the true heir of the legendary Aeneas, Valerius presents Vespasian's military achievement in deliberate contrast with Julius Caesar's failure (*Argonautica* 1.7–9). Thus, by implication, the emperor and his successors become the true heirs of the heroes and demigods of the legendary *Argo*.

Another element worthy of comment is Valerius's introduction of the theme of civil war, a theme wholly absent from Apollonius's Hellenistic version of the legend. Here again, the poet's interest appears to coincide with an important theme in Flavian propaganda. The legend *Roma resurgens*, which appeared on Flavian coinage and celebrated a new Flavian era marked by a regeneration of traditional Roman values and renewed prosperity, also implied that the certitude of Roman ascendancy and destiny is demonstrated in its having overcome adversity, rather than through an eternal condition of peace and tranquillity. In contrast to the *Thebaid,* therefore, the theme of civil war is treated apologetically in the *Argonautica*, becoming almost a benign element in Fate's plan. The battles that take place within Aeetes's kingdom do not overwhelm the protagonists. Rather, they merely serve as additional obstacles enabling the heroes to temper their spirits and prove their valor.

By poetic analogy, Valerius depicts the legendary heroes of the *Argo* as distant precursors of the Flavian emperors who, through their battles and triumphs, are also redefining the boundaries of the civilized world. His work is, therefore, a serious attempt to transpose Virgil's masterful exposition of a national salvation history into a new metaphorical language that will be more meaningful for the late-first-century empire. Like the *Aeneid* (and in contrast with the *Thebaid*), the *Argonautica* of Valerius Flaccus seeks to place Rome at the center of a saving history with cosmic dimensions. Jupiter's response to a worried Sol (*Argonautica* 1.498–593) is drawn in careful parallelism to Jupiter's response to a troubled Venus (*Aeneid* 1.257–79). In speeches placed in the opening books of both epics, Jupiter is the guarantor of a grand design in which the Roman people ultimately emerge as the lasting rulers of a just and peaceful world order.

---

cating that this claim was part of Vespasian's earliest propaganda, see Arnaldo Momigliano, "Panegyricus Messellae and 'Panegyricus Vespasiani,'" *JRomS* 40 (1950): 39–42.

64. Philip R. Hardie, *The Epic Successors of Virgil: A Study in the Dynamics of a Tradition* (Cambridge: Cambridge Univ. Press, 1993), 83.

The *Aeneid* views cosmic history from a perspective in which Saturn's paradisial reign has receded into the distant past. The purpose and fervently anticipated goal toward which its poetic prophecy points is the restoration of this idyllic condition, manifested in human history in the reign of Augustus. In the Flavian epic of Valerius Flaccus, however, it would no longer serve to have history's goal accomplished in the Augustan past, especially since the intervening years from Tiberius to Vespasian and his successors had not always been idyllic. Perhaps for this reason, Valerius begins his epic at the very outset of Jupiter's reign. Jupiter himself, who had gained supremacy over the world by defeating Titans and Giants, becomes the model and prototype for an indefinite age of heroic endeavor in which the overcoming of obstacles is the path to glory outlined by destiny. In this revision of Virgil's eschatological timetable, the focus of human history shifts from a restoration of paradisial peace to the emulation of Jupiter's heroic achievements. Jason and the Argonauts and, by poetic extension, Vespasian and his successors, overcome numerous obstacles on their journey to the stars. Thus, although its message is partially obscured by the medium of Archaic Greek legend, Valerius Flaccus's epic represents a serious effort on the part of this late-first-century Latin writer to reassess the meaning of the divine promises to Rome within an altered framework of time and history.

SILIUS ITALICUS'S *PUNICA*: HISTORICAL EXTENSION OF VIRGILIAN MYTHOLOGY

If little is known about the author of the *Argonautica*, this is not the case for the author of the *Punica*, the last important Latin epic successor to the *Aeneid*. T. Catius Silius Italicus (ca. 25–100 CE), although not a particularly talented poet, apparently was a man of some wealth and importance. He had been politically active during the reigns of three emperors: Nero, Vitellius, and Vespasian. Indeed, he had been consul in 68, witness to and participant in the civil and military turbulence of 69, governor of the province of Asia during Vespasian's reign, and, for many years, a prominent forensic orator.[65] It was not, however, until he had retired from public life that he began work on his lengthy epic,[66] a project that probably consumed most of the last twenty years of his life. Thus, at least with respect to Silius, it can be assumed that mere flattery or the

---

65. The primary references for Silius's life and career include the following: Martial *Epigrammata* 6.64.9; 7.63.7–8; Pliny *Epistulae* 3.7; Tacitus *Historiae* 3.65.2.

66. Although it has come down to us in seventeen books, many critics assume that the author had originally intended eighteen.

enhancement of the emperor's public image was not the primary concern of the author.[67]

In contrast to both the *Thebaid* and the *Argonautica,* the theme of the *Punica* is historical rather than mythological. It is a narrative account of what Livy had called Rome's most memorable war,[68] the Second Punic War (218–201 BCE), beginning with Hannibal's attack on Saguntum, highlighting the heroic efforts and bitter struggles surrounding the Roman defeat at Cannae as well as Hannibal's retreat from the walls of Rome, and ending with Rome's glorious victory at Zama.[69]

If it is evident that Silius relied extensively on Livy for historical detail and on Ennius for his annalistic paradigm,[70] it is equally clear that he is most indebted to Virgil. Not only is the *Punica* steeped in Virgilian parallels and allusions,[71] but its entire historical situation is presented as the inevitable outcome of the mythical events narrated in the *Aeneid*. In particular, it is Dido's curse called down upon Aeneas and his descendants (*Aeneid* 4.622–29), rather than historical issues of *Realpolitik*, that is presented as the root cause of Hannibal's relentless pursuit of Rome. Indeed, it has been observed that whereas Virgil historicized myth, Silius has mythologized history.[72] While this distinction is essentially true, both epics—albeit with widely diverging levels of skill and artistry—were written with the intention of probing Roman his-

67. On the other hand, it would probably be naive to assume that such considerations were wholly absent.

68. Livy *Ab urbe condita* 21.1.

69. One of the most important recent critics of the *Punica* has argued that the circumstances attending the Roman defeat at Cannae are the dramatic core of the epic. He interprets Cannae as "at one and the same time the high-water mark and the low ebb of Rome's fortunes," inasmuch as her people never came closer to annihilation nor ever achieved greater heroism (Frederick Ahl, Martha Davis, and Arthur Pomeroy, "Silius Italicus," *ANRW* 2.32.4 [1986]: 2505). Because Ahl believes that the theme of noble defeat is central to the poem, he asserts that the *Punica's* most important structural division is tripartite, with books 8–10, which treat the battle of Cannae and its immediate aftermath, forming the keystone (ibid.; see also, 2508–9). From a structural perspective, however, the epic falls just as neatly into halves, the first half ending on the eve of disaster at Cannae (book 8) and the second half, reversing the results of the first half, ending with the victory at Zama. This latter structural division makes the Flavian theme of *Roma resurgens* (Rome rising) the central concern of the epic.

70. For further parallels between Ennius and Flavian poets, see William J. Dominik, "From Greece to Rome: Ennius'*Annales*," in *Roman Epic*, ed. Boyle, 48–50.

71. For example, *Punica* 1.81–122; 2.395–457; 13.650–53, 719–23, passim.

72. Marcus Wilson, "Flavian Variant: History. Silius' *Punica*," in *Roman Epic*, ed. Boyle, 218.

tory's underlying meaning and investing historical events with the weight of cosmic significance.[73]

The epic genre is exceedingly tolerant of the blurring of boundaries that normally define and limit history, boundaries that close off the present from the future and the past, as well as the mortal from the immortal world.[74] In the *Punica*, as is the case in the *Aeneid*, both of these aspects of dramatic freedom are explored extensively. Although the historical drama takes place in the comparatively recent past, in Silius's epic it becomes, nevertheless, the narrative point where gods and heroes still meet. Thus, it is the goddess Juno who arranges the appointments of important military commanders such as Flamininus and Minucius (*Punica* 4.708–10; 7.511–24), just as it is Jupiter who aids in the crucial selection of Scipio (*Punica* 15.143–47). Indeed, the gods themselves insist on the preservation of Rome (*Punica* 12.707–11), even as it was they who willed the destruction of Troy (*Aeneid* 2.589–623).[75] Conversely, all of the important mortal protagonists are depicted as approaching heroic stature with respect to virtue and accomplishment, and every significant Roman leader is described in terms approaching divinity (*Punica* 7.19, 49; 10.308; 12.278; 14.680).[76] Even the collective protagonist—the Roman senate—meeting to consider action over Saguntum "matches the gods in virtue" (*aequantem superos virtute senatum; Punica* 6.11); and Hannibal, the poem's superhuman antihero, rivals the accomplishments of Hercules (*Punica* 4.4–5).

Because of its rather anachronistic mingling of mythological deities in the narration of recent history, it is frequently suggested that the *Punica* was written for a limited audience of those who happened to share Silius's antiquarian interests and that the poet makes no significant attempt to relate his version of the past to the wider concerns of a contemporary Flavian audience.[77] This assumption, however, ignores the rather suggestive literary parallels with contemporary leaders, which the author insinuates into his descriptions of the

---

73. Indeed, it is this particular characteristic of contemporary Roman epic that provides the most fundamental hermeneutical correspondence between the methods and intentions of its authors and the methods and apparent intentions of the author of Luke-Acts.

74. Wilson, "Flavian Variant," 229–30.

75. This parallelism is noted by Ahl et al., "Silius Italicus," 2500.

76. See Wilson, "Flavian Variant," 227.

77. Carlo Santini, *Silius Italicus and His View of the Past* (Amsterdam: Gieben, 1991), 8. See also, Conte, *Latin Literature*, 491–92; Albrecht Dihle, *Greek and Latin Literature of the Roman Empire: From Augustus to Justinian*, trans. Manfred Malzahn (London/New York: Routledge, 1994), 176.

leading characters.[78] For Silius, the Second Punic War is the crucible of adversity and triumph out of which the heroic qualities of the Roman people reemerge after years of inactivity and obscurity (*Punica* 3.575–90). These republican heroes are depicted as Romans who are truly worthy to be called successors of the founding hero, Aeneas (hence they are repeatedly referred to as "the Aeneadae").

As has previously been noted, epic tends to diminish the importance not only of spatial barriers but also of temporal distinctions. Whereas history generally views events retrospectively, epic has the dramatic means to determine events prospectively as well. Thus the *Aeneid* can bridge the temporal distance between the time of the story line and the time of Augustus by employing divine omens and prophecies. In the *Punica*, time has been refined one step further. The story line is positioned along a temporal continuum that extends into the past all the way back to the time of Aeneas, even as it extends into the narrative future to the time of the author and his audience.[79] From a narrative perspective, the time of the Second Punic War represents the center of time, that

78. For example, Silius's portrait of the republican hero Fabius Maximus Verrucosus, whose caution and concern for the well-being of Rome transcended his desire for personal glory, contains elements that bring to mind some of the character traits and propaganda claims associated with Vespasian (*Punica* 7.217–52). Moreover, just as Virgil's protagonist, Aeneas, resembled more than one contemporary Roman leader (for example, *Aeneid* 4.261–64, in which Aeneas resembles the Mark Antony of Augustan propaganda), Silius's depiction of Scipio takes on different colorings in different dramatic settings and situations. Often he resembles Aeneas, whose reputation for *pietas* he shares and perhaps surpasses. (Like Aeneas, Scipio is reputed to have saved his father's life in the stress of war [Livy *Ab urbe condita* 21.46; *Punica* 4.62–71].) But just as Silius's hero, Scipio, by means of his resemblance to Aeneas, creates a link with the legendary past, so also is he used by the poet to suggest other parallels. Thus, for example, in the final scene of the last book, a victorious Scipio rides in triumphal procession (*Punica* 17.625–54). He is depicted as a worthy successor to Bacchus and to Hercules, as well as a worthy offspring of Jupiter. In his regal garb and youthful splendor, however, preceded by captives of the peoples he has subdued, he also resembles Titus, as he is depicted in Josephus's narration of the Jerusalem triumph (*Bellum Iudaicum* 7.132–57) and on the reliefs of Titus's triumphal arch. Indeed, this portrait of Scipio may be intended to serve as an idealization of all the Flavian emperors, whom Silius extols elsewhere in the *Punica* as the worthy successors to the heroes of the republican past (*Punica* 3.594–611).

79. The *Punica*'s utilization of time in the recent historical past as a means of joining the legendary world of Aeneas with the immediate world of contemporary Rome certainly provides an apt parallel for Luke's unique portrayal of the apostolic mission, the literary means by which Luke joins the remote events narrated in the early chapters of the Gospel to the late-first-century Greco-Roman world of Luke's audience.

is, the time of the rebirth, growth, and spread of the heroic spirit throughout the Roman people (*Punica* 12.306–19) as well as their collective acceptance of the burden of destiny.

In his concern over the visibly corrupting effects of wealth and leisure on the national character, and in his desire to urge the Roman people to remain worthy of their destiny and the Roman emperors to be worthy of future divinity, Silius Italicus was interested in addressing the fundamental social and political issues of his times. To that end, he endeavored to write an inspiring and edifying account of a time in the relatively recent past, when gods still spoke directly with human beings and mortals could still transcend the limitations of their common humanity to perform extraordinary deeds—not for themselves, but for Rome, its mission, and its destiny.

THE LEGACY OF LATIN EPIC AND ITS RELEVANCE FOR LUKE-ACTS

Virgil's *Aeneid* was Rome's great foundational epic and its only lasting salvation history. Because of the poet's superb artistic skills and keen insight into the human condition, the *Aeneid* did and does speak for all generations. Inasmuch, however, as it pointed to a specific historical era—the Augustan era—as the goal and end of history, it could not continue to speak to the specific hopes and fears of future generations. Therefore, despite the widespread popularity and reverence in which the *Aeneid* continued to be held by Roman citizens throughout the empire, it was perhaps inevitable that it would be amended by subsequent writers from a variety of social, political, and philosophical perspectives.

Probably as a response to Nero's abusive rule, Lucan's *De bello civili* sought to overturn the *Aeneid*'s hold on the national imagination by calling into question its fundamental assumptions of Julio-Claudian legitimacy and national mission. Statius's *Thebaid*, in its effort to establish the new legitimacy of Flavian rule, inadvertently accomplished nearly the same results. In differing ways, however, both Valerius Flaccus and Silius Italicus endeavored to build upon the political and religious claims first introduced by the *Aeneid,* each continuing to view Romans as Fate's chosen people. Perhaps as a subtle rejection of Domitian's new dynastic assertions, however, both sought to replace the *Aeneid*'s realized eschatology by narrating stories in which history again points to an open-ended future.

Whereas the *Thebaid* is perhaps best understood as a literary response to historical and ideological issues raised by early Flavian propaganda, the *Argonautica* and especially the *Punica* appear to be, at least in part, responses to Domitian's bold attempt to appropriate for himself Augustan eschatology and the material and symbolic trappings of the *aureum saeculum* mythology. Although these poets primarily addressed a Roman audience, the definition of that term had broadened considerably during the course of the first hundred years of the Principate. Consequently, Domitian's appropriation of the trappings of Augustan salvation history and his obsessive concern with the orchestration and promulgation of the literary and iconographical elements of this powerful ideological claim may well have provoked epic responses beyond the immediate walls of the capital city. Thus, it is by no means impossible that a relatively literate Pauline Christian residing in Rome or in a cosmopolitan provincial city such as Ephesus, Corinth, Antioch, or Philippi, where Christianity was beginning to attract increasing numbers of pagan converts, decided to recast his community's sacred traditions in a style and manner that would make the Christian claim a powerful and appealing rival to the ubiquitous and potentially seductive salvation claims of imperial Rome.

4

THE DRAMATIC UNFOLDING OF PROPHECY AND HISTORY IN LUKE-ACTS

LUKE'S ROLE IN THE DEVELOPMENT OF EARLY CHRISTIAN TRADITIONS

While in no way seeking to undermine the veracity and authority of the early Christian tradition on which previous narratives such as that of Mark were based, Luke nonetheless begins his own writing with a hint of dissatisfaction with the work of his predecessors.[1] Indeed, Luke's desire to assure a smooth transition from Israel's scriptural past to the rapidly emerging gentile Christianity of his own time merely emphasizes the pivotal role that the Lukan community played in a process of interpretive development that had been under way for some time.

Because, like Rome, the early church had no glorious antiquity to which it could lay exclusive claim, from the beginning it had sought to place Jesus within the context of the sacred narratives of Israel's past: Israel's own national epic, broadly defined.[2] The original community for which Israelite epic had gradually been compiled and eventually canonized was the southern kingdom of Judah, which alone survived after the destruction of the northern kingdom in the eighth century BCE. The southern kingdom was the self-proclaimed heir to the collective traditions and name of Israel, and already by the end of

---

1. Ἐπειδήπερ (Luke 1:1) is probably best translated "Although." While acknowledging the efforts of previous narrators, Luke nevertheless finds the need to offer his own account to the reader; cf. François Bovon, *L'Évangile selon Saint Luc 1–9*, CNT 3a (Geneva: Labor et Fides, 1991), 36–37; Joseph A. Fitzmyer, *The Gospel According to Luke*, vol. 1 (Garden City, N.Y.: Doubleday, 1981), 290; Gregory E. Sterling, *Historiography and Self-Definition: Josephos, Luke-Acts, and the Apologetic Historiography* (Leiden: E. J. Brill, 1992), 343.

2. See the discussion in chapter 1.

the seventh century its cult was centered exclusively in Jerusalem and its temple. Even war, destruction, and captivity did not diminish the importance of the civic and religious ideal of the Jerusalem temple state within Israelite society.

The Hellenistic period, however, brought grave new challenges both to the Jerusalem temple and to the religious identity of Israelite society. One challenge centered on Samaria. After its destruction by Alexander the Great and its subsequent refounding as a Greek colony, devout Samaritans built their own temple on Mt. Gerizim, near the Samaritan city of Shechem. Although this rival to the Jerusalem temple was subsequently destroyed by the Hasmonaean ruler John Hyrcanus late in the first century BCE, there was another internal challenge that proved much more difficult for the Jerusalmem establishment to fend off.

Probably already by the third century BCE,[3] the seductive but ultimately corrupting influence of Hellenism had begun to create severe divisions within Israelite society, divisions that led to confrontations between royal court and temple and that were invariably resolved in favor of the royal court. Although the Maccabean War (167–164 BCE) was heralded in court propaganda as a great victory for the restoration of the sanctity of the temple,[4] in fact, the Hasmonean rulers only sullied its reputation further by naming themselves to the high priesthood.[5] With Rome's conquest of Jerusalem in 63 BCE and the subsequent restoration of Hyrcanus II to the high priesthood, the temple's preeminence in Israel's civic life was once more reaffirmed, but at a very high price.[6]

The result of this long history of political brokering was that, although the Jerusalem temple remained the center of the national cult and of civic life, the religious ideal of the temple state had been seriously compromised. A further

---

3. Elias J. Bickerman, *The Jews in the Greek Age* (Cambridge, Mass./London: Harvard Univ. Press, 1988), 69–80.

4. See, for example, 1 Maccabees.

5 As a result of this action on the part of Jonathan and Simon, the younger brothers of Judas Maccabeus, it is believed that the Zadokite priest, known only as the Righteous Teacher, together with a group of like-minded followers, established a sectarian community on the shores of the Dead Sea. See Geza Vermes, *The Dead Sea Scrolls: Qumran in Perspective* (Philadelphia: Fortress Press, 1977), 137–42. For a more complete evaluation of the events of this period in the light of the power politics of the Hellenistic rulers, see Peter Green, *Alexander to Actium: The Historical Evolution of the Hellenistic Age* (Berkeley: Univ. of California Press, 1990), 497–524.

6. E. Mary Smallwood, *The Jews Under Roman Rule: From Pompey to Diocletian*, 2d ed. Studies in Judaism in Late Antiquity 20 (Leiden: E. J. Brill, 1981), 21–43.

result of the undermining of this foundational communal ideal was that it led to the reinterpretation of Israel's scriptures from a variety of new social, political, and religious perspectives. The *Book of Jubilees,* the *Sibylline Oracles,*[7] parts of *Ethiopic Enoch,*[8] many of the Qumran writings,[9] the Wisdom of Solomon,[10] and the major works of Philo[11] illustrate the ubiquity as well as the variety of new biblical interpretations developed during this late Hellenistic/early Roman period. Redefining the meaning of the Israelite past, therefore, was an old and widely practiced tradition long before the earliest followers of Jesus began the process from their own particular perspective.

Nevertheless, it was the Jewish War of 66–70 CE that was the definitive catalyst for a number of new literary reflections on the meaning of Israel's history, from the despair of *2 Baruch* and *4 Ezra,* to the strong affirmation of Israel's chosen status in Pseudo-Philo's *Biblical Antiquities,* to the pragmatic reform efforts of the Pharisaic reflections and codifications begun at Jamnia. As many commentators have observed, however, it was the early Christian evangelist known as Mark who, in conjunction with his writing of the story of Jesus' mission, took the unprecedented step of linking the destruction of the Jerusalem temple to the rejection and crucifixion of Jesus at the hands of the Jews.[12] In this effort, Mark made use of a number of earlier traditions in order to establish the context in which Jesus' preaching would emerge as the harbinger of God's new vision, and his suffering death would prove to be the climactic event leading to God's victory over the cosmic forces of evil. Moreover, Mark's Gospel characterizes Jesus preeminently as God's Son and anointed agent for change in both the cosmic and earthly spheres. In this new endeavor, Israel's people, particularly its leaders and cultic institutions, appear in either passive or openly hostile opposition and, therefore, are deserving of divine destruction. Conversely, Mark formulates the locus of Christian hope in Jesus' vindication as Son of God and the promise of his imminent return as Son of Man.

7. For example, *Sibylline Oracles* 3.702–30.

8. For example, "Apocalypse of Weeks" (*1 Enoch* 93:1–10, 12–17); "Animal Apocalypse" (*1 Enoch* 89:73–74).

9. For example, 1QapGen; 4Q159; 4Q180; 1Q22; 4Q166–67; 1QpHab.

10. Especially, Wisdom 10–19.

11. For example, *De Abrahamo; De Josepho; De decalogo; De vita Mosis.*

12. See, for example, Adela Yarbro Collins, *The Beginning of the Gospel: Probings of Mark in Context* (Minneapolis: Fortress Press, 1992), 88–89. However, Robert T. Fortna (*The Gospel of Signs: A Reconstruction of the Narrative Source Underlying the Fourth Gospel* [Cambridge: Cambridge Univ. Press, 1970]) and, more recently, Lawrence M. Wills (*The Quest of the Historical Gospel* [London: Routledge, 1997]) have made compelling arguments that this task was already achieved by an earlier Christian writer.

Of the two subsequent revisions of Mark's narrative, Matthew's Gospel is the first to cast Jesus within the context of Israelite narrative traditions.[13] For Matthew, Jesus' role parallels that of Moses. Not only his presentation of Jesus' teachings but even the details of the Matthean birth narrative consciously echo the salient features of the Exodus saga. Jesus is portrayed as God's anointed, who reinterprets the Torah and redefines the people's covenant obligations uniquely, profoundly, and definitively. Moreover, the Matthean Gospel ends with the risen Jesus commissioning the rehabilitated disciples to promulgate to the nations the teachings of his earthly ministry under the continuing guidance of his glorified presence (Matt 28:19-20). Thus, unlike Mark, whose Gospel pointed to an apocalyptic finale of salvation history,[14] Matthew merely turned its course in a new direction.[15]

As had Mark and Matthew, Luke portrayed Jesus within the long tradition of God's divinely appointed and inspired agents. According to all three evangelists, however, Jesus' place among these divine agents was exalted and unique, because only in him was the manifestation of God's Spirit and power complete and undiluted. Luke further developed the theme that it was the presence of the Spirit that united Jesus' life and ministry with the earlier traditions of Israel's scriptural past. Indeed, after Jesus' crucifixion and ascension, it was the guidance of the Spirit in the mission of the disciples and the presence of the Spirit in the ongoing life of the church that linked Luke's audience to the power and vision of Jesus' original mission.

Moreover, it is generally accepted, particularly with respect to the opening segments of both the Gospel and Acts, that Luke consciously employs the language and style of the Septuagint in an effort to clothe his work in the legitimacy and authority of Israel's scripture,[16] an effort that is particularly evident

13. M. D. Goulder, *Midrash and Lection in Matthew* (London: SPCK, 1974), 33–34.

14. Collins, *Beginning of the Gospel,* 34–35.

15. New, that is, in its exclusively messianic focus and its abandonment of circumcision, of the literal observance of the purity and holiness codes, and even of a strict interpretation of the Sabbath observance, all of which Matthew takes over from his sources, Mark and Q.

16. See, for example, two classic articles: J. de Zwaan, "The Use of the Greek Language in Acts," and William K. L. Clarke, "The Use of the Septuagint in Acts." Both appear in *The Beginnings of Christianity: Acts of the Apostles,* ed. F. J. Foakes-Jackson and Kirsopp Lake, vol. 2 (London: MacMillan, 1922), 30–65, 66–105. See also Thomas L. Brodie, "Greco-Roman Imitation of Texts as a Partial Guide to Luke's Use of Sources," in *Luke-Acts: New Perspectives from the Society of Biblical Literature,* ed. C. H. Talbert (New York: Crossroads, 1984), 48; and Eckhard Plümacher, *Lukas als hellenistischer Schriftsteller: Studien zur Apostelgeschichte,* SUNT 9 (Göttingen: Vandenhoeck & Ruprecht, 1972), 59–64; 72–78.

in his extensive use of ancient prophecy as a means of heralding its fulfillment in the life and death of Jesus. Although in his development of this literary motif, Luke follows an already well established tradition of early Christian exegesis, several Lukan interpreters have observed that there is far more to Luke's use of prophecy than the redirection of ancient Israelite prophetic tradition for Christian theological ends. Indeed, François Bovon has argued that, in addition to the motif of fulfillment of Hebrew prophecy, Luke has incorporated numerous new prophecies, which are presented either by Jesus himself, by angelic messengers, or by reliable human agents on whom the divine Spirit rests. Some of these prophecies are presented clearly and fulfilled almost immediately; others are not fulfilled within the narrative itself but would have been considered fulfilled by Luke's late-first-century audience.[17] Bovon also argues that Luke creates some prophecies in a deliberately ambiguous manner, which not only adds subtlety and complexity to his narrative but also invites the reader to participate in the interpretive task.[18]

Bovon's hypothesis concerning prophetic ambiguity is complemented by the further observations of Charles H. Talbert. In an article published independently of Bovon's, Talbert also argues that the function of prophecy in Luke-Acts cannot be reduced simply to an elaboration of the early Christian theme of the fulfillment of scriptural promise.[19] After listing the numerous instances of new prophecy in Luke-Acts, Talbert concludes that the function of prophecy by no means was limited to the emphasizing of continuity between the early Christian church and the traditions of Israel. Indeed, the Lukan concern with new prophecy and its fulfillment appears to be directed toward the Greco-Roman world, in which the fulfillment of prophecy played an important legitimizing role in contemporary political and religious propaganda.[20]

Therefore, even though the dependence of Luke-Acts upon Israel's scriptural themes is considerable and remains the starting point of nearly all interpretive analyses, concentration solely on the metaphors, motifs, and typologies borrowed from Israel's past provides only a limited understanding of Luke's composition. For just as traditional Virgilian scholarship at one time had focused

---

17. François Bovon, "The Effect of Realism and Prophetic Ambiguity in the Works of Luke," in *New Testament Traditions and Apocryphal Narratives*, Princeton Theological Monograph Series 36, trans. J. Haapiseva-Hunter (Allison Park, Pa.: Pickwick, 1995), 97.

18. Ibid., 101.

19. Charles H. Talbert, "Promise and Fulfillment in Lucan Theology," in *New Perspectives,* ed. Talbert, 94.

20. Ibid., 99.

almost exclusively on Homeric influence, neglecting the importance of the Alexandrian themes and perspectives that many interpreters now consider to be substantive,[21] so, too, has traditional Lukan scholarship tended to focus too narrowly on scriptural typologies and motifs, ignoring the more immediate influence of Greco-Roman religious, political, and literary paradigms.[22]

LUKE AND THE HISTORICAL CONTEXT OF LUKE-ACTS

As is the case with many early Christian authors, historical knowledge of the author of Luke-Acts remains sketchy at best. His identity is unknown, and both the date and the location of his composition remain open to speculation. However, because of numerous points of contact between Luke-Acts and the deutero-Pauline letters of Colossians and Ephesians,[23] this study assumes a dating of between 90 and 100,[24] and a location in a major metropolitan center of the Greco-Roman world, such as Ephesus, Philippi, Corinth, Antioch, or even Rome itself.[25]

21. And, therefore, crucial to the interpretation of Virgil's work. See, for example, Wendell Clausen, *Virgil's* Aeneid *and the Interpretation of Hellenistic Poetry* (Berkeley: Univ. of California Press, 1987).

22. In addition to the notable exceptions to this generalization that were cited in chapter 1, I should also mention a number of smaller studies by Dennis MacDonald pointing to the influence of Homeric epic on specific passages in Luke-Acts. See, for example, "The Shipwrecks of Odysseus and Paul," *NTS* 45 (1999): 88–107; "The Ending of Luke and the Ending of the *Odyssey*," unpublished paper; "Earthquakes and Prison Breaks," unpublished paper; and "Young Men Falling to their Deaths," unpublished paper.

23. For example, the exalted Lord, Col 1:18–20; 2:10, 19; 3:1–4; Eph 1:3, 10, 20–21; 2:6; 6:9; Paul's persecutions completing those of Christ's for the sake of the church, Col 1:24; Jews and gentiles described as those "near" and "far off," respectively, Eph 2:12–17; the spread of the gospel and the growth of the church throughout the civilized world, Col 1:6, 23.

24. This time frame is compatible with the later end of the spectrum of 80–100 CE commonly assumed by NT scholars. For example, A. Wikenhauser and J. Schmid, *Einleitung in das Neue Testament,* 6th ed. (Freiburg: Herder, 1973), 272; Dennis C. Duling and Norman Perrin, *The New Testament: Proclamation and Parenesis, Myth and History,* 3d ed. (New York: Harcourt Brace, 1994), 369; Hans Conzelmann, *Acts of the Apostles,* Hermeneia (Philadelphia: Fortress Press, 1972), xxxiii; Bovon, *L'Évangile 1–9,* 28; Fitzmyer, *Luke,* vol. 1, 57.

25. Although the focus of the "we" passages on Philippi and its surrounding area make this city an intriguing possibility (see Bovon, *L'Évangile 1–9,* 27–29), I am inclined to favor a more truly cosmopolitan location. Philippi was an important center of Pauline influence and a Roman colony; however, I find Ephesus the most plausible choice, because Luke designates the church elders of this wealthy and influential city as the guardians of the Pauline gospel.

Despite the high degree of speculation that still surrounds the location and dating of Luke-Acts, however, some details regarding the author are less controversial. For example, that the author of Luke-Acts, whom tradition names "Luke," was either a fairly literate, Greek-speaking gentile or a thoroughly Hellenized Jew is an assumption that has received broad scholarly acceptance.[26] That Luke's community included a number of women, was socially and economically diverse, and was largely gentile are further assumptions that have also received broad acceptance. That this community may have included a number of Roman citizens has also been suggested by some.[27] Although this latter suggestion is based largely on the internal evidence of the text itself, such a possibility is greatly increased if the Lukan community was indeed located in Rome, Ephesus, Corinth, or any one of a number of cosmopolitan, wealthy, and commercially active provincial cities.[28] Highly relevant also to any profile of the author of Luke-Acts is the inference, alluded to earlier, that Luke is a third-generation Christian and a member of a church nurtured in the Pauline tradition.

Finally, the issue of Luke's attitude toward the fate of the Jews remains hotly contested. Although this issue will be discussed in greater detail later in this chapter, some preliminary opinions may be stated at the outset. Luke was writing in a period when it is widely argued that a majority of Christians had separated from the local synagogues, either voluntarily or forcibly.[29] That an

---

26. Favoring the first possibility is the strong gentile bias of Luke-Acts. Favoring the second possibility is the thorough familiarity with the Greek Bible that characterizes this work. I am inclined to favor the former hypothesis, because even gentile Christians might be expected to have acquired considerable knowledge of the Septuagint, especially if they had belonged to the church since youth.

27. For example, Duling and Perrin, *The New Testament,* 371.

28. Corinth and Philippi were Roman colonies, and Ephesus was a major commercial port as well as the provincial capital for the very important senatorial province of Asia.

29. Recent opinion has tended to discount the significance of the *Birkat ha-minim* for Jewish Christians in the late first century CE, arguing that the Yavnean rabbis had more important issues with which to contend (see the discussion in Stephen G. Wilson, *Related Strangers: Jews and Christians, 70–170* CE [Minneapolis: Fortress Press, 1995], 178–83). On the other hand, the situation within the diaspora, where any sort of standardized rabbinic authority appears to have been minimal at this time, was considerably different. Whether or not Hellenistic Judaism actively proselytized, the substantive archaeological evidence regarding godfearer and gentile benefactions for Jewish synagogues leaves little doubt that late-first-century Christian communities located in the Greek provinces of the Roman empire would have been well aware of the competition posed by neighboring Jewish communities.

inevitable rivalry existed between Jews and Christians, each actively engaged in mission and each claiming the authority and legitimacy of the same ancient scriptures, is also maintained by a number of historians.[30] Although an equal number of scholars stand in either partial or total disagreement with this view,[31] the text of Luke-Acts, particularly Acts, suggests that such a rivalry did, at the very least, exist in the mind of its author. Indeed, it is likely that some degree of rivalry with contemporary diasporan Jewish groups prompted Luke to present his thoroughly distinctive interpretation of Christian origins. The Pauline churches of the late first century stood at the cultural intersection of diasporan Judaism and Greek provincial life under Roman imperial dominion. It is hardly surprising, therefore, that Luke-Acts reflects an innovative mode of narrative combining biblical typologies and motifs with significant dramatic and stylistic elements from the literary and cultural milieu of the Roman imperial world. Nor should it be surprising that Luke-Acts contains many points of contact with the contemporary Latin epic literature that anticipated the ultimate renewal of the mythological Golden Age and celebrated the Roman people as the new elect.

30. For example, Paul Trebilco, *Jewish Communities in Asia Minor* (Cambridge: Cambridge Univ. Press, 1991); Joyce Reynolds and Robert Tannenbaum, *Jews and Godfearers at Aphrodisias: Greek Inscriptions with Commentary*, Cambridge Philological Society Supp. 12 (Cambridge: Cambridge Philological Society, 1987); Folker Siegert, "Gottesfürchtige und Sympathisanten," *JSJ* 4 (1973): 109–64; Dieter Georgi, *The Opponents of Paul in Second Corinthians* (Philadelphia: Fortress Press, 1986); Alan F. Segal, *Rebecca's Children* (Cambridge, Mass.: Harvard Univ. Press, 1986); Marcel Simon, *Verus Israel* (Oxford: Oxford Univ. Press, 1986); Louis Feldman, *Jew and Gentile in the Ancient World* (Princeton: Princeton Univ. Press, 1993); and Marianne Palmer Bonz, "The Jewish Donor Inscriptions from Aphrodisias: Are They Both Third-Century, and Who Are the *Theosebeis?*" *HSCP* 96 (1994): 281–99.

31. See Shaye J. D. Cohen, "Was Judaism in Antiquity a Missionary Religion?" in *Jewish Assimilation, Acculturation and Accommodation*, Studies in Jewish Civilization 2, ed. M. Mor (New York: Univ. Press of America, 1992), 14–23; idem, "Adolf Harnack's 'Mission and Expansion of Judaism': Christianity Succeeds Where Judaism Fails," in *The Future of Early Christianity: Essays in Honor of Helmut Koester*, ed. B. A. Pearson (Minneapolis: Fortress Press, 1991), 163–72; Scott McKnight, *A Light among the Gentiles: Jewish Missionary Activity in the Second Temple Period* (Minneapolis: Fortress Press, 1991); Martin Goodman, "Jewish Proselytizing in the First Century," in *The Jews among Pagans and Christians*, ed. J. Lieu, J. North, and T. Rajak (London: Routledge, 1992), 53–78; Martin Goodman, "Nerva, the Fiscus Judaicus and Jewish Identity," *JRomS* 79 (1989):40–44; idem, *Mission and Conversion: Proselytizing in the Religious History of the Roman Empire* (Oxford/New York: Clarendon, 1994).

VIEWING LUKE-ACTS FROM ITS NARRATIVE CENTER: ACTS 2

The unusual degree to which Luke blends biblical motifs with the elements of literary style from the Greco-Roman would occurs throughout Luke-Acts, and nowhere is the evangelist's technique more intriguingly illustrated than in his narration of the dramatic events attending Pentecost. Moreover, the Pentecost event, with its interpretation as disclosed in Peter's speech, the reaction of the people, and the formation and growth of the early community under the guidance and protection of the Spirit, appears in the very center of Luke's two-part work, contains *in nuce* (in a nutshell) his theological message, and touches upon nearly every important theme of his narrative composition. Acts 2 will serve, therefore, as a useful introduction to the examination and interpretation of Luke-Acts as a whole and will illustrate how its author may have been influenced in his literary presentation by elements of Greco-Roman epic in general and by examples from Virgil's *Aeneid* in particular.

The specific elements from contemporary Greco-Roman epic tradition that will come into play in this chapter focusing on Acts 2 and related passages include the following: (1) the use of literary allusion to add complexity and ambiguity to the surface level of the narrative, (2) the use of descriptive embellishments that are intended to be interpreted proleptically and symbolically, and (3) the dramatic presentation of the central theme in terms of a divinely ordained mission that finds its ultimate resolution in the reconstitution of the people of God.

A Preliminary Word on Sources and Structure

The problem of discerning Luke's sources in Acts 2 reflects the source problem evident throughout the entire second half of his composition. Although Luke undoubtedly made use of sources, three of which have been identified for the Gospel,[32] their detection and isolation in Acts is generally acknowledged

---

32. Although Luke's use of Mark and Q can be determined with a fairly high degree of precision, scholars differ on the extent of Luke's use of the L source. Determining what should be attributed to this source and what has been composed by Luke himself is much more subjective. Consequently, no scholarly consensus has yet been reached. For example, although chapters 1–2 are generally attributed to L, broadly defined, Bovon (*L'Évangile 1–9*, 25, 72, 83, passim) observes that most of this material has been thoroughly reworked by Luke. That this makes separation of source from redaction highly problematic is typically illustrated in Luke 2:29-32, 34-35. With respect to verses 29-32, Bovon (*L'Évangile 1–9*, 143) argues that Luke composed them. Raymond E. Brown (*The Birth of the Messiah* [New York: Image Books, 1979], 454) believes that Luke added these verses after the completion of his original composition; Gerhard Lohfink (*Die Sammlung Israels: Eine Untersuchung zur lukanischen Ekklesiologie*,

to be problematic.[33] Since the identification of Luke's sources must depend on indirect criteria, such as style, word usage, or variations and contradictions in conceptuality and theological viewpoint, judgments are highly subjective and appear to be contingent upon the specific preconceptions of the individual interpreter. Thus, even with respect to Acts 2, there is no consensus concerning Luke's use of sources.[34] Indeed, although Eduard Lohse believes that Luke is making use of a quasihistorical source in verses 1-4 and verse 13, he also acknowledges that "both linguistically and stylistically the account is wholly Lucan."[35] It is not surprising, therefore, that some interpreters doubt that Acts 2 reflects the significant use of any traditional source or sources.[36]

On the other hand, the literary structure of Acts 2 is relatively clear. The chapter begins with the Pentecost event, verses 1-13. Thereafter follows Peter's speech, verses 14-36. This in turn prompts a dramatic response from the assembled people, verses 37-41, the chapter closing with a Lukan summary of the early life of the community under the Spirit, verses 42-47.

SANT 39 [Munich: Kösel, 1975], 29) attributes them to L. Conversely, Bovon (*L'Évangile 1–9,* 143–44) attributes verses 34–35 to L, whereas Brown (*Birth,* 454) attributes them to Luke. Indeed, even setting chapters 1–2 aside, there is no unanimity on the character or extent of L. The vocabulary and style-oriented research of Friedrich Rehkopf (*Die lukanische Sonderquelle: Ihr Umfang und Sprachgebrauch* [Tübingen: Mohr/Siebeck, 1959], 89) has led him to define a coherent L source which, along with Luke's other sources (Mark, Q, and the source behind the birth narratives), may be distinguished from Luke's redaction. On the other hand, Helmut Koester's form-critical research (*Ancient Christian Gospels: Their History and Development* [London/Philadelphia: SCM/Trinity Press International, 1991], 337) has led him to conclude that L is really a composite of a number of disparate materials.

33. Jacques Dupont, *Les sources du livre des Actes: État de la question* (Paris: Desclée de Brouwer, 1960), 159–62; Conzelmann, *Acts,* xxxviii.

34. For example, according to A. Harnack, chapter 2 reflects a legendary source of which Luke also made use in chapter 5; Jackson and Lake also attribute chapter 2 to one of two major sources behind Acts 1–5; H. W. Beyer believes that Acts 2:1-13 reflects the juxtaposition of two sources, but that verses 6-10 were composed by Luke himself; J. A. Findlay attributes chapter 2 to a Caesarian source, also responsible for part of chapter 5 as well as chapters 7–8. Étienne Trocmé suggests that most of chapter 2 is based on one source, with verses 22-36 relying on a special documentary source, and verses 7-11 composed by Luke himself. All of the above are cited in Dupont, *Les sources,* 35–90.

35. Eduard Lohse, "πεντηκοστή," *TDNT* 6 (1968): 48.

36. Richard Zehnle, *Peter's Pentecost Discourse,* SBLMS 15 (Nashville: Abingdon, 1971), 113.

Intentional Ambiguity in Lukan Biblical Motifs: Acts 2:1-13

The account begins (verse 1) with a temporal expression of theological significance: "When the day of Pentecost had come ..."[37] That the coming of the Spirit is accompanied by a resounding noise (ἦχος, verse 2) identifies this new event with the scriptural tradition of theophany.[38] Richard Zehnle sees etiological motivation at work in Luke's description of the tongues of fire (verse 3), which depicts the descent of the Spirit as resting on the disciples' heads. He further notes that the precision of the description of the divine action, which triggers the inauguration of the community's ministry, seems designed to evoke comparison with the laying on of hands, connected in Acts with the conferring of the Spirit (Acts 8:17; 9:17; 19:6) and of missionary authority (Acts 6:6; 13:3).[39] On a more immediate level, the divided "tongues of fire" of verse 3 quickly become the "other tongues" of individualized speech (verse 4), an interpretation that is subsequently confirmed in verse 8, with the substitution of διάλεκτος for γλῶσσα.[40]

Acts 2:5 marks the beginning of the second part of Luke's narrative of the Pentecost event itself, as the focus shifts from the events inside the house to their impact and significance for those gathered outside. Although Ernst Haenchen interprets the meaning of this contrast as the immediate distinction between speakers and hearers,[41] it is likely that Luke's interest in this physical juxtaposition also harbors a metaphorical connection between the spread of the proclamation from those inside to those outside the house of Israel, a connection that will be discussed in more detail subsequently.

Verse 5 also invites controversy on another level. What is the meaning of the phrase εἰς Ἰερουσαλὴμ κατοικοῦντες Ἰουδαῖοι? If the phrase refers to religious pilgrims merely gathered for the Pentecost feast, it strains the meaning of κατοικέω. On the other hand, to speak of Jews dwelling in Jerusalem seems excessively clumsy for a writer of Luke's general level of literary skill. Although

---

37. Literally, "as the day of Pentecost was being fulfilled." Jacques Dupont ("The First Christian Pentecost," in idem, *The Salvation of the Gentiles: Essays on Acts of the Apostles* [New York: Paulist Press, 1979], 36–37) notes that the use of the present tense (συμπληροῦσθαι) emphasizes the "now" of this event; compare Lohse, "πεντηκοστή," 50.

38. For example, Jer 28:16 LXX; Philo *Decal.* 33. Typically, however, the Septuagint uses φωνή, a synonym for ἦχος, in theophany scenes (compare Exod 19:16, 19; Deut 4:12; 1 Kgs 18:26, 27, 29, 41).

39. Zehnle, *Discourse,* 118.

40. Ernst Haenchen, *The Acts of the Apostles: A Commentary* (Philadelphia: Westminster, 1971), 167–68.

41. Ibid., 168.

scholarly opinion remains divided on the meaning of this phrase,[42] its ambiguity is of less interest than the fact that, in Luke's telling, these Jews represent all the nations of the world, and an outpouring of the Spirit has miraculously enabled a group of Galileans to proclaim the wonderful deeds of God so that every listener may understand their proclamation in his own linguistic idiom.[43] The real question, therefore, is whether Luke intends verses 5-11 to refer explicitly to Jews dwelling in other lands or whether he has inserted this detail to signal proleptically the universal mission encompassing not only diasporan Jews but especially gentiles. Haenchen believes that this first Lukan Pentecost makes no such allusion to gentiles, arguing that such an interpretation would jeopardize the carefully drawn historical progression, which he believes to be the essence of Luke's composition.[44]

In contrast to Haenchen, however, many others interpret Luke's presentation of the Pentecost miracle as primarily symbolic—as, for example, the counterpart of the confusion of tongues in Babylon (Gen 11:1-9). L. Cerfaux argues that the inspired languages of Pentecost appear as a prophetic sign of the preaching to the gentiles and that the Pentecost event is seen by Luke as signaling the reversal of the dispersion of peoples in Deuteronomy 32:8.[45] Lohse agrees that the miracle of languages was intended by Luke as a proleptic expression of world mission, which Luke wants to identify with the church at its very inception.[46] Étienne Samain, Richard Zehnle, and Jacques Dupont agree, Dupont emphasizing that the function of these particular Jews is purely symbolic.[47]

The catalogue of nations (Acts 2:9-11) presents another minor problem for exegetes. Although the combined efforts of Franz Cumont, F. C. Burkitt, Stefan Weinstock, and J. A. Brinkman succeeded long ago in presenting a fairly plausible explanation as to the original source from which Luke's list is derived, this accomplishment has been of little help in determining the purpose of Luke's redactional modifications or his reason for including such a list at all. Because catalogues are a prominent style characteristic of Greco-Roman epic, a more detailed investigation of this problem will also be undertaken subsequently.

---

42. Haenchen, *Acts*, 175; *contra* Dupont, "Pentecost," 56; Étienne Samain, "Le récit de Pentecôte," *Foi et Vie* 70 (November 1971): 56.

43. Zehnle, *Discourse*, 119.

44. Haenchen, *Acts*, 175.

45. L. Cerfaux, "Le symbolisme attaché au miracle des langues," *EThL* 13 (1936): 257–58.

46. Lohse, "πεντηκοστή," 50–52.

47. Samain, "Pentecôte," 67; Zehnle, *Discourse,* 122; Dupont, "Pentecost," 55.

The narration of the Pentecost event ends with a reference to a division in the people, some being amazed or perplexed, others scoffing (Acts 2:12-13). Although Haenchen attributes Luke's incorporation of these verses to his need for creating a narrative bridge to Peter's speech,[48] Hans Conzelmann believes that these verses are a variant of the source quoted in verse 7.[49] It should be pointed out, however, that the theme of a division among the people when confronted by divine revelation is a significant and pervasive theme in Luke's composition, which begins with Luke 2:34-35 and is repeated in a variety of ways throughout Luke-Acts. Thus, although these verses do serve as a narrative bridge to what follows, they also serve as a climax to what has preceded.

The first interpretive problem inviting closer examination is whether Luke's description of the descent of the Spirit upon those gathered in the house is consciously depicted with the Mt. Sinai theophany in mind. Many scholars have argued that it is and that Luke's purpose for this element of the narrative is to call particular attention to the institution of the old covenant and law as background for his presentation of the new law of the Spirit. Other scholars disavow this interpretation, arguing that Luke only wants to evoke the concept of theophany in the most general way and intends no specific contrast between the events that occurred on Mt. Sinai and the events that he wishes to relate. Although both positions have some degree of merit, neither position is entirely acceptable.

Proponents of the hypothesis that the Mt. Sinai theophany is clearly evoked in the Lukan narration of Pentecost begin with a number of examples of similarities from the tradition that they believe cannot be attributed to coincidence. First, the repetition of the Greek words of sound and fire ($\mathring{\eta}\chi o\varsigma$ [$\phi\omega\nu\acute{\eta}$], $\pi\acute{u}\rho$) in Luke's Pentecost theophany is also found in the Septuagint's narrative accounts of the Mt. Sinai theophany.[50] Second, in the later development of the tradition as seen in Philo,[51] the parallelism between the Mt. Sinai theophany and Luke's Pentecost theophany is strengthened in that Philo's elaboration envisions the divine flame becoming articulate speech, in language that is intelligible to its hearers.[52] Third, rabbinic midrash on the events at Sinai, albeit dating to the mid–third century CE,[53] provides a further elaboration to that found in Philo, namely, that "God's voice divided into seven voices and then

48. Haenchen, *Acts*, 175.
49. Conzelmann, *Acts*, 15.
50. For example, Deut 4:12 LXX; Samain, "Pentecôte," 60.
51. Philo *Decal.* 33, 44–46.
52. Ibid., 46.
53. Dupont, "Pentecost," 42.

again into seventy voices or tongues, as many tongues as there were peoples."[54] Although it cannot be said with certainty precisely when the tradition developed to this particular level, Cerfaux suggests that "the fact that a parallelism between the two theophanies exists" indicates that such an interpretation was indeed known to Luke.[55]

Not all proponents of the Sinai hypothesis would go so far, however. They prefer to emphasize instead that the linking of the Jewish feast of Pentecost with the events on Mt. Sinai was indeed known in the time of Luke's writing. Furthermore, although there is no literary evidence of the connection of the Mt. Sinai event with the celebration of Jewish Pentecost until the middle of the second century CE, this complete acceptance would have been preceded by a long period of partial acceptance. Luke, therefore, may well have known of it.[56] Zehnle goes on to suggest that even though there is no systematic covenant theology in Luke-Acts, "the importance of Pentecost among certain Jewish groups, and its natural plausibility for the opening of the mission, probably induced Luke to choose it as the date of the descent of the Spirit."[57]

On the other hand, because of the evident parallelism drawn between Mt. Sinai and the granting of law and covenant, Dupont argues that it was Luke's intention to imply that the prescriptions of the law were being replaced by the gift of the Spirit, creating the basis for a new covenant.[58] Samain is in general agreement with Dupont, arguing that whereas Jewish celebration of Pentecost had focused on the gift of law and covenant, Luke's Pentecost narrative describes the inauguration of a new covenant and the promulgation of a new law. Furthermore, that Luke is aware of and consciously makes use of the parallel to the Jewish Pentecost is shown by his placing of this important narrative event fifty days after Easter.[59] Only tangentially related to this line of thought, however, is Samain's further observation that Luke's depiction of the Pentecost event reflects the inauguration of the eschatological community. Thus, an equally evocative symbol of this aspect of Jewish tradition, as expressed in prophetic writings from Third Isaiah to Zechariah, was the eschatological assembly on Mt. Sinai:[60]

54. Ibid., 42.
55. Cerfaux, "Le symbolisme," 259.
56. Zehnle, *Discourse*, 114.
57. Ibid., 115.
58. Dupont, "Pentecost," 44.
59. Samain, "Pentecôte," 56–59.
60. Ibid., 53.

For . . . I am coming to gather all the nations and tongues; and they shall come and shall see my glory, and I shall lay a sign upon them. From them I will send survivors to the nations. . . .

Isa 66:18b-19a LXX[61]

Although Haenchen appears to accept the hypothesis of a conscious parallelism between the Mt. Sinai theophany and the descent of the Spirit at Luke's Pentecost, Conzelmann, following Lohse, discounts the theory, arguing that the linking of the covenant to the Jewish celebration of Pentecost is a later tradition.[62] Étienne Trocmé agrees with Lohse and Conzelmann. While acknowledging similarities with Philo regarding the description of God's voice, Trocmé states that the differences between Philo's scene and Luke's are so great that Luke cannot be interpreted as recounting the gift of the new law.[63]

A more recent expression of dissent comes from Mark Strauss, who rejects the notion that the Pentecost event or the ascension statement in Peter's speech (Acts 2:33) is intended by Luke to recall the Jewish Pentecost tradition of the giving of the law at Mt. Sinai, thus casting Jesus in Mosaic colors. Strauss repeats the objections of Conzelmann and Trocmé, arguing that Luke's real intention in his narration and interpretation of Pentecost is to emphasize Jesus' role as messianic king, now enthroned in heaven.[64]

The problem with the arguments of both the proponents and the opponents of the Mt. Sinai theophany hypothesis is their joint assumption that if Luke consciously evokes the Mt. Sinai theophany, this parallelism must be determinative for the interpretation of the entire Pentecost pericope. Samain is unusual in his realization that Luke may, in fact, be inviting multiple associations in the minds of his audience. Yet this multivalent quality is usually the way in which the device of literary allusion is designed to enhance a narrative. A parallel for Luke's use of this technique and its desired results can be

---

61. ἔρχομαι συναγαγεῖν πάντα τὰ ἔθνη καὶ τὰς γλώσσας, καὶ ἥξουσι καὶ ὄψονται τὴν δόξαν μου. καὶ καταλείψω ἐπ' αὐτῶν σημεῖον, καὶ ἐξαποστελῶ ἐξ αὐτῶν σεσωμένους εἰς τὰ ἔθνη. . . .

62. Haenchen, *Acts*, 174; Conzelmann, *Acts*, 16; cf. Lohse, "πεντηκοστή," 48–49. Although Lohse believes that the linking of Sinai to Pentecost occurred shortly after 70 CE, he also believes that Luke's Pentecost narrative rests on earlier Christian tradition.

63. Étienne Trocmé, *Le livre des Actes et l'histoire*, Études d'histoire et philosophie religieuses 45 (Paris: Presses Universitaires de France, 1957), 203.

64. For example, Acts 2:29–35; Mark L. Strauss, *The Davidic Messiah in Luke-Acts*, JSNTSup 110 (Sheffield: Sheffield Academic Press, 1995), 145–47.

readily found in two epics of the Hellenistic and early Roman periods that were discussed in chapter 2.[65]

As may be recalled, Apollonius Rhodius's *Argonautica* (mid–third century BCE) consciously evokes the world of Homeric epic in its adaptation of incidents from the *Iliad* and the *Odyssey*, as well as in its use of Homeric language and simile. Yet, running as a counterpoint to this literary tendency is a very different dynamic, one betraying the social sensibilities and literary refinement of the more contemporary Alexandrian school. These Alexandrian interests are revealed in the epic's studied thematic correspondences and verbal reminiscences, as well as in its assimilation of Hellenistic themes of love and of heroes with moral flaws.

The creation of texture and complexity in the *Argonautica*'s narrative is achieved by the conscious synthesis and layering of Alexandrian themes and perspectives upon Homeric language and motifs. The result is not a one-to-one correspondence or parallelism with any specific Homeric incident, but rather the creation of something entirely new out of the studied borrowing and synthesis of a multiplicity of older motifs, combined with Apollonius's own more contemporary perspectives.

An illustration of this point may be seen in a brief résumé of an incident from the *Argonautica* that has been described in greater detail in chapter 2. In the seduction scene, Apollonius consciously evokes the famous military arming scenes from the *Iliad* as the ironic backdrop against which the reader perceives Jason's elaborate preparations for the sexually and politically advantageous conquest of Queen Hypsipyle.

The Homeric allusions deliberately created by Apollonius actually operate on two levels, however. On a superficial level, Apollonius places his characters and draws his narrative situation in a manner analogous to characters and situations found in Homer's *Odyssey*. Jason's landing on the island of Lemnos and his brief affair with Hypsipyle are rather similar to Odysseus's arrival on the island of Aiaia and his affair with Circe, thus bringing to the reader's mind the possible danger that the situation presents for the hero and for the successful completion of the voyage. Lying just beneath this surface correspondence, however, are the military allusions drawn from Homer's *Iliad*. Their contribu-

---

65. In his work, *Luke the Literary Interpreter* (Rome: Pontifica Studiorum Universitas A. S. Thomas Aq. in Urbe, 1987), Thomas L. Brodie not only describes a number of methods and stylistic techniques by which textual rewriting could be carried out, but he also argues that by the first century of the common era many of these literary techniques had begun to find their way from the poetic genres into various prose genres. Epic poetry, however, continued to maintain its paradigmatic status.

tion to the narrative is quite different. Through them the reader is warned of Jason's predatory nature, a latent element of the plot that only gradually emerges but is of equal, if not greater, importance to the interpretation of Apollonius's story.

In Virgil's *Aeneid*, an even more diverse mixture of literary allusions is skillfully interwoven. In addition to extensive allusions to incidents and motifs from Homeric epic, Virgil also incorporates elements of Alexandrian irony and artistic refinement, all overlaid upon his own nationally and religiously motivated literary scheme. Thus, to an even greater degree than was true of Apollonius Rhodius's epic, Virgil creates scenes and narrative episodes with several different facets or levels of meaning. For example, in the opening scene of the narrative proper, Aeneas and his followers find that their ships and indeed their very lives are threatened by a violent storm. The dramatic description is deliberately drawn by the poet to call to the audience's mind the famous storm scenes of the *Odyssey*. When the survivors finally reach shore and make camp, Aeneas, feigning a hopeful expression that he clearly does not feel, reminds his crew of their divinely ordained mission and urges them to persevere.

Although this reference to Aeneas's face as a mask for his inner feelings (*Aeneid* 1.205–6) is consciously drawn and reveals Virgil's indebtedness to Alexandrian literary technique, here the great Roman poet uses Alexandrian artistry to add subtlety and complexity to his appropriation of Homeric themes. In this scene and others like it, according to Thomas L. Brodie, Virgil intends for his audience to recognize the Homeric allusion and then be struck by the nuanced disparities that he has introduced. Indeed, the *Aeneid* consciously "synthesizes and reshapes" a variety of literary sources in its skillful and sophisticated appropriation of the most important traditions of Homer for Roman political and religious ends.[66]

In the epics of both Apollonius Rhodius and Virgil, the literary allusions are lightly drawn and deliberately complex. They are generally not designed to invite one-to-one correspondences, nor do they lend themselves to interpretation on the basis of direct analogy. Rather, they exist in combinations of varying complexity, and their purpose is more to suggest to the audience or to bring to its remembrance similar episodes in different contexts—collecting, combining, and, above all, transforming insights borrowed from the treasured past.

---

66. Brodie, "Greco-Roman Imitation of Texts," 23. Brodie recognized that Virgil's use of Homer was analogous to Luke's appropriation of material from the Septuagint. It was, of course, Richard Heinze (*Vergils epische Technik* [Leipzig/Berlin: Tübner, 1915]) who extensively analyzed Virgil's appropriation of Homer.

Returning to the Pentecost narrative in Acts 2, its interpretation can be better understood if Luke's technique is perceived as a synthesis of a variety of scriptural allusions, rather than as an attempt to create a direct link to one particular scriptural typology. Although there are too many elements of correspondence with the Mt. Sinai theophany as it had developed in Luke's inherited tradition for these details to have been coincidental, the disparities are also significant, suggesting that a direct comparison with the bestowal of the covenant was not Luke's primary objective.

Therefore, although the proponents of the Mt. Sinai theophany hypothesis are justified in drawing attention to Luke's conscious allusion to this tradition, it is perhaps an overstatement to assert that Luke's primary intention is to depict the Christian Pentecost as a celebration of the new covenant, or as the replacement of the Mosaic law with a new law of the Spirit. Such an interpretation not only introduces theological themes largely ignored elsewhere in Luke-Acts, but it also fails to recognize the equally strong Lukan allusions to royal messianic traditions critical to Peter's interpretation of the Pentecost events (Acts 2:29-35) and to the eschatological ingathering of the nations and its attendant call to mission (Acts 2:3-11; cf. Isa 66:18-19). Employing a literary technique that is most typical of Greco-Roman epic, therefore, Luke suggests a variety of scriptural themes or motifs, the synthesis of which is intended to integrate and encompass the rich and relatively complex theological message of Acts 2.

The Proleptic and Symbolic Use of Catalogues (Acts 2:9-11)

Another element that deserves further scrutiny for the possible influence of contemporary Greco-Roman epic tradition on Luke's composition is Luke's incorporation of the catalogue of nations and its contribution to the important Lukan theme of universalism. It has already been suggested that in Acts 2:5-11, Luke's true intention, thinly veiled beneath the surface of his apparently historical presentation of the events of Pentecost, is to foreshadow the ultimate outcome of God's plan. The climax of this most important segment of the Pentecost event, therefore, must be the catalogue of nations in verses 9-11. That most interpreters fail to note the importance of this catalogue can be attributed to the fact that the details of its composition and the purpose of its incorporation have proven so unyielding to meaningful explanation.

This persistent lack of understanding has not been, however, from want of trying. In 1909, Franz Cumont published an article examining the ancient doctrine that divided or apportioned the regions of the world according to the astrological signs of the zodiac. Among the relevant evidence cited by Cumont was a copy of an early Hellenistic list of astrological signs and their corresponding regions, which had later been incorporated by Paulus Alexandrinus in his fourth-century CE work on astrology entitled Εἰσαγωγή εἰς τὴν ἀποτελεσματικήν (*Introduction to Astrological Matters*).[67] When F. C. Burkitt subsequently read Cumont's article, he jotted down notes (in Latin) alongside the margins of the Paulus Alexandrinus list, suggesting a close relationship between this list of countries or regions and the list of regions and peoples in Acts 2:9-11.

It was Stefan Weinstock, however, who developed and expanded Burkitt's unpublished discovery.[68] Although there are several significant deviations, the two lists exhibited a substantial enough agreement to suggest to both Burkitt and Weinstock that Luke was working from some variant of the same source as that used three centuries later by Alexandrinus.[69] Weinstock concludes from his analysis that Luke meant to use this astrological list to convey to his audience the idea of "the whole world," a concept clearly paralleled in the geographical distribution of the regions of the world under the signs of the zodiac.

A somewhat more recent study by J. A. Brinkman has attempted to provide further refinements regarding Luke's adaptation of the source in Acts 2:9-11 as previously outlined by Weinstock. First, Brinkman observes a slightly crude chiastic literary pattern in Luke's arrangement of his list:

> Πάρθοι καὶ Μῆδοι καὶ Ἐλαμῖται
> καὶ
> > τὴν Μεσοποταμίαν,
> > Ἰουδαίαν[70] τε καὶ Καππαδοκίαν,
> > οἱ κατοικοῦντες Πόντον καὶ τὴν Ἀσίαν,
> > Φρυγίαν τε καὶ Παμφυλίαν,
> > Αἴγυπτον καὶ τὰ μέρη τῆς Λιβύης
> > τῆς κατὰ Κυρήνην,
> καὶ
> οἱ ἐπιδημοῦντες Ῥωμαῖοι, Ἰουδαῖοι τε καὶ προσήλυτοι
> Κρῆτες καὶ Ἄραβες

---

67. Franz Cumont, "La plus ancienne géographie astrologique," *Klio* 9 (1909): 263–73.

68. Stefan Weinstock, "The Geographical Catalogue in Acts II, 9–11," *JRomS* 38 (1948): 43–46.

69. Ibid., 44. Weinstock's comparative list appears in appendix C.

70. Judea is viewed by Weinstock ("Catalogue," 44) as a scribal substitution for Armenia, which Luke had copied from his source unaltered; cf. Tertullian *Adv. Jud.* 7. Haenchen (*Acts*, 170) thinks that Judea is simply a scribal interpolation, whereas Conzelmann (*Acts*, 14) thinks that Judea has been added by Luke himself.

However, all efforts to detect a logical system or pattern in regard to the content of this catalogue have thus far met with frustration. According to Brinkman, the catalogue appears to be designed to approximate the progression of the countries of the world from east to west, but he is forced to admit that this rationale breaks down after Pamphylia.[71] He concludes, therefore, that the internal logic of the list of the astrological source had ceased to matter for Luke, whose subsequent emendation yields no particular message beyond that of a somewhat whimsically conceived expression of the whole world.[72] Most scholars are in general agreement with this conclusion, although they differ in their emphases. Observing the lack of discernible logic in the Lukan list, Dupont remarked: "This enumeration has always amazed commentators by what it includes, and even more by what it omits. . . . It corresponds so little with Luke's own geographical horizons that he surely did not compose it himself."[73]

It should be noted, however, that if Cerfaux is correct in his suggestion that one of Luke's allusions in his Pentecost narrative is to the eschatological ingathering of the nations, then Luke's appropriation of an astrological list, which no doubt was still in contemporary usage, may well have been intentional. According to scriptural tradition, when God divided the nations he apportioned them among the angels and allotted the sun, moon, and stars, so that the nations might worship them.[74] This assertion was part of a larger polemic in which Israel claimed superiority over the nations of the world by virtue of its exclusive relationship to God himself.[75] Luke's appropriation of the astrological list, therefore, would enrich the universalizing significance of the Pentecost narrative by consciously calling attention to this reversal of the biblical past. The nations, which were once apportioned to the oversight of the relatively unimportant stars, are now to be drawn directly into God's eschatological plan of salvation. If the inclusion of Judea is original with Luke, the list further serves to emphasize the denial of Judea's pride of place. It is henceforth just one among the nations.

Consistent with their perception of Luke's narrative as historiography, neither Haenchen nor Conzelmann is entirely convinced by Weinstock's hypothesis. Conzelmann argues that Luke's dependence is probably upon a list

71. J. A. Brinkman, "The Literary Background of the 'Catalogue of the Nations,'" *CBQ* 25 (1963): 419.

72. Ibid., 424–25.

73. Dupont, "Pentecost," 56–57.

74. Cf. Deut 32:8; Sir 17:17; Dan 10:13.

75. Hermann Strathmann, "λαός," *TDNT* 4 (1967): 35.

,of nations reflecting some prior political or geographical situation, and he points out that such lists are frequently found in the works of Hellenistic historians.[76] If this is so, however, no commentator, including Conzelmann, has thus far been able to specify what particular political or geographical configuration such a list might actually describe. As Haenchen had noted, the Parthians were contemporary enemies of Rome in Luke's own time, whereas the Medes and Elamites (mentioned in the Septuagint) had faded from political significance by the sixth century BCE.[77] Wisely bowing to the intractability of the evidence, Haenchen advises Lukan interpreters not to dwell on the tradition behind the list of Acts 2:9-11, but rather to "make due allowance for a theological writer's sense of effective composition."[78]

Although seldom taken to heart by Lukan interpreters, Haenchen's advice has considerable merit. Catalogues of heroes, forces, and nations are found not only in Hellenistic histories but also in Greco-Roman epics. Indeed, the catalogue as a literary form originated in Homeric epic and has been a characteristic feature of the genre ever since. The *Aeneid* incorporates at least five, two of which are particularly relevant for explaining the function and significance, even if not the content, of the list in Acts 2:9-11.[79]

In the *Aeneid*, Jupiter reveals to Venus the prophecy of Rome's glorious future. His prophecy is programmatic for Aeneas's mission and indeed for the entire epic drama. The catalogue of heroes that Aeneas views on his trip to the Underworld is one of the great proleptically climactic moments in the *Aeneid*. Here, personified in a parade of unborn heroes, is revealed the eschatological fulfillment of the glorious march of Roman history, set forth by Jupiter and the Fates at the beginning of the epic. The pageant begins with the earliest kings of Alba Longa and ends with a review of important military leaders of the republican era. This rather orderly chronological progression is, however, deliberately undermined by Virgil, who at the center of the list places Augustus, described as the son of a god, the second founder of Rome, and the leader destined to bring the world to eschatological fulfillment, extending his empire beyond the boundaries of the known world (*Aeneid* 6.792–96).

Although bearing little resemblance to the catalogue of nations in Acts 2:9-11, either in scale or in content, Virgil's catalogue of heroes does bear an important resemblance in its literary function. Like the catalogue in Acts 2, Virgil's

76. Conzelmann, *Acts*, 14.

77. Haenchen, *Acts*, 170.

78. Ibid., 169–70, n. 5.

79. In addition to those in books 6 and 8 discussed below, there are catalogues in books 5, 7, and 10.

catalogue is used to give detail and an impression of historical concreteness to the proleptic expression of the eschatological fulfillment pointed toward by the epic's narrative. Thus, unlike the lists of nations found in historical works, which simply provide additional historical detail for an event that has already taken place, the catalogues in *Aeneid* 6 and Acts 2 function *symbolically* and *proleptically*.

A more important parallel to the catalogue in Acts 2, however, appears in *Aeneid* 8. Virgil's final visual synthesis of prophecy and history occurs at the close of this book, when Venus presents Aeneas with a divinely crafted shield to take into the battles that must be won to accomplish the ultimate fulfillment of the mission. On this shield, which displays not only the art but also the wisdom of the gods, is etched a series of tableaux depicting the triumphal moments of Rome's future history.

As with the prophetic pageant of book 6, the shield depicts a number of scenes which—from the perspective of Virgil's audience—represent Rome's development from the Archaic past to the most recent climactic events of the Roman present, with Augustus again occupying pride of place. At the center of the shield Virgil depicts the battle of Actium, placing Augustus Caesar in the stern of a ship leading the civic fathers and people into battle. The scene is drawn in careful parallelism to Aeneas's departure from Troy, which Virgil describes at the beginning of book 3. Thus, by means of the shield's central tableau, the victory of Actium becomes the symbolic and proleptic fulfillment of the quest begun with Aeneas's exile from Troy. Closely linked to this portrayal of Rome's glorious victory over the impious and barbarous forces of the East (*Aeneid* 8.685–88), Augustus is depicted reviewing a parade of conquered peoples, who penitently lay down their arms before him. The triumph of peace over the forces of chaos is thereby expressed not merely in national terms but also is extended to include the entire world. With this *ex eventu* (after the fact) prophetic vision of eschatological fulfillment, the central section of the poem ends.

This catalogue of conquered peoples (*Aeneid* 8.722–28) is similar both in length and in general structure to that of Acts 2:9-11. Its ten names are structured into four balanced groupings: two names, followed by three names; then three more names, followed by two final names. Thus, Virgil's list exhibits the carefully crafted chiastic balance that Acts somewhat crudely approximates. The names themselves bear no discernible correlation with those listed in Acts 2, so there is no question of Luke's having actually used the *Aeneid*'s list as his source.

What the Augustan epic prototype has in common with Luke's reworked version of his source, however, is a studied *lack* of any immediate political, geographical, or theological coherence. For example, Virgil's reference to the

Leleges and Carians singles out people from what was evidently an obscure region of Asia Minor in the early Augustan era. Their placement within the catalogue was probably more directly related to their inclusion in Homer's *Iliad*, where they were mentioned in conjunction with certain allies of Troy.[80] Similarly, Luke's inclusion of the Medes and Elamites doubtless owes to their mention as foreign powers in the Septuagint. Conversely, like the Parthians of Luke's list, Virgil's inclusion of the Morini and the Nomades could conceivably reflect historically and politically relevant peoples and regions in Rome's recent past.[81] Generally speaking, however, the enumeration of areas and peoples, such as the Gelonians and the Dahae, as with the majority of the regions mentioned in Luke's list, seem merely symbolic of a collection of peoples from the farthermost ends of the known world.[82]

Thus, the catalogue of nations at the close of book 8 concludes Virgil's final description of the proleptic fulfillment of the prophecies set forth at the beginning of his epic, and it does so in a manner of presentation and for compositional reasons that are strikingly similar to the presentation and function of the catalogue of nations in Acts 2:9-11. Most characteristic of the lists in both Acts 2 and *Aeneid* 8 is their haphazard, eclectic quality, which seems intended to purposely defy both temporal and geographical categories. As with Virgil's list, Luke's list functions as symbolic and proleptic evidence of the eschatological fulfillment of a divinely ordered mission and of promises of the establishment of a kingdom without temporal or spatial limits.[83]

Indeed, Dupont has emphasized the theological, rather than the historical or geographical nature of Luke's interest in the spread of the apostolic mission "to the ends of the earth." He notes the close connection between Jesus' command that the message of repentance and the forgiveness of sins be preached in his name "to all the nations" (εἰς πάντα τά ἔθνη; Luke 24:47) and "to the ends of the earth" (ἕως ἐσχάτου τῆς γῆς; Acts 1:8). This connection is subsequently clarified in the climax of Paul's Pisidian Antioch speech (Acts 13:47), in which the purpose of the mission is presented as the fulfillment of the divine plan already revealed in scriptural prophecy: "I have set you to be a light for the nations" (τέθεικά σε εἰς φῶς ἐθνῶν) "so that you may bring salvation to the ends of the earth" (τοῦ εἶναί σε εἰς σωτηρίαν ἕως ἐσχάτου τῆς γῆς).[84]

---

80. C. J. Fordyce, *Virgil: Aeneid VII–VIII* (Bristol: Bristol Classical Press, 1977), 286.
81. Ibid., 286–87.
82. Ibid.
83. Cf. *Aeneid* 1.278–79; Luke 1:32-33.
84. Compare Isa 49:6b LXX.

Inasmuch as Simeon had linked the fulfillment of this prophecy based on Second Isaiah with the birth of Jesus (Luke 2:32), the theme of the divinely ordained mission and its expansion from Jerusalem to the ends of the earth may be considered the central, unifying theme of Luke-Acts. That Paul's arrival in Rome may be taken as the proleptic or symbolic fulfillment of the mission's ultimate goal is explained by Dupont:

> The expansion of Christianity "to the ends of the earth" is not merely a geographic movement, but involves a passage out of the Jewish world into the Gentile world. So Rome, as the capital of the pagan world, is really situated "at the ends of the earth," but the reasoning implicit in this expression is more religious than geographic.[85]

More recently, however, Robert L. Brawley has rightly noted that proleptic fulfillment nevertheless implies an element of incompletion within the narrative proper.[86] In this regard also, the *Aeneid* presents an instructive literary parallel. Although the prophecy assuring the founding of Rome remains unfulfilled at the end of Virgil's narrative, Aeneas's defeat of Turnus establishes the dramatic certainty of the prophecy's ultimate fulfillment, which takes place outside the narrative limits of the poem. In short, therefore, what Luke's list has in common with the conquered people's catalogue in Virgil's *Aeneid* is the theological nature of the geographical conquests to which both lists give symbolic witness.

The Continuation of Jesus' Mission and the Reconstitution of the People of God: Acts 2:14-41

Peter's speech contains Luke's interpretation of the meaning of his Pentecost narrative. It also reveals the Lukan perspective concerning the fate of the house of Israel and the importance of the incorporation of the gentiles in the reconstituted people of God. It is the dramatic presentation of this theme of the reconstitu-

---

85. Jacques Dupont, "The Salvation of the Gentiles and the Theological Significance of Acts," in idem, *Salvation*, 19. See also, William S. Kurz (*Reading Luke-Acts: Dynamics of Biblical Narrative* [Louisville: Westminster John Knox, 1993], 29) and Mikeal C. Parsons (*The Departure of Jesus in Luke-Acts*, JSNTSup 21 (Sheffield: Sheffield Academic Press, 1987], 157), who likewise emphasize the fulfillment of the mission in its arrival and success within the wider gentile world, without, however, qualifying this fulfilment as only proleptic.

86. "Because . . . the plot development in Acts discloses witnesses to the ends of the earth only partially, this trajectory never reaches its complete resolution. [It is] . . . a foreshadowing that anticipates fulfillment beyond the end of the literary work" (Robert L. Brawley, *Centering on God: Method and Message in Luke-Acts* [Louisville: Westminster John Knox, 1990], 18).

tion of the people as the eschatological fulfillment of the divine plan that affords the most significant agreement between Virgil's presentation and Luke's.

Peter begins his reply by addressing the people as 'Ιουδαῖοι. Luke here places 'Ιουδαῖοι in parallelism with 'Ισραηλῖται (verse 22) and with ἀδελφοί (verse 29).[87] Following the salutation of verse 14, Peter begins with the present situation, explaining the events of Pentecost as the fulfillment of scriptural prophecy concerning the outpouring of the Spirit in the last days (verses 17–21). On the one hand, through his incorporation of this passage within the larger context of the miraculous phenomena of wind and fire related at the beginning of the Pentecost narrative, Luke transforms the apocalyptic overtones of this passage from Joel. On the other hand, the eschatological meaning is heightened by the substitution of ἐν ταῖς ἐσχάταις ἡμέραις ("in these last days"; Acts 2:17a) for μετὰ ταῦτα ("after this"; Joel 3:1a LXX). Accordingly, within its new Lukan context, the implication of this prophecy from the tradition is that now begins the time of judgment and redemption. The gift of the Spirit is the harbinger of the new age.[88]

The πᾶσαν σάρκα of verse 17 reinforces the interpretation of verses 5–11 as a proleptic or symbolic reference to the universal scope of the mission.[89] This universalist interpretation is reinforced by verse 21. As Dupont has shown, in Luke's incorporation of this Joel passage, he appears to be working from a written source of scriptural citations, based on the Septuagint's translations but collected and edited for Christian apologetic purposes. Therefore, the "Lord" to which verse 21 refers is now Jesus,[90] although this is definitively clarified only in verse 36.

With the new address in verse 22, Peter begins a new phase of his argument. Although Jesus' crucifixion was part of God's larger plan of salvation,[91] Israel is[92] nonetheless responsible for his death (verse 23)[93] and guilty of disobedience

---

87. Although the term 'Ιουδαῖοι becomes a pejorative as the narrative progresses, its use here, as well as earlier in verse 5, is synonymous with 'Ισραηλῖται. Conversely, there is nothing inherently positive in this latter term. Peter accuses those he has just addressed as 'Ισραηλῖται of being responsible for Jesus' death (verse 23); likewise it is men who have just been addressed as 'Ισραηλῖται who drag Paul from the temple (Acts 21:30).

88. Conzelmann, *Acts*, 20.

89. *Contra* Haenchen, *Acts*, 179.

90. Jacques Dupont, "Apologetic Use of the Old Testament," in idem, *Salvation*, 151–52.

91. Haenchen, *Acts*, 186; Conzelmann, *Acts*, 20.

92. Literally, "Israelites are."

93. Haenchen, *Acts*, 179; Conzelmann, *Acts*, 20.

to God (verse 22). Despite this breach between God and people, however, the divine plan has continued to unfold in Jesus' resurrection (verse 24). Luke now quotes Psalm 16:8-11 (15:8-11 LXX) as proof that Jesus' resurrection had been prophesied by David (verses 25-28). As Strauss points out, not only is David depicted as having spoken *about* the Messiah, he is also depicted as speaking prophetically *in the voice of* the Messiah.[94]

With the third and final address to the assembled people (verse 29), Peter launches into the dramatic conclusion of his arguments. Knowing that God has promised that a Davidic descendant would one day be seated on his throne, the revered Israelite king had spoken prophetically of the resurrection (and exaltation) of Jesus. Through the words of Peter, Luke interprets Psalm 16 in light of that scriptural promise. The promise statement in verse 30 is a scriptural allusion most likely drawn from Psalm 132:11 (131:11 LXX).[95]

In verses 32-33, the resurrection, exaltation, and enthronement of Jesus are collapsed into one climactic event.[96] Indeed, the outpouring of the Spirit is the indirect, but nonetheless definitive, proof of Jesus' exaltation at the right hand of God.[97] Verse 34 quotes Psalm 110:1 (109:1 LXX). In this instance, Jesus is inserted into a Davidic enthronement psalm, a hermeneutical move again made possible by the Septuagintal translation, which has been reinterpreted by the compiler of Luke's early Christian source.[98] The purpose is to identify Jesus as the exalted Lord who sits at God's right hand.[99]

The climax of the entire speech lies in verse 36, which provides a fourth and, this time, indirect summons to the entire house of Israel (πᾶς οἶκος Ἰσραήλ). It is a more forceful and succinct paraphrase of verses 22-23, in which Peter again apprises the Israelites of the fateful crisis in which their own acts have placed them. Haenchen asserts that, from a literary point of view, Peter's making such a charge before this gathering of devout diasporan Jews is

---

94. Strauss, *Messiah*, 137.

95. (ὤμοσεν. . . . ἐκ καρποῦ. . . . ἐπὶ τὸν θρόνον) Strauss, *Messiah,* 138. But Strauss also notes affinities to a broader range of promise tradition passages (e.g., 2 Sam 7:12-16; Ps 89, etc.).

96. Conzelmann, *Acts*, 21; Strauss, *Messiah*, 139.

97. Strauss, *Messiah*, 144; *contra* Haenchen, *Acts*, 186, who reverses the emphasis.

98. Conzelmann, *Acts*, 21.

99. Although Luke is merely expanding and refining the messianic claims found in the tradition that he has inherited, his work may also have been influenced by the parallel claims that Virgil had made concerning Augustus's relationship to Aeneas and Hercules. Note also the claims that Statius and Martial had made on behalf of Domitian, and, negatively, Lucan's depiction of Julius Caesar as the prototype for Nero in *De bello civili*. See the discussion of this question in chapter 3.

inept.[100] If, however, the scriptural promises are understood by Luke as pertaining to the entire house of Israel, then so also must the guilt for the Messiah's death be laid at its collective doorstep.

Only repentance can return the people of Israel from the brink of destruction. Moreover, since Jesus has been identified through scriptural proof as Lord and Messiah, it is *his* name on whom Israel must call in order to be saved.[101] Thus, after the death and resurrection of Jesus, the restoration of Israel requires repentance of a very radical nature. Indeed, this is precisely what Peter asks of the Israelites in verse 38. Only repentance and baptism make possible the descent of the Spirit, the power by which the fallen people may seek redemption and transformation.[102]

In verses 40-41, we are told that the people's response to Peter's testimony was substantial but nonetheless partial. Thus, from this point on, although Christian baptism becomes the distinguishing mark of the "true Israel," it also signifies entrance into a new community of the saved, a community that is no longer identical to "the house of Israel," which continues to be the immediate object of the apostles' mission. Indeed, the house of Israel is depicted by Luke as profoundly divided, even at the outset of the apostolic witness (cf. verses 12-13). Since a house divided cannot stand, the message of Luke's Pentecost narrative has far-reaching implications for the continued unfolding of his plot; the gathering of the true Israel will necessitate the collapse of the house of Israel as that "house" was formerly conceived.

If verse 36 is the climax of Peter's remarks concerning the house of Israel, however, verse 39 is considered by many to be the most important statement in the Pentecost narrative regarding the promise of salvation for the gentiles. Opinion is sharply divided, nevertheless, and hinges on the interpretation of the phrase καὶ τοῖς τέκνοις ὑμῶν καὶ πᾶσιν τοῖς εἰς μακράν ("and for your children, and for all who are far away"). Both Haenchen and Conzelmann interpret the phrase as describing the promise of salvation to Israel, which is extended both in time (καὶ τοῖς τέκνοις ὑμῶν) and in space (καὶ πᾶσιν τοῖς εἰς μακράν), and they cite Sirach 24:32 and Isaiah 57:19 in support of this interpretation.[103]

According to Dupont, however, whose research in this particular area Conzelmann has generally accepted and incorporated into his commentary,[104]

---

100. Haenchen, *Acts*, 183.

101. Dupont, "Apologetic Use," 138.

102. That the gift of the Spirit as a means of redemption does indeed necessitate transformation, cf. Ezek 11:19; 36:26.

103. Conzelmann, *Acts*, 22; Haenchen, *Acts*, 184.

104. Conzelmann, *Acts*, 19, n. 4; 21, n. 17.

verse 39 is a further reference to the Joel passage cited in Acts 2:17-21. But whereas in the earlier references from the prophet, Luke has Peter quote from Joel 3:1–5a, in verse 39 Peter reflects on Joel 3:5 in its entirety:

καὶ ἔσται πᾶς, ὃς ἂν ἐπικαλέσηται τὸ ὄνομα κυρίου, σωθήσεται· ὅτι ἐν τῷ ὄρει Σιὼν καὶ ἐν Ἰερουσαλημ ἔσται ἀνασῳζόμενος, καθότι εἶπεν κύριος, καὶ εὐαγγελιζόμενοι, οὓς κύριος προσκέκληται.

And then whoever should call on the name of the Lord will be saved, for on Mt. Zion and in Jerusalem will be those who are being saved [lit., "will be the one who is being saved"], as the Lord has said, and those to whom glad tidings are announced whom the Lord has called.[105]

Dupont suggests that in place of "the one(s) on Mt. Zion and in Jerusalem" Luke has substituted "you and your children and all those who are far off."[106] Indeed, the phrase "those who are far off," found in Isaiah 57:19 in the context of a promise of peace "for those who are far off and for those who are near," either had been reinterpreted in early Christian exegesis prior to Luke's composition, or it was being interpreted anew within the Pauline churches of Luke's own time. Ephesians 2:13-17 repeatedly and unambiguously identifies "those who are far off" with gentiles, while "those who are near" are understood to be Jews.[107] It has already been argued that Luke has close theological affiliations with the writings of Colossians and Ephesians, so it is quite reasonable to assume that Luke's use of the phrase in Acts carries the same meaning as it does in Ephesians. Moreover, in Acts 22:21, Paul relates a vision granted him in the temple, in which Jesus ordered him to leave Jerusalem with the words, "for I will send you to the gentiles, far away."

Although both Haenchen and Conzelmann understand this reference as supporting their interpretation of the phrase as relating solely to distance, they seem to ignore the fact that it is placed here in apposition with the phrase "the gentiles." Nor can it be plausibly argued that ἔθνη here refers to "nations" in some collective sense that includes diasporan Jews. The closest parallel to Paul's words in Acts 22:21 occurs at the end of Acts 28, when Paul contrasts the deafness of "this people" with the willingness with which τὰ ἔθνη will listen (Acts 28:27-28). Thus, in Acts 22:21, those who are "far away" are clearly and specifically the gentiles.

---

105. Joel 3:5 LXX; see Dupont, "Apologetic Use," 151.
106. Dupont, "Salvation," 22–23.
107. Ibid., 23; Zehnle, *Discourse*, 124.

Further examples of the metaphorical use of the phrase "far away" (μακράν) as a reference to gentiles can be found in the parable of the prodigal son (Luke 15:11-32), the composition of which is attributed to Luke's special source (L).[108] The community behind this special tradition to which Luke is heir, therefore, may already have understood the repentant younger son who becomes the object of the father's compassionate forgiveness, while he is still "far off" (Luke 15:20) as an allusion to God's surprising call of the gentiles (cf. Luke 15:13).[109] Finally, in Luke's emendation of the parable of the great banquet (Luke 14:15-24), those brought in to replace the previously invited guests make up two groups: (1) the poor, the crippled, the blind, and the lame from the streets and alleys within the town (Luke 14:20-21); and (2) those brought in from the roads and hedges (οἱ φραγμοί) beyond the town (Luke 14:22-23).[110] This latter group should also be identified as gentiles.[111]

Zehnle, following Dupont, further concludes that the point of Acts 2:39 is its allusion to the universal mission. Moreover, whereas the wording of the original passage in Joel has the final verb in the perfect tense ("whom the Lord has called," προσκέκληται), in Acts 2:39, the verb "to call" has the force of continuing action.[112] Thus, Luke implies that the group for whom salvation is to be given is still in the process of being defined.[113]

The Immediate Aftermath of Pentecost: Acts 2:42-47

Although verse 41 serves as the immediate conclusion to Peter's Pentecost speech, it also serves as the transitional sentence for the more detailed summary (Acts 2:42-47) that brings the entire Pentecost narrative to its dramatic close.[114]

---

108. Although, by default, this parable is commonly attributed to Luke's special source, Bovon (*L'Évangile selon Saint Luc 15–24*, CNT 3c [Geneva: Labor et Fides, 2000]) is certain that the parable was originally composed by this same special source—albeit drawing indirectly upon earlier tradition. Thus, according to Bovon, the original language and conceptuality are primarily Greek, not Semitic.

109. The further development of this interpretation is illustrated in Eph 2:12-17.

110. The words οἱ φραγμοί also appear in Eph 2:14 as the term for the barrier that formerly separated the gentiles from salvation. Indeed, its only other appearance in the NT is Mark 12:1 (= Matt 21:33). Here also it designates the boundary of God's vineyard, Israel.

111. David Tiede, Introduction and Notes on the Gospel of Luke in *Harper Collins Study Bible: New Revised Standard Version* (London: Harper Collins, 1993), 1989 (notes).

112. Inasmuch as it is part of the protasis of a present general conditional sentence.

113. Zehnle, *Discourse*, 124.

114. Gregory E. Sterling ("'Athletes of Virtue': An Analysis of the Summaries in Acts [2:41-47; 4:32-35; 5:12-16]," *JBL* 113 [1994]: 679–96) has argued for the formal inclusion of verse 41; see also, Luke T. Johnson, *The Literary Function of Possessions*

In addition to the theme of the spectacular success of the apostolic preaching (verses 41, 47) and the awe-inspiring power of the apostles to perform signs and wonders (verse 43),[115] this summary section describes the faithful performance of communal rituals and the unrestricted mutuality of material possessions.

Although Haenchen concluded that this summary (as well as that in Acts 4:34-35) was from Luke's own hand,[116] and Conzelmann emphasized its purely rhetorical function,[117] more recent interpretations have not been content to let these rather "summary" treatments of these verses stand. While acknowledging that both linguistic and stylistic evidence argue strongly for the Lukan composition of Acts 2:42-47, a number of interpreters point out that this does not preclude some historical basis for Luke's description. Dupont, for example, observes the affinity of ideas on the mutual sharing of possessions with classical Greek speculation regarding the Golden Age, as well as with the somewhat later Hellenistic topos of sharing within a society of friends.[118] At the same time, however, he notes affinities with certain biblical texts, particularly Deuteronomy 15:4, and he concludes that, while Luke may be guilty of some exaggeration, his description characterizes the historical reality of at least the most exemplary members of this earliest community of believers.[119] Moreover, Luke's purpose in composing this narrative summary is to hold up the example of the earliest community of Jerusalem believers "as an example for the church of his own day."[120]

More recently, S. Scott Bartchy has sought to further Dupont's suggestion of a historical basis for these verses by employing the sociocultural model of the "fictive kin group" to argue for the historical plausibility of the Lukan summaries regarding the sharing of possessions in Acts 2, 4, and 5. Moreover, his contention is aided by reference to the practice of historically contemporary and ethnically related religious communities, such as the Jewish sectarian community at Qumran. According to Bartchy, a mixture of Greek utopian language

---

in *Luke-Acts*, SBLDS 39 (Missoula: Scholars Press, 1977). Most interpretations, however, still assume verse 42 to be the formal beginning of the summary. Since both positions have their merit, it is, perhaps, best to consider verse 41 as intentionally transitional.

115. ἐγίνετο δὲ πάσῃ ψυχῇ φόβος ("and awe was in everyone").

116. Haenchen, *Acts*, 195.

117. Conzelmann, *Acts*, 24: "It is meant as an illustration of the uniqueness of the ideal earliest days of the movement."

118. Jacques Dupont, "Community of Goods in the Early Church," in idem, *Salvation*, 88–92.

119. Ibid., 92–94.

120. Ibid.

with clear biblical allusions is employed by Luke to describe "recognizable social realities."[121]

Whereas Bartchy thereby follows and expands upon the element of historical reality suggested by Dupont, Alan C. Mitchell is more interested in the practical application of the Lukan verses concerning the mutuality of possessions. In Mitchell's view, Luke depicts the early Jerusalem church in terms of the well-established and widely known Hellenistic philosophical topos of a community of friends in order "to show how friendship can continue across status lines and the poor can be benefited by the rich."[122] Mitchell contends, however, that Luke's interest in narrating these verses pertains chiefly to the historical situation of his own time, rather than to that of the original Jerusalem community.

The most recent variation of the essentially historical line of argument initiated anew by Dupont is an incisive article by Gregory E. Sterling. Sterling argues that the most historically pertinent literary model for the Lukan verses on the common life of the early Jerusalem community is derived from the description of religious or philosophical groups representing some outstandingly virtuous group within a larger ethnic community. He compares the descriptions of a number of such groups, including two Jewish sects that would have been contemporaries of the earliest Jerusalem community of believers—the Essenes and the Therapeutae. Based on a detailed comparison of several historical groups, Sterling develops a model of an exemplary group within a group, and he is able to show that the description in Luke-Acts shares many elements with this hypothetical model.

As with Dupont, Bartchy, and Mitchell, Sterling interprets the summaries of Acts 2:41-47; 4:32-35; and 5:12-16 as essentially historical in nature and function. But whereas both Dupont and Mitchell saw the function as hortatory, Sterling argues primarily for an apologetic function. By presenting the exemplary moral behavior of the early Jerusalem community as the embodiment of Christian values, the churches of Luke's own day could present themselves in a favorable light to their pagan neighbors and to future converts.[123]

Well researched and well argued as all of these studies are, they appear to suffer from at least one common flaw. None of them takes into account the pervasive element of the miraculous that is central to the entire narrative of Acts 2.

---

121. S. Scott Bartchy, "Community of Goods in Acts: Idealization or Social Reality?" in *The Future of Early Christianity: Essays in Honor of Helmut Koester,* ed. B. A. Pearson (Minneapolis: Fortress Press, 1991), 309–18, esp. 312–15.

122. Alan C. Mitchell, "The Social Function of Friendship in Acts 2:44-47 and 4:32-37," *JBL* 111 (1992): 255–72, esp. 272.

123. Sterling, "'Athletes of Virtue,'" 679–96, esp. 695–96.

The outpouring of the Holy Spirit is accompanied by a plethora of signs and wonders. The initial image of tongues of fire (verse 3) dissolves into the portrayal of many linguistic tongues (verse 4), which, in turn, results in the miracle of mutual understanding (verses 7-11). By means of Peter's modified version of the Joel prophecy (verses 17-21), Luke further emphasizes the eschatological nature of this momentous event. Following Peter's speech and the conversion of the first new members of the community of believers, Luke's summary (verses 42-47) closes with another miraculous occurrence: the miracle of spontaneous mutual understanding with which the chapter opened is balanced by the miracle of an equally spontaneous and harmonious sharing of possessions with which the chapter closes.

The emphasis throughout Acts 2, therefore, from the first verse to the last, is on the extraordinary presence of the grace of God, mediated through the power of the Spirit. The birth of the church and the ideal unity of its initial phase of existence rest entirely on the earthly presence of the divine power of the Spirit and its special potency in these early days.

Indeed, the rhetorical nature of Acts 2:42-47 is highlighted by Luke T. Johnson, who has recognized the significance of the inconsistencies in the summary passages of Acts 2, 4, and 5. Only in the initial summary of Acts 2 are there "no sour notes, no hint of division."[124] As the narrative recedes further in time from the eschatological epicenter of the Pentecost, conflict gradually emerges once again, and the miraculous phenomenon of the mutuality of possessions becomes an early casualty of the church's movement into the world. The most valuable aspect of Johnson's study, however, is his insistence that in Luke–Acts possessions function primarily (although not exclusively) on a symbolic level.[125] The full theological importance of this insight will be discussed at greater length in the next chapter.

Acts 2 closes with the apostles and the Pentecost converts gathered together, forming the nucleus of a new community of the saved, the true descendants of Abraham, the faithful remnant of the house of Israel. As has been illustrated in the preceding analysis, Luke's development of the divine plan for the reconstitution of the people of God at the dawn of the new age consists of two separate thematic strands that frequently intertwine: the theme of profound division within the house of Israel and the theme of the extension of the mission to receptive gentiles. Although the theme of the gentile mission quickly rises to a position of dominance within Acts, the problem of the division of Israel is the more pronounced theme within the first half of Luke's composition.

124. Johnson, *Literary Function of Possessions*, 190.
125. Ibid., 221.

"THE HOUSE OF ISRAEL" AND THEMES OF DIVISION AND REVERSAL

Indeed, the situation with respect to Israel receives great attention from the very beginning of the Gospel. The term *Israel* appears ten times within this first half of Luke-Acts, seven of which occur in the Gospel's first two chapters. Although he probably made use of sources, the composition of these opening chapters has been thoroughly reworked by Luke.[126] Of the remaining three instances of the term *Israel*, the one occurring in Luke 24 is probably an editorial addition (Luke 24:21), whereas the other two references originated in the tradition that Luke inherited (Luke 7:9; 22:30). Since the term *Israel* also appears fifteen times in Acts, the concern with the identity and role of Israel in God's salvation plan, which figures prominently in both halves of Luke-Acts, is clearly Luke's own.

The first mention of Israel occurs in Luke 1:16, in the context of the angel's prophecy to Zechariah regarding God's purpose for John the Baptist. Although the statement is mentioned in the positive—"he will turn many of the people of Israel to the Lord their God"—the implication that many of Israel's people are unfaithful cannot be ignored. Even with this first mention of the house of Israel, therefore, the implications are not unambiguously positive.[127] Israel is again mentioned in the concluding strophe of the second part of the Magnificat (Luke 1:54-55), which also forms the climax of this hymn of praise spoken by Mary. The Magnificat appears to have been composed by Luke out of a wealth of biblical hymnic traditions.[128] Its lyrical emphasis on God's coming to the aid of his people is closely allied with the soteriological tone of the great majority of the Psalms. Verses 54-55, which doubtless represent Luke's own theological summary, appear to unambiguously affirm that the promise of salvation for Israel is eternally valid because God is merciful and because he is faithful.[129]

The next two references to Israel are relatively unimportant.[130] With respect to the development of the theme of the identity and function of "Israel" in the

126. Bovon, *L'Évangile 1–9*, 25, 72, 83, passim; see also, Pierre Benoit ("L'enfance de Jean-Baptiste selon Luc i," *NTS* 3 [1957]: 169–94), who argues even more strongly for Lukan creativity in chapters 1–2.

127. Although Bovon (*L'Évangile 1–9*, 58) emphasizes the aspect of individual responsibility, he also recognizes the passage's corporate implications: "l'idée de l'endurcissement n'est pas loin" ("the idea of hardening is not far off").

128. Ibid., 83.

129. Ibid., 92.

130. The opening line of the canticle of Zechariah, "blessed be the Lord, the God of Israel" (Luke 1:68), is a formulaic benediction taken from early Jewish-Christian tra-

concluding episode of the divine salvation drama, however, it is Simeon's oracles, delivered in the temple, that serve as the climax of the overture of Luke's
composition and point toward the future development of this theme throughout Luke-Acts. That Simeon's two prophecies are delivered against a backdrop
of pious observance of the Mosaic law and of cultic sacrifice within the temple serves to legitimize the words that he is about to speak. Moreover, Simeon's
words are delivered under the direct inspiration of the Spirit (Luke 2:25).[131]
Luke's entire portrait of Simeon as a man under the Spirit, who longs for the
messianic salvation, is consciously drawn to evoke the spirit of the Psalms and
of Isaiah.[132] He describes Simeon as "righteous and devout, looking forward to
the consolation of Israel." As Bovon notes, the connotation of παράκλησις in
this context is clearly eschatological and corporate.[133] As with the reference to
Israel in Luke 1:16, here also Simeon's pious hope for Israel's future suggests
its decadent or degraded present state.

In the first oracle, Simeon praises God for the salvation that will be revealed
in Jesus and that is already perceived by the prophet with the inspired aid of
the Holy Spirit (verse 30). Most importantly, that salvation is here acknowledged to be universal in scope (verses 31-32). Whether these verses are the
work of Luke himself or are derived from an early Christian collection of
scriptural citations, this oracle is steeped in allusions to verses from Second
Isaiah.[134] Whereas in these verses' original context, however, their universalistic theme was subordinated to the uniqueness and importance of Israel's role,[135]
in the transition from Second Isaiah to Luke the universalistic theme has gained
supremacy and pride of place over that of Israel (verse 32).[136]

---

dition (ibid., 101). Luke's summarizing statement pointing to John's future public
appearance in Israel (Luke 1:80) is of slightly more importance, in that it further
strengthens the impression that the drama between God and Israel is about to unfold
its final act.

131. Brown, *Birth,* 453.

132. Werner Bieder, "πνεῦμα, πνευματικός," *TDNT* 6 (1968): 370.

133. Bovon, *L'Évangile 1–9,* 141.

134. Ibid., 143. Bovon argues that Luke composed these verses. Gerhard Lohfink (*Die
Sammlung Israels: Eine Untersuchung zur lukanishcen Ekklesiologie,* SANT 39 [Munich:
Kösel, 1975], 29) thinks that they come from L source.

135. At least to the extent that the restoration of Israel is the servant's primary task
(Isa 49:5). The extension of salvation to the nations is mentioned only afterward (Isa
49:6).

136. Bovon, *L'Évangile 1–9,* 142; *contra* Lohfink (*Die Sammlung,* 29), who argues that
Luke makes no change in the original biblical thought or formulation in this respect.
In his opinion, the gentile mission in Luke-Acts remains wholly subordinate to the goal
of salvation for Israel.

Bovon has also observed that the glory to be reflected on Israel may be a literary allusion to the glory that, in an earlier time, was reflected on Moses' face.[137] If that is true, then the surface meaning, which is clearly positive with respect to Israel, would be undercut by the knowledge that, in the case of Moses, the reflected glory visible on his face was only temporary. Although this hint of warning for Israel should not be dismissed, in the narrative present the first oracle of Simeon is clearly meant to be viewed both optimistically and inclusively; the salvation that Jesus brings will be brought before all peoples.

If, however, this first oracle offers the hope of salvation both to the nations and to Israel, the second oracle undercuts that hope with respect to Israel alone.[138] That Jesus will cause the falling and rising of many in Israel (verse 34c) is the prophecy of the division within the house of Israel already commented upon in the discussion of Acts 2.[139] By means of this prophecy, Luke emphasizes that the division reflects the explicit will and plan of God. Moreover, the prophecy suggests that the degraded or fallen condition of Israel will get much worse before it gets better.

The final segment of the verse (verse 34d) completes the theme of division expressed in verse 34c: Jesus will be a sign that will arouse opposition.[140] Luke's use of the verb ἀντιλέγω is significant, in view of the other instances within the narrative in which this verb appears. Indeed, it appears only one other time within the Gospel. In the context of the last days of Jesus' public ministry, when he is teaching in the temple and is confronted by the opposition of Jerusalem's leaders, the Sadducees are described as those who speak against (ἀντιλέγω) the resurrection (Luke 20:27). Thus, the Sadducees and, with them, the scribes, chief priests, and elders may be identified with the nucleus of the opposition group within Israel.

The next occurrence of ἀντιλέγω is in the reaction of the synagogue audience to Paul's Pisidian Antioch speech (Acts 13:26–47). Although their reaction is initially favorable, when the synagogue becomes overrun with interested gentiles residing in this city, the synagogue members are described by Luke as "filled with jealousy" and as "speaking against" (ἀντιλέγω) what was preached

---

137. Bovon, *L'Évangile 1–9*, 142.

138. Again opinion seems to be divided as to whether Luke wrote these verses or took them from a source. Brown (*Birth*, 454) thinks that he wrote them; Bovon (*L'Évangile 1–9*, 143–44) does not.

139. See, for example, Brown, *Birth*, 460. However, Brown is certainly mistaken in his identification of these two groups as Jews and gentiles. Luke is speaking of two distinct groups of Israelites; see also, Lohfink, *Die Sammlung*, 30.

140. Literally, "that will be spoken against."

by Paul (Acts 13:45). Thus, the third use of this verb serves as a dramatic marker in the narrative; the rift within Israel has widened from a relatively small coterie of leaders (Luke 20:27) to include large numbers of the former people of God, now generally referred to as οἱ Ἰουδαῖοι.

The last two references to ἀντιλέγω occur in Acts 28, in the same scene in which the last reference to Israel also appears. In relating his arrest in Jerusalem to his audience in Rome (Acts 28:17-22), Paul draws a picture of Jewish guilt and reluctant Roman complicity in his sufferings that roughly parallels Peter's summary of Israelite guilt and reluctant Roman complicity in Jesus' persecution and crucifixion (Acts 2:22-23). In this later recapitulation, Paul remarks that although the Romans had wanted to release him, the Jews had spoken against him (ἀντιλεγόντων δὲ τῶν Ἰουδαίων; Acts 28:19). That he attributes his present circumstances to his efforts "for the sake of the hope of Israel" (ἕνεκεν γὰρ τῆς ἐλπίδος τοῦ Ἰσραήλ) is deliberate Lukan irony. Within the context of Acts 28, this last remark must refer to Paul's final, futile attempt to save the house of Israel from destruction.

Luke emphasizes that Paul's efforts with regard to Israel have largely been in vain, when he employs the last instance of ἀντιλέγω in Acts 28:22. Here, the Jews of Rome make their reply with respect to the believing segment of divided Israel: "for concerning this sect, we know that everywhere it is spoken against" (μὲν γὰρ τῆς αἱρέσεως ταύτης γνωστὸν ἡμῖν ἐστιν ὅτι πανταχοῦ ἀντιλέγεται).

Thus, in this concluding segment of Luke's composition, Simeon's second oracle has been fulfilled with disastrous results. The opposition that Jesus, his message, and his mission have aroused within Israel has become so widespread that faithful Israel represents only a fraction of those formerly known as the house of Israel. This, however, is only one strand of Luke's story of the reconstitution of the people of God. To enable a comparison between Luke's transition from the "house of Israel" to the "true Israel" on the one hand, and Virgil's transition from Trojans to Romans on the other, it is necessary to review two additional passages.

Prelude to Calamity: Division and Reversal in Luke 4:14-30

If Simeon's second oracle warned of the coming division in Israel, in which rejection of God's chosen emissaries would bring its people to the brink of annihilation, Simeon's first oracle held out the hope of a reconstituted people in which gentiles would assume the dominant place among the recipients of salvation. Luke subsequently incorporates key references to this theme of the spread of salvation to the gentiles in the chapters that follow. For example, in

John the Baptist's inaugural address to Israel, only Luke among the synoptic writers has lengthened the scriptural paraphrase of Isaiah 40 so as to include the words "all flesh will see the salvation of God" (καὶ ὄψεται πᾶσα σὰρξ τὸ σωτήριον τοῦ θεοῦ; Luke 3:6).[141]

In an ironic counterpoint to this universalistic emphasis, however, Luke stages Jesus' inaugural discourse in a synagogue at Nazareth.[142] Just as Simeon's oracles had been delivered against the backdrop of the temple with its cultic trappings, at Nazareth Jesus' words are delivered within the context of the synagogue liturgy.[143] In several important respects the scene at Nazareth actualizes, at least proleptically, both of Simeon's oracles. Because of this and because Jesus sets forth the terms of the mission as the fulfillment of the divine plan revealed in scriptural prophecy, his speech is programmatic not only for the Gospel but for the entire composition of Luke-Acts.[144]

Initially, Jesus' speech activates the bright promise contained in Simeon's first oracle. Luke narrates that Jesus addresses his hearers by reading from the prophet Isaiah. The text itself is a modified version of Isaiah 61:1-2, with an addition from Isaiah 58:6,[145] as well as several omissions from the former text.[146] This prophecy—which announces a general program of redemption and liberation and which Isaiah had identified with the eschatological promise of the reign of God—Jesus announces as fulfilled in his presence. Thus, the promise of messianic salvation about which Simeon spoke following Jesus' birth is on the brink of fulfillment, albeit proleptically, with the inauguration of Jesus' mission.

If, however, Jesus' speech actualizes the hope and promise of Simeon's first oracle, the people's incredulity and Jesus' harsh response to their questioning dramatically confirm the warning contained in Simeon's second oracle. Jesus will provoke opposition and division within Israel. In verses 25-27, Luke moves the plot beyond the mere verification of the Simeon oracles by suggesting that

141. Dupont, "Salvation," 14–15; Zehnle, *Discourse*, 130.

142. Despite the general similarities between Luke's account and that found in Mark 6:1-6 (= Matt 13:53-58), the differences are significant. Not only is the story greatly expanded in Luke, but it is also completely reinterpreted. Whereas in Mark the point of the story is the offense caused by Jesus' wisdom and mighty works, in Luke the point of the story is the offense caused by Jesus' claim to be the messianic agent of the eschatological time of fulfillment and the rejection with which that messianic claim is met by his compatriots; cf. Strauss, *Messiah*, 219.

143. Étienne Samain, "Le discours-programme de Jésus à la synagogue de Nazareth," *Foi et Vie* 70 (1971): 25–43.

144. Ibid., 40.

145. "To let the oppressed go free" (ἀπόστελλε τεθραυσμένους ἐν ἀφέσει).

opposition and rejection within Israel will be linked to the bestowal of the eschatological gifts upon gentiles. Indeed, Jesus' allusion to the gentile-oriented nature of Elijah's and Elisha's miracles provokes a united response of rage among his pious synagogue hearers (καὶ ἐπλήσθησαν πάντες θυμοῦ) who, in their nearly successful attempt to kill him, not only provide a narrative preview of the passion[147] but also disclose with a rather skillful display of dramatic irony how the people's actions will one day draw the entire house of Israel to the brink of destruction. Thus, Luke depicts Jesus' inaugural encounter with his people as a prelude to calamity that anticipates the problem of the entire composition. This dramatic technique corresponds on a stylistic level to Homer's depiction of the plague, with which the *Iliad* opens, and Virgil's depiction of the storm, with which the *Aeneid* begins.[148]

The veiled hope for Israel's continuation lies in Jesus' pronouncement of the verses from Isaiah (Luke 4:18-19). The mission will succeed in Israel among those currently viewed as outsiders: the sick, the poor, and the penitent sinners. These are the people from whom the mass of Israelites will divide, and these are the ones whom God has willed to save from the midst of a sinful people. They will form the nucleus of a new people of God, joined by a large influx of gentiles, to create the eschatological Israel according to God's will and plan.

Out of the Ruins: The Emergence of the "True Israel"

Although the hints of division within Israel and of the importance of the gentiles to the final stage of the divine plan of salvation can be traced from the birth narratives to the inauguration of both John's and Jesus' missions, and although the development of this dual theme is proleptically fulfilled in the Pentecost narrative and its interpretation in Peter's speech, the ultimate composition of the people of God in accordance with his divine will is revealed most clearly in the first section of James's speech before the apostolic council in Jerusalem (Acts 15:14-18).

Dupont has argued that verses 16-18, which are a slightly modified version of the Septuagint's translation of Amos 9:11-12,[149] are closely linked to the

---

146. "To heal the broken heart" (ἰάσασθαι τοὺς συντετριμμένους τῇ καρδίᾳ); "and the day of vengeance" (καὶ ἡμέραν ἀνταποδόσεως).

147. Samain, "Le discours," 37; Bovon, *L'Évangile 1–9*, 209–10.

148. Viktor Pöschl, *The Art of Virgil: Image and Symbol in the* Aeneid (Ann Arbor, Mich.: Greenwood Press, 1986), 12–14; see discussion in chapter 2.

149. The major modifications that Luke makes are: (1) the addition of ἀναστρέψω ("I will return"); (2) the replacement of the two instances of ἀναστήσω ("I will raise up") with ἀνοικοδομήσω ("I will build up"), and the resulting necessity of adding the synonym ἀνορθώσω ("I will restore, rebuild"); (3) the addition of τὸν κύριον and the

composition of verse 14. Moreover, because verse 15 is only a transitional link, verses 14–18 form an integrated compositional unit, all elements of which presuppose the use of the Septuagint.[150] Thus, the declaration in verse 14, ὁ θεὸς ἐπεσκέψατο ("God looked favorably"), while not a direct biblical quotation, is nonetheless a literary allusion to a specific complex of Septuagintal passages in which the phrase λαὸς / λαὸν....παρὰ πάντα τὰ ἔθνη / ἀπὸ πάντων τῶν ἐθνῶν appears.[151] Dupont suggests that, whereas all of these passages also include the adjective περιούσιος ("special, peculiar"), Luke has substituted τῷ ὀνόματι αὐτοῦ ("for his name"), the substitution having been suggested by the inclusion of a variation of the phrase in the Amos text quoted in verse 17.[152]

Based on this literary analysis, Dupont concludes that Luke wants to emphasize that the people whom God established will not only be his possession in *opposition* to the nations, but a people whom he has chosen from *among* those very nations. They will be a new people set apart as his possession. Thus, Dupont finds the Exodus analogy to be particularly appropriate.[153] Fallen Israel has become just another ἔθνος, from which emerges the nucleus of the new λαός.[154]

In response to Dupont's interpretation, which stresses the primacy of the gentiles in the reconstituted people of God, Nils Dahl has argued that the literary allusion in verse 14 is not linked to the complex of passages Dupont has cited but refers instead to Zechariah 2:15: "and many peoples shall be *added to* the people of the Lord at this time, and they shall be a people before me" [emphasis mine]. Dahl is able to make this connection by arguing for a close relationship between Amos 9:11-12 and Zechariah 2:14-17, as both passages have been worded in the Septuagint.[155] According to Dahl, therefore, the meaning of Acts 15:14 is that, despite the fact that "the majority of Jews have disinherited themselves,"

---

addition of γνωστὰ ἀπ' αἰῶνος at the conclusion of verse 18. For a detailed comparison of the text of Amos 9:11-12 with that of Acts 15:16-18, see Earl Richard, "The Creative Use of Amos by the Author of Acts," *NovT* 24 (1982): 44–48.

150. Jacques Dupont, "ΛΑΟΣ 'ΕΞ 'ΕΘΝΩΝ," *NTS* 3 (1956–57): 47.

151. That is, Deut 7:6; 14:2; Exod 19:5; 23:22. Conzelmann (*Acts*, 17), however, argues that Luke has no specific allusion in mind and is just imitating biblical style.

152. Dupont, "ΛΑΟΣ," 48.

153. Ibid., 49.

154. As opposed to Strathmann's view ("λαός," 54) regarding Acts 15:14-18, that another λαός now takes its place along with Israel, but on a different basis: "Within Israel only those who meet the decisive conditions belong to *this laos.*"

155. Nils A. Dahl, "'A People for His Name,'" *NTS* 4 (1957–58): 324.

the status of Israel as the people of God is not questioned; it is only said that in addition to the people to whom the promises were given God has also taken "from the Gentiles [some] people for His name."[156]

Closely allied with the position of Dahl is that of Gerhard Lohfink, who argues that it is verses 16-17, taken together, that provide the key to a true understanding of Luke's perspective on the relationship of the gentile church to Israel. Whereas Dupont's interpretation focuses on verse 17, treating verse 16 as irrelevant prologue,[157] Lohfink believes that verse 16 has primary importance for Luke because it is the gathering and rebuilding of Israel that not only precedes but, more importantly, makes possible the very existence of the gentile mission. Indeed, it is because this gathering and rebuilding of the true and believing Israel out of the old people of God has already taken place (Acts 2–5) that the gentile mission is enabled to go forth.[158]

Although Lohfink's interpretation is possible, it places too little emphasis on the importance of the participial phrases modifying τὴν σκηνὴν Δαυίδ, namely, τὴν πεπτωκυῖαν ("the fallen dwelling of David") and τὰ κατεσκαμμένα αὐτῆς ("out of its ruins").[159] In Luke's eyes, the gathering and rebuilding of the true Israel takes place out of the *ruins* of the old people of God. Indeed, whereas Lohfink implies a smooth transition from the former composition of Israel to its eschatological composition, Bovon emphasizes that along with continuity there is also an important element of "rupture." He concludes by saying,

> it seems clear to me that Luke saw in the primitive community not only the legitimate continuation of the people of Israel, but also a new creation of God in the midst of a fallen people.[160]

---

156. Ibid., 324, 326.

157. Lohfink, *Die Sammlung*, 59.

158. Ibid., 59.

159. The weight of the NT textual evidence favors this reading. Moreover, although the variant reading of κατεστραμμένα, witnessed in uncials B and ℵ does appear as a variant reading of the original Amos passage, it is not attested by manuscripts that have a likelihood of reflecting first-century CE Palestinian readings (see Dominique Barthélemy, *Études d'histoire du texte de l'Ancien Testament*, OBO 21 [Göttingen, Ger.: Vandenhoeck & Ruprecht, 1978], 1–157, passim). Therefore, in the unlikely event that the original Lukan text read κατεστραμμένα, it would indicate that Luke had somewhat softened the wording of his source without, however, changing its essential meaning.

160. François Bovon, "Israel, the Church, and the Gentiles in the Twofold Work of Luke," in *New Testament Traditions* (1995): 89.

A somewhat different approach, based on that formerly espoused by Haenchen,[161] has been developed in the recent study by Strauss. According to him, the belief that the entrance of the gentiles into the church was initiated and preordained by God is one of the most important themes of Luke-Acts and has become the work's central focus by Acts 15.[162] Strauss agrees that James's speech is the focal point of chapter 15, and he argues that the key interpretive problem of verses 16-18 is the following: To what does the phrase ἡ σκηνὴ Δαυίδ refer? What has fallen and what is restored or rebuilt that makes possible the salvation of the gentiles?[163]

According to Strauss, σκηνὴ Δαυίδ refers to the Davidic dynasty and reflects the retrospective interpretation of Hellenistic Judaism on the inherent fragility of the now defunct Davidic dynasty. Thus, Strauss argues, the rebuilt tent (tabernacle, dwelling) of David does not refer to the church as the "true Israel." In Acts 15, the true Israel is still in the process of being formed, whereas the statement in verse 14 presupposes that this rebuilding has already occurred. Rather, it is the reestablishment of the fallen Davidic dynasty, accomplished in the death, resurrection, and exaltation of Jesus, that is the restoration out of ruins to which James alludes.[164]

Although Strauss's interpretation attempts to avoid the vexing issue of the changing composition of the people of God, it has a serious weakness. If by ἡ σκηνὴ Δαυίδ, Luke was actually referring to the Davidic dynasty, restored through Jesus' resurrection and exaltation, he would have had no reason to delete the two references to ἀνίστημι from the Amos citation in the Septuagint. That Luke has taken care to replace the references to this theologically loaded verb indicates that, whatever else his intended meaning may have been, it was not primarily a reference to the risen and exalted Jesus as the restoration of the Davidic dynasty.[165]

The σκηνὴ Δαυίδ must therefore refer to the "house of David," in the sense of the "house of Israel," as that term is used in Acts 2:36: the house that, in Luke's opinion, has been brought to the brink of ruin through its culpability in Jesus' death and by the continued rejection of the apostolic witness by so many of its people. Indeed, already in Acts 2, it had become a house divided to its very foundations. From the ruins of this former people, however, has

161. Haenchen, *Acts*, 448.
162. Strauss, *Messiah*, 181.
163. Ibid., 184–87.
164. Ibid., 187.
165. Of the nine times that the verb ἀνίστημι appears in Acts, seven of them are references to Jesus' resurrection.

emerged a faithful remnant, who now form the nucleus of the new people of God. To this faithful remnant from the former house of Israel will be added a great number of gentiles, whom the Lord shall call. Together they will constitute the true Israel, called by a new name and ultimately destined to form a new cultic center in the very heart of the Roman world. Moreover, as Peter's speech had proclaimed (Acts 15:7-11) and as Luke's addition of γνωστὰ ἀπ' αἰῶνος further emphasizes (Acts 15:17b-18), the inclusion of gentiles is no afterthought. Rather, that which is now becoming manifest has indeed been "known" for a long time.[166]

Thus, just as the gods who had willed the destruction of Troy also ensured the survival of a faithful remnant, so also does Luke portray the division and ultimate collapse of the house of Israel as a result of the expressed will and plan of God. The faithful remnant, the true descendants of Abraham who are obedient to the divine Spirit, form the nucleus of a new community. To this core, a great number of gentiles are added, just as in Virgil's narrative the Trojan remnant is led by divine guidance to merge with the numerically superior Latin peoples, taking a new name. Even though the Trojans will relinquish their native language and customs, their nobility and courage, the true virtues of ancient Troy will live on in their Roman descendants. In an analogous manner, even though the identity and cultic practices of the eschatological people of God will reflect their new cultural and ethnic composition,[167] Luke takes care throughout his narrative to emphasize that it is within this new people of God that the true spirit of ancient Israel lives on.

The preceding discussion of Acts 2 and key related passages in Luke's two-part composition has not only revealed the evangelist's use of certain themes and dramatic devices borrowed from the repertoire of Greco-Roman epic, but it has also pointed to the very strong possibility that Luke composed his work as a unified dramatic whole, rather than simply as a narrated series of historical and quasihistorical events. The final chapter will examine the structure and composition of Luke-Acts in its entirety, in an effort to show that the literary tendencies already revealed do indeed apply to the whole of Luke-Acts.

166. That is, it has been knowable through a proper understanding of the prophets. The implication is that it has been part of God's plan from the very beginning.

167. Negatively, in its abandonment of circumcision and other cultic exactions of the Mosaic law, but also positively, in its adoption of new cultic practices that are more congenial with a Hellenistic milieu.

5

LUKE-ACTS RECONSIDERED

A SUITABLE INTRODUCTION FOR LITERATE GREEK PROSE: LUKE 1:1-4

Structurally independent of the Lukan narrative, the prologue (Luke 1:1-4) sets forth the audience and the fundamental objective of Luke-Acts. Many scholars also insist that it clearly signals Luke's intended genre. Indeed, it is frequently assumed that, by the particular form of his prologue, Luke signals his intention to write in the manner of Hellenistic historians. This assumption, however, appears to go beyond the evidence afforded by an examination of Luke 1:1-4.

For example, although Cadbury believes that Luke is inspired by the example of Hellenistic historians, he also acknowledges that Luke's use of stylized words such as ἐπειδήπερ and πολλοί are primarily indications of Luke's desire to achieve a manner of presentation that may be deemed worthy of Greco-Roman literary style *in general* and that the formal elements of his prologue are broadly imitative of the literary prologues of nearly all types of literate Greek prose.[1] W. C. van Unnik, after noting the anomalous brevity of the Lukan prologue in comparison to those found in the works of Greco-Roman historians, is nonetheless certain that it has been patterned after the prologue of Flavius Josephus's apologetic treatise, *Contra Apionem*.[2]

Both Joseph A. Fitzmyer and Loveday Alexander, however, agree with Cadbury in stressing the multigeneric nature of the Lukan prologue, which,

---

1. Henry J. Cadbury, "Commentary on the Preface of Luke," in *The Beginnings of Christianity: Acts of the Apostles*, ed. F. J. Foakes-Jackson and Kirsopp Lake, vol. 2 (London: Macmillan, 1922), 492–93.

2. W. C. van Unnik, "The Purpose of Luke's Historical Writing (Luke 1:1-4)," in *Sparsa Collecta: The Collected Essays of W. C. van Unnik* (Leiden: E. J. Brill, 1973), 11.

they note, finds as many parallels among scientific treatises as it does among
Hellenistic histories.[3] Indeed, based on the general consensus of research
regarding Luke 1:1-4, all that may be reasonably concluded is that Luke adopts
a mode of literary presentation that he deems suitable both to his intended
audience and to the importance of his subject matter. Moreover, although the
form of Luke's prologue indicates his intention to conform to the style of
Greek literary prose, nothing in its content precludes the possibility that he
conceived of his project as a prose epic of early Christian origins.

As was mentioned in the previous chapter, Luke begins the prologue by
recalling his literary predecessors and their common narrative task,[4] which
Luke alone defines as the setting forth of an ordered account, not just of events
handed down in Christian tradition by "those who from the beginning were
eyewitnesses and servants of the Word" (οἱ ἀπ᾽ ἀρχῆς αὐτόπται καὶ
ὑπηρέται γενόμενοι τοῦ λόγου, verse 2) but also "concerning events that
have been fulfilled among us" (περὶ τῶν πεπληροφορημένων ἐν ἡμῖν πραγμάτων, verse 1). Van Unnik interprets this latter phrase solely in terms of Jesus'
work of salvation as set forth in Luke's Gospel.[5] However, Luke is clearly think-
ing in the more inclusive terms of *God's* work of salvation and the complete
unfolding of the divine plan,[6] which is accomplished in part through the birth,
ministry, death, resurrection, and ascension of Jesus, but which also continues
in the birth of the church and the growth of the early Christian community
under the guidance of the Spirit.[7]

It is from this wider perspective of the ongoing fulfillment of God's salvation plan that Luke interjects himself as a participant and interpreter[8] of these
events, not "from the beginning" (ἀπ᾽ ἀρχῆς), as was the case with the eye-

---

3. Joseph A. Fitzmyer, *The Gospel According to Luke*, vol. 1 (Garden City, N.Y.:
Doubleday, 1981), 288. See also, François Bovon, *L'Évangile selon Saint Luc 1–9* (Geneva:
Labor et Fides, 1991), 35; Loveday Alexander, "Luke's Preface in the Context of Greek
Preface-Writing," *NovT* 28 (1986): 65.

4. See chapter 4, n. 1.

5. Van Unnik, "Purpose," 14.

6. See, for example, Robert L. Brawley, *Centering on God: Method and Message in Luke-
Acts* (Louisville: Westminster John Knox, 1990), 25; and Robert Tannehill, *The Narrative
Unity of Luke-Acts: A Literary Interpretation*, vol. 1 (Philadelphia: Fortress Press, 1986),
20–22, passim.

7. Cadbury, *Beginnings*, vol. 2, 496; Bovon, *L'Évangile 1–9*, 38-39; cf. Col 1:6, 24-25;
2:19; Eph 1:11-14.

8. παρακολουθέω, "to follow closely with a mind to understand." LSJ, rev. ed.
(Oxford: Clarendon, 1968), 1313b. For an interpretation of the "we" passages as part
of this central literary agenda, see the discussion later in this chapter.

witnesses, but nevertheless "for some time" (ἄνωθεν).[9] Thus, Luke's implicit claim to offer a narrative account of the recent events of salvation history that is superior to that of his predecessors is based not only on the greater inclusiveness of his account but also on his implied access to a deeper or more complete understanding of how these events fulfill God's will and plan for the salvation of humankind. It is to this deeper insight into the meaning and interrelationship of the momentous events of the recent past that Luke obliquely refers by the term καθεξῆς (verse 3).[10]

Even today opinion remains divided as to whether the Lukan addressee, "most excellent Theophilus" is merely symbolic or refers to a historical person. Although a majority of scholars currently favor the latter interpretation,[11] a metaphorical or symbolic reading of this name, which means "friend of God," is more probable on the basis of both the internal as well as the external evidence. First, that Luke is using the name *Theophilus* as a symbolic term encompassing both the Christian believer and the favorably disposed pagan is consistent with other examples of symbolic Lukan names.[12] Second, although those who favor the historical reality of Luke's Theopilus argue that the term "most excellent" (κράτιστος) is an adjective commonly applied to dedicatees of literary works,[13] in point of fact, Luke employs the term on three other occasions (Acts 23:26; 24:3; 26:25), and in each of these instances the context is forensic and the person addressed as κράτιστος appears in the role of a judge. Likewise, the verb ἐπιγιγνώσκω (Luke 1:4), which many translations render

9. Jacques Dupont, *Les sources du livre des Actes: État de la question* (Paris: Desclée de Brouwer, 1960), 104; also in general agreement, Heinz Schürmann, *Das Lukasevangelium,* Herders Theologischer Kommentar zum Neuen Testament, vol. 3 (Freiburg: Herder, 1969), 11; *contra* Cadbury, *Beginnings,* vol. 2, 502–3.

10. As Cadbury (*Beginnings,* vol. 2, 505) observed, καθεξῆς need not imply accordance with an objectively determined chronological or geographical order; see also Bovon, *L'Evangile 1–9,* 41.

11. For example, Cadbury, *Beginnings,* vol. 2, 507–8; Fitzmyer, *Luke,* vol. 1, 287; Bovon, *L'Évangile 1–9,* 41.

12. For example, Lydia, the wealthy merchant of purple cloth from Thyatira (Acts 16:14); Barnabas, virtual embodiment of the dutiful Christian disciple, whose very name means "encouragement" (Acts 4:36–37; 11:22–24, 29–30, passim); and Eutychus, whose name means "Lucky" (Acts 20:9). For this last observation, see Brawley, *Centering on God,* 173; *contra* Ernst Haenchen (*The Acts of the Apostles: A Commentary* [Philadelphia: Westminster, 1971], 585). Even Cadbury (*Beginnings,* vol. 2, 507–8), who does not favor this interpretation, acknowledges that *theophilus* as a generic adjective is attested in this period and that early church fathers tended to interpret Luke 1:4 in this manner.

13. Bovon, *L'Évangile 1–9,* 41.

as "to know," may be translated just as correctly as "to come to a determination," "to decide."[14]

Based upon evidence drawn from the text itself, therefore, it is likely that in this direct address to the symbolic Theophilus, Luke invites his reader to be the judge concerning the validity of the Christian proclamation, but also to make his or her determination based upon Luke's unique presentation of the important events leading up to the birth of the church and continuing into its early missionary endeavors, and his presentation of the particular significance of these events within the divine plan. Finally, the emphatic position of τὴν ἀσφάλειαν ("with assurance" or "with conviction")[15] underscores Luke's central assertion that even though his narrative is only one of several that attempt to set forth the events of the recent Christian past, his is the only one that is sufficiently comprehensive and insightful to inspire the pious reader with unequivocal conviction concerning the true meaning of these events.

THE DRAMATIC OVERTURE: LUKE 1–2

After the formal prologue begins the extended dramatic overture that sets the stage for the narration of the epic proper, the story of Jesus and the divine mission he undertakes.[16] A further argument against interpreting Luke-Acts as historiography on the basis of its formal prologue is the extremely contrived and stylized nature of the extended prologue that follows. Just as Virgil places Aeneas within an imaginary continuation of the story line of Homer's *Iliad,* so also does Luke introduce both John the Baptist and Jesus within the imaginary continuation of the story line of Israel's scriptural past.[17]

Moreover, as has already been mentioned by numerous interpreters, the annunciation stories of John the Baptist and Jesus are presented by Luke in conscious parallelism.[18] These parallel stories are subsequently brought together

---

14. LSJ, 627b.

15. For example, Cadbury, *Beginnings,* vol. 2, 509; van Unnik, "Purpose," 8–9; Fitzmyer, *Luke,* vol. 1, 290.

16. See, for example, William S. Kurz, *Reading Luke-Acts: Dynamics of Biblical Narrative* (Louisville: Westminster John Knox, 1993), 19.

17. Tannehill (*Narrative Unity,* vol. 1, 18) remarks on this point with respect to the Gospel of Luke. I do not mean to suggest, however, that this technique is still unique to epic at this comparatively late period. James Kugel (*Early Biblical Interpretation* [Philadelphia: Westminster, 1986], 47–48) has argued that a similar technique has been applied by writers of the Second Temple period to works both biblical and apocryphal.

18. Bovon, *L'Évangile 1–9,* 209; see also, discussion in chapter 1.

through the narrative technique of *interlacement,* when Mary visits Elizabeth and the two women embrace.[19] The most important feature of these annunciation stories is the complex of divine prophecies that they incorporate. The angel tells Zechariah that John will prepare the people for the arrival of salvation by preaching repentance (Luke 1:16-17), whereas Mary is told that her son will reign over the kingdom of God's people and that of this kingdom there will be no end (Luke 1:32-33). Because this latter proclamation alludes to Nathan's prophecy, which had been addressed to David (2 Sam 7:9-16 = 2 Kgs 7:9-16 LXX), it appears to be straightforward and completely understandable within the context of Israel's salvation history. As will be seen, however, this key Lukan prophecy is deliberately ambiguous and will not be fully understood until its final resolution is achieved proleptically at the close of Acts.

That Jesus' unique and exalted destiny is prophesied by divine messenger is just one of several literary techniques by which Luke endeavors to portray Jesus in the language and imagery of a Hellenistic hero.[20] In obedient compliance with the goal of fulfillment of the prophecy,[21] Jesus subsequently embarks upon a lengthy mission, which momentarily appears to end in failure with his rejection and death in Jerusalem.[22] Following Jesus' resurrection and renewed appearances and instructions to his disciples, however, the Gospel closes with the implied assurance of Jesus' heavenly enthronement (Luke 23:42-43; 24:26). Thus, the first part of Luke's narrative ends with only a partial fulfillment of the annunciation prophecy presented in Luke 1:32-33:

καὶ δώσει αὐτῷ κύριος ὁ θεὸς τὸν θρόνον Δαυὶδ τοῦ πατρὸς αὐτοῦ, καὶ βασιλεύσει ἐπὶ τὸν οἶκον Ἰακὼβ εἰς τοὺς αἰῶνας καὶ τῆς Βασιλείας αὐτοῦ οὐκ ἔσται τέλος.

[A]nd the Lord God will give him the throne of his ancestor David. He will reign over the house of Jacob forever, and of his kingdom there will be no end.

---

19. Every element in Jesus' story, however, is depicted as superior to the corresponding detail regarding John. For example, Elizabeth is a descendant of Aaron, whereas Joseph is a descendant of David, Jacob, and Abraham; John will be filled with the Holy Spirit from before birth, but Jesus will be sired by the Holy Spirit; John will preach repentance and offer forgiveness of sins, but Jesus will bring salvation.

20. Also pertinent to this portrait is Jesus' birth in adverse circumstances but with supernatural fanfare (Luke 2:1-20), as well as his growth in strength and wisdom, possessing the favor of God and human beings (Luke 2:40, 52).

21. With Jesus' symbolic abandonment of the protection of his earthly parents in favor of his involvement in the affairs of his heavenly Father (Luke 2:48-50), the stage is set for the beginning of his mission.

22. The disciples initially perceive it as such (Luke 24:21).

The meaning of this prophecy cannot be fully grasped, however, until the end of Luke's second book. The risen Jesus' original missionary charge to the disciples (Luke 24:47) is reissued in geographical terms in the beginning of Acts (Acts 1:8). The repetition and further elaboration of this command set the course for the second phase of the mission, which, when accomplished, will illuminate the true meaning of this programmatic prophecy.[23]

Although Hans Conzelmann regarded the birth narratives as secondary and essentially irrelevant, more recent interpreters have rightly rejected this assumption.[24] On the contrary, it is quite clear that the first two chapters serve as a kind of overture, not only for the Gospel but for the entire composition, in that these chapters contain a preview of all of the major themes and narrative devices that will subsequently be developed within the body of the text. Indeed, three basic Lukan devices introduced in chapters 1–2 prefigure the scope and structure of Luke-Acts in its entirety.

To begin with, Jesus and John are presented in a series of parallelisms, with Jesus always presented as the greater of the two. Moreover, this parallelism between Jesus and John extends beyond the opening chapters and into the main body of the text: John's annunciation (Luke 1:5-25)/Jesus' annunciation (Luke 1:26-38); John's birth (Luke 1:57-80)/Jesus' birth (Luke 2:1-20); John's initial and programmatic proclamation (Luke 3:1-20)/Jesus' opening and programmatic proclamation (Luke 4:14-30). John brings repentance and forgiveness of sins and thereby represents the prerequisite for the salvation of which Jesus is the bearer and embodiment. On a metaphorical level, therefore, this tandem pattern of John and Jesus extends throughout the entire story of Luke-Acts in the continued linkage of repentance and salvation, first negatively with respect to the motif of the judgment of Jerusalem (Luke 13–24), then positively in the preaching of repentance and salvation in the missionary speeches of the apostles (Acts 2–28).[25]

---

23. Although this prophecy appears to have been drawn from Nathan's words to David (2 Sam 7:9-16 LXX), the substitution of οὐκ τέλος for the ἕως αἰῶνος of 2 Sam 7:16 is justified solely as a means of linking the completion of the mission in Acts to this initial birth prophecy pertaining to the role and destiny of Jesus. Moreover, none of the relevant textual variants for this passage suggest that Luke might have found such a substitution in his source.

24. Paul Minear, "Luke's Use of the Birth Stories," in *Studies in Luke-Acts: Essays Presented in Honor of Paul Schubert,* ed. L. E. Keck and J. L. Martyn (Nashville: Abingdon, 1966), 111–30. See also, Fitzmyer, *Luke,* vol. 1, 163; Tannehill, *Narrative Unity,* vol. 1, 20; Bovon, *L'Évangile 1–9,* 47, to cite just a few.

25. Although John's prefatory role is specifically noted in Peter's report to the Jerusalem church (Acts 11:16), the metaphorical linking of repentance and salvation

A second motif that is prefigured in the opening chapters is the unfolding of the divine plan of salvation. Although fully revealed in scripture, God's purpose remains hidden from human beings, unless and until they receive insight through the Holy Spirit. Thus, Luke fills the opening chapters with a series of ambiguous prophecies, a device that allows the prophecies to remain valid throughout surprising reversals as the narrative plot unfolds. This theme of reversal is introduced in the Magnificat (Luke 1:44-55), and hints of its deeper metaphorical levels of meaning are scattered throughout the prophecies of Luke 1–2. For example, as has already been discussed in the preceding chapter, Simeon's first oracle (Luke 2:29-32), which speaks of the glory conferred upon Israel, may be intended as irony, emphasizing the impermanent nature of both this glory and the election of this people as presently constituted. Almost from the outset of the narrative, therefore, the reader is made to realize that the mission of salvation cannot be accomplished without some sort of reversal in human circumstances.

Finally, amid a shower of blessings both human and divine, Jesus is introduced as the one designated by God to undertake the mission, the goal of which is the fulfillment of God's plan of salvation. Indeed, already in these opening chapters, Jesus is presented in the style and manner of Greek and Roman heroes: birth in adverse circumstances, growth in strength and wisdom, possessing the favor of gods and human beings, and easy access to divine guidance and power.

INAUGURATION OF THE MISSION AND INITIAL OPPOSITION: LUKE 3–12

The themes of reversal and of Jesus as the bearer of the new phase of God's salvation plan, which are already implied in the opening series of parallel stories of John and Jesus, are developed more fully in the parallel missionary speeches of chapters 3–4. John begins his preaching of repentance for the forgiveness of sins with an important speech paraphrasing Isaiah (Isa 40:3-5), which Luke has greatly expanded from its brief reference in his Markan source,[26] partly with material from Q. Even this first public proclamation of Luke's Gospel is not completely free of ambiguity and irony. For although John declares that all flesh

---

appears elsewhere in the speeches of Acts (cf. Acts 2:28; 3:19; 8:22; 17:30-31; 26:20-23). See Tannehill's detailed discussion of John and Jesus (*Narrative Unity,* vol. 1, 47–53).

26. Jacques Dupont, "The Salvation of the Gentiles and the Theological Significance of Acts," in idem, *The Salvation of the Gentiles: Essays on the Acts of the Apostles* (New York: Paulist Press, 1979), 15–16.

shall see the salvation of God (Luke 3:6), the final public proclamation delivered by Paul at the end of Acts completely revises this initial assertion by
adding that, although all may indeed *behold,* many will not truly *see* (βλέψετε
καὶ οὐ μὴ ἴδητε; Acts 28:26). Indeed, John himself immediately follows this
irenic proclamation with a castigation of the crowds seeking baptism from
him, warning them with a vehemence that does not seem to suit the occasion
that they may not be the true descendants of Abraham for whom the fulfillment of the divine promises are intended (Luke 3:8).

Although Conzelmann rightly points out that Luke has John put into prison
before Jesus' public ministry begins, his interpretation of the significance of this
editorial modification appears to be misguided,[27] in view of the carefully
orchestrated parallelism of these two figures in the birth narratives and the continuing parallelism that Luke appears to have consciously created between the
initial missionary proclamations of John and Jesus. This parallelism is all the
more pronounced because Jesus' inaugural discourse also begins with a paraphrasing of material from Second Isaiah:[28]

πνεῦμα κυρίου ἐπ᾽ ἐμὲ οὗ εἵνεκεν ἔχρισέν με εὐαγγελίσασθαι
πτωχοῖς· ἀπέσταλκέν με κηρύξαι αἰχμαλώτοις ἄφεσιν καὶ τυφλοῖς
ἀνάβλεψιν, ἀποστεῖλαι τεθραυσμένους ἐν ἀφέσει, κηρύξαι ἐνιατὸν
κυρίου δεκτόν.

The Spirit of the Lord is upon me because he has anointed me to bring
good news to the poor.
He has sent me to proclaim release of the captives and recovery of sight to
the blind, to let the oppressed go free, to proclaim the year of the Lord's
favor.

Luke 4:18-19 RSV

Virtually every commentator has observed that this proclamation is programmatic for the Gospel, and some have noted its importance for Luke-Acts

---

27. Indeed, the division Hans Conzelmann observes (*The Theology of St. Luke* [1961;
reprint, Philadelphia: Fortress Press, 1982], 21) is no doubt attributable to a very different motive from the one that he assumes (namely, the marking of the separation
between the period of Israel and the period of Jesus). Luke's most plausible motive for
the early imprisonment of John is to remove him from the scene of Jesus' baptism,
thereby eliminating the awkward inconsistency of having John linked with Jesus from
a position of superiority rather than inferiority. Whereas Matthew had attempted to
modify the embarrassing implications of the Markan tradition by creating a verbal dis-
claimer (Matt 3:14-15), Luke chose simply to remove the difficulty through a comparatively minor structural change.

28. A paraphrasing and synthesizing of Isa 52:7 and 61:1.

as a narrative whole. Indeed, it might be looked upon as an inspired blueprint outlining the various phases of the salvation mission. Jesus begins its fulfillment, first on a literal level with the healings and feedings of the miracle stories and in his preaching of the kingdom of God. As has already been observed, however, it is also Jesus' task to bring fulfillment of this mission on a metaphorical level. Indeed, spiritual blindness and captivity to sin are the greater evils driving his mission. Fulfillment of the mission, both on the material level and on the metaphorical level, begins in the Gospel and progresses throughout the continuation of the mission by Jesus' disciples in Acts.

If, however, this first public proclamation of Jesus is truly programmatic for the whole of Luke-Acts, then it must also have been intended by Luke to suggest the repatriation of the gentiles and the importance of their inclusion in the future reconstitution of the people of God. Indeed, the importance of the role of the gentiles in God's saving plan is never far from the center of Luke's story. For the sake of the orderly unfolding of the plot, however, the presence of this theme remains veiled throughout much of the Gospel. As was discussed in the previous chapter, the skepticism with which Jesus' proclamation is met by the people of Nazareth prompts him to recall the examples of Elijah and Elisha, whom God had sent to heal gentiles, ignoring the plight of Israel's own people (Luke 4:25-27). This foretaste of things to come is then further emphasized in the beginning of chapter 7, when Luke places Jesus' healing of the centurion's servant (Luke 7:1-10) directly before his raising of the widow's son (Luke 7:11-17). Although the healing of the centurion's servant is taken from the common tradition Luke shares with Matthew, the vagueness of its allusion to Elisha's healing of a gentile officer (2 Kgs 5:1-14 LXX) is clarified considerably in Luke by its placement immediately before the raising of the widow's son. This latter story is unique to Luke[29] and clearly echoes Elijah's performance of the same miracle on behalf of a gentile (1 Kgs 17:17-24 LXX). It must be concluded, therefore, that it is Luke himself who seeks an explicit comparison between the gentile healings of Elisha/Elijah and those of Jesus.

Lukan Geography Reexamined

It has often been noted that Luke has reworked his Markan source so that Jesus' inaugural discourse can take place in a Galilean synagogue. This seemingly minor redactional change sets in motion one of several organizing principles

---

29. Helmut Koester, *Ancient Christian Gospels: Their History and Development* (London/Philadelphia: SCM/Trinity Press International, 1991), 337; Bovon, *L'Évangile 1–9,* 348; Fitzmyer, *Luke,* vol. 1, 83. All of these scholars attribute the basic story to Luke's special source. Bovon, however, notes that Luke has thoroughly reworked his source.

by which Luke has chosen to structure his composition. Indeed, the literary and theological importance of Luke's geographical outline, first worked out in detail by Conzelmann,[30] has become a commonplace of Lukan interpretive analysis. Although there are many nuances upon which commentators may disagree, Luke's basic geographical outline is manifestly clear. Jesus' ministry begins in Galilee and ends in the temple in Jerusalem. Moreover, the progress from one geographical location to the other is marked by a series of Lukan summaries, each emphasizing Jerusalem as the divinely willed climax of Jesus' journey (Luke 9:51; 13:22; 17:11).[31]

Likewise, the second half of Luke's composition, focusing on the apostolic mission carried out in Jesus' name, begins in Jerusalem and ends in Rome, with a series of Lukan summaries emphasizing Rome as the divinely willed climax of this second major phase of the journey (Acts 19:21; 23:11; 27:24).[32] The symmetry of these two phases of the mission, however, is an element of Lukan composition that is seldom emphasized. Yet it is striking and surely signals an important stylistic principle in Luke's composition as a whole.

Geography, however, is merely a basic structural support for the central theme of the composition, which is the progress and divinely guided evolution of the mission for universal salvation. In geographical terms, the mission proper begins in Galilee with Jesus' inaugural address and progresses to Jerusalem, where Jesus is crucified. In the second half of Luke's composition, the mission resumes in Jerusalem, with the creation of the church under the inspiration and guidance of the Spirit, ultimately concluding in Rome, the symbolic and proleptic fulfillment of the divinely prophesied imperative to reach the ends of the earth.

Indeed, although the division of Luke's composition in accordance with this carefully balanced geographical scheme is an important interpretive key to the literary and theological structure of Luke-Acts, it is not the only one. Each of the two halves of Luke's overall composition is also divided into halves along broadly delineated thematic lines. The first half of the Gospel (Luke 1–12) focuses on the respective roles of John and Jesus, Jesus' initial encounters with the people, and the gathering and instruction of the disciples. The second half of the Gospel (Luke 13–24) focuses on the approaching climax of Jesus' encounter with Israel and its leaders, as well as the themes of judgment and reversal that this encounter sets in motion. Likewise, the second half of Luke-Acts is subdivided into two relatively equal narrative segments: Acts 1–15

30. Conzelmann, *St. Luke*, 18.
31. Dupont, "Salvation," 12.
32. Ibid., 12.

focuses on the formation of the Jerusalem community and its leadership in the early stages of the mission, whereas Acts 16–28 focuses on the spread of the mission under the leadership of Paul to the very heart of the gentile world. These and other compositional schemes that Luke employs to elucidate his rather complex literary web of interlocking narrative themes indicate his awareness of Hellenistic (Alexandrian) principles of literary refinement and his receptivity to Greco-Roman modes of artistic presentation.

In the early stages of Jesus' ministry, Luke has Jesus deliver to the disciples and assembled people a second discourse of major importance. The so-called Sermon on the Plain (SP) deviates from Matthew's Sermon on the Mount (SM) in a number of significant respects but none more strikingly than in its introductory section (Luke 6:20-26 = Matt 5:3-11). This deviation between the two versions of an important early Christian teaching tradition has generally been attributed to the editorial adaptations of Matthew and Luke, each working from a common source, Q. Although diverging on minor points, two prominent Lukan scholars who base their respective analyses upon this fundamental premise argue that it is Luke who has changed the pronouns in the blessings from third person to second person plural in verses 20-21,[33] Luke who has inserted the corresponding woes (verse 24-26),[34] and Luke who has inserted the word νῦν (now) in the two blessings of verse 21.[35]

All but one of these conclusions have also been substantiated by the recent findings of prominent Q scholars, who have argued that neither the woes nor the insertion of the word *now* in the two blessings of verse 21 should be considered as part of the original Q source.[36] Taken together, these redactional changes, which are indeed attributable to Luke,[37] dramatically emphasize the

33. Jacques Dupont, *Les Béatitudes: Le problème littéraire*, vol. 1 (Bruges/Louvain: Abbaye de Saint-André/E. Nauwelaerts, 1958), 297; Bovon, *L'Évangile 1–9*, 291.

34. Dupont, *Béatitudes*, vol. 1, 304–12, 342; Bovon, *L'Évangile 1–9*, 291.

35. Dupont, *Béatitudes*, vol. 1, 308–9; Bovon, *L'Évangile 1–9*, 290.

36. The opinions of John S. Kloppenborg (*Q Parallels: Critical Notes & Concordance* [Sonoma, Calif.: Polebridge, 1988], 24–27) have subsequently been corroborated by a series of reports from the International Q Project. That the second person plurals and νῦν's of Luke 6:21 are secondary, see James M. Robinson, "The International Q Project: Work Sessions 12–14 July, 22 November 1991," *JBL* 111 (1992): 501–2; that the woes of Luke 6:24-26 are secondary, see Milton C. Moreland and James M. Robinson, "The International Q Project: Work Sessions 23–27 May, 22–26 August, 17–18 November 1994," *JBL* 114 (1995): 478.

37. Hans Dieter Betz (*The Sermon on the Mount*, Hermeneia [Minneapolis: Fortress Press, 1995]), however, has recently published a major study that challenges the fundamental premise upon which Dupont, Bovon, and a number of other scholars have based their respective analyses. Carefully grounding the beginning stages of his argument in

theme of reversal in this opening segment of the discourse by making the ultimate fate of those who *now* possess an abundance of material goods, personal contentment, and inclusion within the fabric of social and religious community as much of an issue as the ultimate fate of those currently lacking these basic categories of human longing. Since, therefore, it is Luke who has consciously and dramatically heightened the element of reversal in this opening segment of the SP, the theme of reversal that this literary segment so emphatically advances must be regarded as genuinely significant for the interpretation of the literary strategy and theological message of Luke-Acts. Although at this early stage in Luke's composition, this theme of reversal is deliberately confined to the literal level of social and economic reversal, the evangelist is carefully laying the literary foundation for the later stages of the narrative, in which these categories expand to encompass spiritual and eschatological dimensions.

a lengthy and skillful review of the history of relevant scholarship, Betz sets forth the interesting hypothesis that SM and SP "constitute textual units composed by pre-synoptic redactors" that were then incorporated into different recensions of Q (p. 42). These pre-synoptic discourses were produced from a common stock of early Christian teachings, which accounts for the similarity of their overall plans of composition and educational function (p. 44). In their original *Sitz im Leben* (setting in life), they were akin to philosophical *epitomai* (abridgements, catechisms) intended for the training of early Christian disciples. One version (SM) was intended for the instruction of Jewish converts; the other version (SP) was edited for the instruction of Gentile converts, thereby accounting for their many divergences (p. 88). Indeed, Betz's detailed analysis leads him to conclude that all of the major changes in Luke 6:20–26, which Dupont and Bovon have attributed to the evangelist, are actually the work of a pre-synoptic redactor, who has tailored traditional material for a Greek audience (pp. 44–45, 82, 574–75, 583–84, passim). Although Betz's hypothesis is based on extensive research and possesses admirable internal consistency, it overlooks certain important details, at least with respect to Luke 6:20–26. Except for the qualifying term *pre-synoptic*, Betz's theory parallels that expressed by Dupont et al. The critical distinction, of course, is that these other scholars specify Luke himself as the redactor who has tailored traditional material for a Greek audience. In order for Betz's argument to be convincing, therefore, he would need to demonstrate an absence of Lukan style characteristics in these verses. For example, both Dupont and Bovon base their conclusions on the extensive incorporation of Lukan vocabulary (Dupont, *Béatitudes*, vol. 1, 308–9; Bovon *L'Évangile 1–9*, 291), as well as on elements consistent with Lukan style (Dupont, *Béatitudes*, vol. 1, 311; Bovon, *L'Évangile 1–9*, 291). Betz, however, does not appear to give these elements sufficient consideration. For example, even though he remarks that the verb σκιρτάω (leap for joy) in Luke 6:23 is rare, he fails to note that within the New Testament this verb appears only in Luke, who uses it twice in his opening chapter (Luke 1:41, 44). Moreover, as Dupont has observed, verse 27a is clearly an editorial bridge, which is more likely the work of Luke than of a pre-synoptic redactor (Dupont, *Béatitudes*, vol. 1, 189–90).

Following the introductory speech of John the Baptist and the two programmatic teachings of Jesus, the initial segment of the Gospel narrative having to do with the respective roles of John and Jesus closes with the formal end of John the Baptist's role and a concluding summary of his importance, which is delivered by Jesus himself (Luke 7:28-35). Moreover, the entire segment (Luke 7:18-35), taken from Q, forms a concise *inclusio*, thereby achieving the desired effect of definitively integrating John's prophetic role into Luke's central theme of the unfolding plan of God for the salvation of many.

The story of the sinner and the Pharisee (Luke 7:36-50) provides a brief interlude before a new thematic segment begins in chapter 8. Moreover, this story also serves a metaphorical function in Luke's narrative, inasmuch as it provides the evangelist's rationale for why it is that outsiders will most readily come to repentance and acceptance of the gospel. Because of their long history of special favor with God and because of their scrupulous attention to the demands of the scriptures, many of the leading Israelites will have great difficulty accepting the peculiar logic of the gospel, which enables all people to stand before God on a basis of equality, despite widely differing past histories of ethical standards or religious observance.[38]

That the next segment will be dominated by the instruction and empowerment of the disciples is anticipated by the introductory statement in Luke 8:1-3, which not only mentions that Jesus was traveling in the company of the twelve (καὶ οἱ δώδεκα σὺν αὐτῷ), but also names some of the women in the entourage who helped to provide for the needs of the entire group subsequently engaged in missionary activity (verse 3).[39] Following a series of preliminary teachings (Luke 8:4-21), Jesus sends out the twelve with power and authority to heal diseases and to preach the inauguration of God's reign (Luke 9:1-6). Peter's confession of Jesus as the Messiah (Luke 9:18-20) is followed by Jesus' instruction that he must suffer and that this particular price of the mis-

38. Although both Fitzmyer (*Luke*, vol. 1, 6, 84–85) and Bovon (*L'Évangile 1–9*, 378–79) assume that this story, originally rooted in oral tradition, reached Luke through his special source, Bovon adds that, in its present state, it thoroughly reflects Lukan style and language.

39. Although the manuscript tradition divides almost evenly between the singular αὐτῷ and the plural αὐτοῖς, as the recipients of the women's service and support, there is little doubt that the plural form is original. See, for example, Bruce M. Metzger, *A Textual Commentary on the Greek New Testament* (Stuttgart: United Bible Societies, 1971), 144; Bovon, *L'Évangile 1–9*, 390, n. 30. Furthermore, Tannehill (*Narrative Unity*, vol. 1, 210) emphasizes the connection of the women to the entire group of the disciples (and not just to Jesus) by noting this as a Lukan theme.

sion's fulfillment will almost certainly be shared by those disciples who identify themselves with his cause (Luke 9:21-24).

Furthermore, Luke's particular adaptation of the transfiguration tradition
serves to emphasize two specific Lukan themes. First, his introduction of new
material in verses 30b-32 revises the Markan interpretation of the transfiguration as a prefiguring of the parousia. In Conzelmann's opinion, the purpose
of Luke's revision is to transform this pericope into an announcement of the
passion. Although mindful of the apparent compositional inconsistency created
by this interpretation, in view of Jesus' prior announcement of the passion
(Luke 9:22), he credits this inconsistency to Luke's thoughtlessly having
retained the transfiguration pericope in its Markan order. Thus, according to
Conzelmann, Luke simply failed to take into account his subsequent editorial
changes and their impact on the consistency of his narrative.[40]

Bovon, however, softens Conzelmann's charge of apparent incompetence on
the part of the third evangelist by arguing that, even though Jesus' "departure"
(ἔξοδος) primarily refers to the passion, it also encompasses the entire sequence
of salvation events: crucifixion, resurrection, and ascension.[41] Although Bovon's
analysis of Luke's adaptation of the transfiguration story moves in the right direction, it does not go far enough. Indeed, in view of Luke's introduction of the
phrase καὶ ἰδοὺ ἄνδρες δύο into his account of the transfiguration (verse 30)
and the likelihood of his having incorporated the enveloping cloud from the
transfiguration tradition into his ascension narrative (Acts 1:9), it is readily apparent that Luke's primary interest in modifying the transfiguration account received
from his Markan source is to point to the ascension, which, from Luke's narrative perspective, is the climax of the Jerusalem events involving Jesus.

In addition to pointing proleptically to the ascension, the transfiguration also
points to the disciples' future roles as authoritative witnesses. Peter, James, and
John see and presumably also hear Moses and Elijah speaking with Jesus (Luke
9:30-31); they behold all three in their glory (Luke 9:32). Moreover, Luke closes
his version of this story from the tradition with a note that the disciples' proclamations of such momentous events would be reserved for a later time (Luke
9:36). These redactional changes indicate that one of Luke's concerns is to
employ the transfiguration as another proleptic symbol of the disciples' ultimate
roles in the divine mission begun by Jesus. Indeed, in addition to dramatically
marking a new phase of Jesus' christological consciousness, the transfiguration
narrative and the attendant passion predictions that both precede and succeed it
are deliberately presented by Luke within the wider narrative context of the

40. Conzelmann, *St. Luke,* 57.
41. Bovon, *L'Évangile 1–9,* 484–85; see also Fitzmyer, *Luke,* vol. 1, 794.

preparation and instruction of the disciples for their future role in the mission.[42]

This juxtaposition of the themes of Jesus' ordained suffering in Jerusalem and the future role of the disciples as witnesses to its victorious outcome continues throughout the next several chapters. The first of the three Lukan geographical summaries (Luke 9:51) is followed by a brief pericope on discipleship taken from Q. This, in turn, is followed by the sending and return of the seventy-two (Luke 10:1-23).[43] Yet it is not the divine power conferred upon them for the performance of their mission in which they are to rejoice. Rather, it is their aid in the fulfillment of the divine purpose that assures their inclusion in the kingdom and enables them to see what others cannot (Luke 10:24).

That both the mission of the twelve and the mission of the seventy-two prefigure the two stages in the disciples' continuation of the mission in Acts[44] makes it highly unlikely that Luke would place them in separate narrative segments. Indeed, Jesus' instruction of the disciples continues throughout this early phase of the journey toward Jerusalem, with the stories of the good samaritan (Luke 10:25-37) and Mary and Martha (Luke 10:38-42), the teaching of the Lord's Prayer (Luke 11:1-14), the warnings to the disciples against hypocrisy (Luke 12:1-3), the strengthening of their resolve to witness fearlessly (Luke 12:4-12), warnings against excessive attachment to possessions (Luke 12:13-34), and warnings of the necessity for vigilance (Luke 12:35-53). Verses 54-56 apply the theme of vigilance to the crowds (οἱ ὄχλοι), and the preceding tone of warning approaches that of a threat. These verses serve, therefore, as a narrative bridge to the next thematic section.

THE JUDGMENT OF JERUSALEM: LUKE 13–24

Although the followers of Conzelmann find no major narrative break before the geographical reference to Jerusalem in 19:28,[45] from a thematic perspective the

42. See, for example, Luke 8:1-21; 9:1-6, 23-27, 46-50, 57-61; 10:1-12, 17-24, 38-42; 11:1-13, 33-35; 12:1-12, 22-53.

43. The arguments for the reading of *seventy-two* rather than *seventy* rest on both textual and contextual grounds. For the textual arguments, see Metzger, *Textual Commentary*, 150–51. For a good summary of the contextual evidence, see Tannehill, *Narrative Unity*, vol. 1, 233. In support of the reading of *seventy-two*, see François Bovon, "Évangile de Luc et Actes des Apôtres," in *Évangiles synoptiques et Actes des Apôtres*, Nouveau Testament 4, ed. Joseph Auneau, François Bovon, Étienne Charpentier, Michael Gourgues, and Jean Radermakers (Paris: Desclée, 1981), 220.

44. That is, the preliminary mission of Peter and the other disciples in and around Jerusalem, followed by Paul's mission to the nations of the world.

45. For example, according to Fitzmyer (*Luke*, vol. 2, 1004), this is just another stage in the ongoing travel narrative.

most decisive break in the narrative of the Gospel half of Luke–Acts occurs at the beginning of chapter 13. At this point begins a more concentrated focus on Jerusalem and a heightening of the tension between the proclamation of the gospel and the blind obstinacy of the house of Israel, particularly of its leaders. The conflict will reach its climax in the crucifixion of Jesus and its joyous resolution in his resurrection and the assurance of his enthronement.

Chapter 13 begins with the report concerning Galilean rebels who were executed by Pilate. This report is interpreted by the Lukan Jesus as a sign and a warning to the crowds[46] that their failure to repent of their sins will lead to far greater disaster (Luke 13:1-5). This brief but ominous episode is followed by a parable of judgment, the story of the fig tree that will be cut down if it does not bear fruit (Luke 13:6-9). On a more positive note, Jesus reenacts his pledge to release the captives (Luke 4:18) by healing a woman whom Satan had bound for eighteen years (Luke 13:10-17). Even this story, however, is set within the context of the opposition of religious leaders;[47] however, for the moment, Jesus retains the approval of the crowds (Luke 13:17). Two parables of growth imply that the kingdom will continue to grow *despite* the people's opposition, a theme that gains force and definition in Acts. There follows a collection of sayings from the tradition that again throws into question whether the members of the house of Israel are necessarily the true descendants of the patriarchs and the prophets (Luke 13:22-30). Jesus then makes an allusion to his coming death in Jerusalem (Luke 13:31), followed by the first of several laments over the city (Luke 13:34-35).

The atmosphere of judgment and crisis continues in the next several chapters, where it is merged with the dramatic element of *reversal*, an element first introduced on a material level in Luke's narrative of the SP but now expanded to suggest an eschatological dimension. Chapter 14 begins with Jesus' chiding of lawyers and Pharisees for their obstruction of his saving work because of its interference with Sabbath observance (Luke 14:1-6).[48] This is followed by a long discourse on the theme of the reversal of the exalted and the humble, a theme that is brought to a momentary climax in the parable of the great ban-

---

46. οἱ ὄχλοι remain the primary recipients of Jesus' warnings as chapter 13 begins.

47. What begins as one leader (ὁ ἀρχισυνάγωγος; Luke 13:14) soon swells to many (οἱ ἀντικείμενοι αὐτῷ; Luke 13:17).

48. An introductory segment that Luke constructs from a variety of disparate sources. For one of the most detailed recent source analyses, see Bovon, *L'Évangile 9, 51–14, 35*, 413–16.

quet (Luke 14:15-24). As was noted in the previous chapter, Luke modifies this Q parable to suggest the substitution of the originally invited guests with outcasts from within the town and outsiders dwelling beyond the town (Luke 14:24). In this and the parables that follow in chapters 15–16, Luke, augmenting theological tendencies already present in his special source, further develops his theme of surprising reversal, which may be interpreted on several levels: literal, spiritual, and indeed eschatological.

In their parabolic dramatization of the theme of surprising reversal, the three parables of chapter 15 afford instructive insight into Luke's creative use and development of source material in pursuit of theological and dramatic ends. He begins the chapter with three introductory verses that establish the context for all of the parables that follow.[49] Luke's Jesus continues to speak on behalf of sinners and outcasts; these groups are again designated as the primary targets of God's mercy precisely because of their precarious worldly status.

After the editorial introduction of verses 1-3, Luke presents the parable of the lost sheep (verses 4-7), a Q parable found also in Matthew and in the *Gospel of Thomas*. According to Bovon, however, Luke's version of the parable has been filtered through his special source, and Luke himself has edited the parable even further to enhance his particular theological perspective.[50] This parable, in turn, is followed by the brief parable of the lost coin, which gives every evidence of Lukan literary creativity, both in its tailor-made complementarity to the preceding parable and in its provision of the necessary narrative bridge to the more important parable that follows.[51]

Although controversy regarding the degree of Lukan redactional activity present in the parable of the prodigal son (Luke 15:11-32) reached a certain intensity in the late 1960s and early 1970s—with serious challenges to its literary unity[52] as well as formidable challenges to its authentic origins within primitive Christian tradition[53]—these challenges thus far have not met with

---

49. That these verses are essentially Lukan is accorded almost universal agreement. See, for example, even Joachim Jeremias, "Tradition und Redaktion in Lukas 15," *ZNW* 62 (1971): 172–89, esp. 185–89.

50. François Bovon, *L' Évangile selon Saint Luc 15–24* (Geneva: Labor et Fides, 2000).

51. Ibid.

52. Most notably, Jack T. Sanders, "Tradition and Redaction in Luke XV. 11-32," *NTS* 15 (1968–1969): 433–38.

53. Luise Schottroff, "Das Gleichnis vom verlorenen Sohn," *ZThK* 68 (1971): 27–52. More recently, Schottroff's hypothesis has been modified by Heikki Räisänen, "The Prodigal Gentile and His Jewish Christian Brother, Lk 15, 11–32," in *The Four Gospels: Festschrift for Frans Neirynck*, ed. F. van Segbroeck, C. M. Tuckett, G. van Belle, and J. Verheyden, vol. 2 (Louvain: Peeters, 1992), 1617–36.

widespread acceptance. Even if one rejects the arguments of these earlier studies, however, the more methodologically and theologically conservative Bovon, in his analysis of chapter 15 in general, and of the parable of the prodigal son in particular, offers little comfort to the prevailing status quo, which accepts the parable as quintessentially authentic to the tradition stemming from Jesus and acknowledges only a very limited degree of Lukan redaction.[54]

For his part, Bovon upholds both the literary unity and the essential authenticity of this parable, which is so beloved by the church. Nevertheless, he also demonstrates through detailed and sophisticated analysis that this particular parable, in its earliest written form, has been thoroughly shaped by Luke's special source,[55] and that two key verses (verses 24 and 32) have been composed by Luke himself.[56] Accordingly, when Bovon's conclusions regarding the parable of the prodigal son are added to his previous analysis of the opening parables of chapter 15, at the very least, one can reasonably conclude that Luke's redactional contributions are so thoroughgoing that, in their present state, they constitute a carefully crafted reflection of Lukan theological and soteriological concerns. Furthermore, in regard to the story of the prodigal son in particular, there is little doubt that in its thorough reformulation by Luke's special source, what may have begun as a genuine parable has become an early church allegory in which the gentile believers of Luke's own community identify with the younger son, who, by a seemingly miraculous reversal in divine providence, has been redeemed by God.

Thus, as part of a larger literary segment shaped by Luke, the opening parables of chapter 15—the lost sheep and the lost coin—in addition to expressing God's concern for the poor and for sinners, may also allude to God's decision to reclaim those farthest away from the Israelite elect. That the mention of these "far away" ones is indeed a veiled reference to gentiles is clearly implied in the parable of the prodigal son.[57] In Luke's eyes, an allusion to the

---

54. Joachim Jeremias ("Tradition und Redaktion") remains the most prominent defender of this prevailing tide of opinion. But see also, for example, J. J. O'Rourke, "Some Notes on Luke XV. 11–32," *NTS* 18 (1971–72):431–33; and Charles Carlston, "Reminiscence and Redaction in Luke 15:11–32," *JBL* 94 (1975): 368–90.

55. Thereby already reflecting literary and linguistic patterns that are essentially Greek.

56. Bovon, *L'Évangile 15–24.*

57. As Räisänen has noted ("Prodigal Gentile," 1625), the description of the younger son as having departed to a far-off country (εἰς μακράν χώραν) is hardly accidental in view of the application of the adjective/adverb μακράν as a means of distinguishing gentiles in Acts 2:39; 22:21; and in Eph 2:13, 17. The fact that the term is repeated in verse 20, also in reference to the younger son, further emphasizes its importance as

justification of the exclusion of the unbelieving majority of Israelites is readily provided by the parable's depiction of the elder brother, who allows his petty
jealousy to cause him to refuse the celebration to which he also was invited
(ὠργίσθη δὲ καὶ οὐκ ἤθελεν εἰσελθεῖν; Luke 15:28a).

Indeed, both the parable of the dishonest manager (Luke 16:1-8) and the
parable of the rich man and Lazarus (Luke 16:19-31) condemn the abuse of
trust and privilege by those formerly placed in this special position by God.
Luke's redaction of the latter parable introduces a further dimension to this traditional tale of greed and divine judgment. With his insertion of a new ending, the theme of ungrateful and unworthy Israel is incorporated into the traditional typology of the sinful rich man.[58] Thus, it is not the rich man but rather
the outcast Lazarus who dwells in heaven with Abraham. This new dimension
of the story is created by the addition of the last two verses, in which the rich
man asks Abraham to warn his brothers[59] so that they won't make his fatal mis-
take. Abraham's response in verse 31 is telling: "If they do not listen to Moses
and the prophets, neither will they be convinced, even if someone rises from
the dead" (εἰ Μωυσέως καὶ τῶν προφητῶν οὐκ ἀκούσιν, οὐδ' ἐάν τις ἐκ
νεκρῶν ἀναστῇ πεισθήσονται). The meaning of these added verses is that
an unbelieving Israel that failed to understand the true message of its prophets
will also fail to recognize its Messiah.

The next two chapters continue to advance the themes of unbelief, judgment, and reversal, particularly as these themes relate to Jerusalem and its
inhabitants. Thus, Luke places the story of the healing of the ten lepers (Luke
17:12-19) immediately following his final geographical summary (Luke 17:11).
In this story, nine Jewish lepers and one Samaritan leper are healed by Jesus,

---

a term of identification for this son. See also Eduard Schweizer, "Antwort," *ThZ* 5
(1949): 232, n. 3.

58. Again, Bovon's forthcoming book (*L'Évangile 15–24*) presents a detailed analysis
of this parable, in which he argues that verses 27-29 must be attributed to Luke's special source and have been inserted to provide a second ending tacked on to the original story; and verses 30-31, attributed to Luke himself, provide a third ending. See also,
for example, Jack T. Sanders, "The Jewish People in Luke-Acts," in *Luke-Acts and the
Jewish People*, ed. J. B. Tyson (Minneapolis: Augsburg, 1988), 64.

59. Although, in his discussion of this parable, Luke T. Johnson (*The Literary Function
of Possessions in Luke-Acts*, SBLDS 39 [Missoula: Scholars Press, 140–44]) does not
comment on the metaphorical meaning of ἀδελφοί, as Luke's narrative progresses the
term is used almost exclusively to refer to fellow members of an ethnic group or of a
religious community. See, for example, Acts 1:14, 15; 2:29, 37; 7:2, 23; 8:17, 22, and so
forth.

but only the Samaritan, the outsider, responds with repentance and worship.[60] The parable of the Pharisee and the tax collector (Luke 18:9-14) repeats the theme of the coming reversal in the fortunes and destinies of the smugly self-righteous and the truly repentant. When placed within this distinctly Lukan context, even the traditional story of Jesus' blessing of the little children (Luke 18:15-17) serves as a variation of the same basic theme: the proud and self-important will find themselves excluded from the kingdom, while the humble and obedient will be welcomed in their place.

With Jesus' triumphal entry into Jerusalem via the temple (Luke 19:28), the "judgment of Jerusalem" enters its final and climactic phase.[61] As will be discussed at length later in this chapter, the Jerusalem temple plays a central role in Luke's development of the theme of judgment, a theme that unifies both halves of his composition. Already here, in the final segment of the Gospel, the force of the possessive regarding Jerusalem switches from a primarily *objective* genitive to a primarily *subjective* genitive concerning the judgment that is about to be rendered upon Jerusalem, although both meanings play a part in the closing scenes of Luke's Gospel. Jesus' entry into this city of destiny also inaugurates a series of events which, taken together, represent the center of time from Luke's narrative perspective. Jesus' trial, death, resurrection, and promised exaltation will bring to a close the Gospel half of Luke's two-part epic. The narrative will continue, however, with the disciples gathered in Jerusalem, where the church is subsequently formed under miraculous circumstances and the mission is resumed under the guidance of the Spirit. Not until the trial and death of Stephen will the mission again be propelled beyond the city limits.

Thus, the momentous events that occur in Jerusalem not only represent the center of time from a Lukan theological perspective, but they also occupy the center of the narrative structure, unifying the two great halves of his epic story. Again, the degree to which Luke's formation of the dramatic structure of his composition appears to emulate the structural principle of Greco-Roman epic in general and Virgil's *Aeneid* in particular should be emphasized.

More than either of his synoptic predecessors, Luke portrays Jesus' entry into Jerusalem as a triumphal homecoming. A great crowd of disciples echo the

---

60. Although this story is frequently attributed to Luke's special source, Fitzmyer (*Luke*, vol. 2, 1149) emphasizes that Lukan redaction is so heavy and thoroughgoing as to make the question of source irrelevant.

61. Conzelmann (*St. Luke*, 77) emphasizes the importance of the redactional changes whereby Luke has Jesus enter directly into the temple. By incorporating two chapters of teaching material into this segment of the narrative, Luke deliberately expands the period of Jesus' ministry to include this final temple phase.

angelic chorus at Jesus' birth: Jesus is God's Messiah, the harbinger of heavenly peace (Luke 19:38). Yet, by having Jesus again express his anguish over Jerusalem's ever more certain fate (Luke 19:41-44), Luke continues to stress that divine intervention is not good news for everyone. Indeed, the fact that Luke qualifies as "disciples" (οἱ μαθηταί) the crowd of well-wishers who welcome Jesus to his rightful domain provides symbolic confirmation of the events that are about to take place in Jerusalem. On the one hand, therefore, Jesus' successful teaching in the temple (Luke 19:45—21:38) is a misleading narrative interlude, created by Luke to increase suspense and heighten the drama concerning Israel's fate. On the other hand, Luke's narration of a period of extended teaching, which marks the close of Jesus' public ministry and serves as a prelude to the passion, inaugurates an important subtheme involving the temple and the rejection of God's emissaries. This theme will be discussed in more detail in conjunction with the shutting of the temple doors (Acts 21:30).

Luke's distinctive account of the Last Supper (Luke 22:15-19b)[62] clearly alludes to the Passover meal[63] and thus provides further insight into Luke's view of the role of the passion in Christian proclamation. Far from negating its importance, the Lukan allusion to Passover in this context reinterprets the passion as the indispensable inauguration of a chain of events that will ultimately lead to the deliverance of the true Israel.[64] From Luke's perspective, some twenty years later than Mark's, Jesus' death is no longer an end in itself

---

62. Although a majority of Lukan scholars currently accepts verses 19c-20 as authentic (see Metzger, *Textual Commentary*, 173–77), the shorter version, as one of the most notable of the Western noninterpolations, is still to be preferred. This is all the more the case in view of the fact that the new-covenant theology of verse 20 is not characteristic of Lukan theology in general. Nor is the excessively sacramental interpretation of the passion (verses 19c-20). The sacramental interpretation of the passion, in particular, argues for the lack of authenticity of these verses.

63. For example, the explicit reference in verse 15 and the unusual order of cup, bread, [cup].

64. This view supports J.-D. Kaestli (*L'eschatologie dans l'oeuvre de Luc, ses caractéristiques et sa place dans le développement du christianisme primitif* [Geneva: Labor et Fides, 1969], 88), who further recognizes that for Luke these events mark only the fulfillment of God's plan *in nuce* (in a nutshell); ultimate fulfillment is a process continuing into the Lukan present and beyond. Ulrich Wilckens (*Die Missionsreden der Apostelgeschichte*, 3d ed., WMANT 5 [Neukirchen-Vluyn: Neukirchener, 1974], 194–200), Haenchen (*Acts,* 92), and Conzelmann (*St. Luke,* 201) also stress that Jesus' death in and of itself has no saving significance for Luke. Unlike that of Kaestli, however, their interpretations lack sufficient appreciation of the dynamic dimension of Lukan soteriology and eschatology.

but is one of several divinely ordained stages that must be accomplished in the fulfillment of the salvation plan, the ultimate goal of which is the establishment of the kingdom of God. Thus, the allusion to the Passover is both artistically and theologically appropriate in that it informs and dramatizes the meaning of the events that are about to take place. If, on the other hand, verses 19-20 are original in their entirety, Luke's narration of the Last Supper would then be seen in terms of the superimposition of the Christian words of cultic institution upon the traditional pericope's primary literary allusion to an ancient celebration of deliverance and remembrance.[65] Indeed, in this special sense, Luke's version of the Last Supper serves as a fitting prologue to the entire series of events that are about to take place in Jerusalem.

As has also been noted frequently, Luke's trial account increases the tradition's emphasis on the guilt of the people—particularly its leaders—by inserting an extra trial appearance before Herod and by adding that Jesus' death sentence reflected the expressed and repeated urgings of the Jerusalem priests, leaders, and people (Luke 23:6-13). Moreover, by having Jesus, as he is being led away for his execution, admonish the "daughters of Jerusalem" to weep for themselves and for their children, Luke again links Jesus' death to the fate of Jerusalem. The city's destruction will serve as divine judgment against the great majority of its people (Luke 23:28-31).

Tannehill interprets the words of Jesus to the mourning women as a tragic (and unacceptable) reversal of the oracles of salvation directed at Jerusalem in Isaiah 40–66.[66] Tragic perhaps, but Luke's interpretation also includes more than a little deliberate irony, especially in view of the number of prophecies from Second Isaiah that resound throughout the opening chapters of Luke's Gospel. Although at this point in the narrative the tragic reversal of Israel's destiny may appear to be an unresolved problem in the Lukan drama, by the end of Acts Luke intends to make it manifest to every reader that the destruction of the former house of Israel and the exclusion of the majority of its members from the reconstituted people of God had been foreseen and, therefore, intended by God from the very beginning.

Nevertheless, from a narrative perspective, as the final chapter of the Gospel opens, the great mission on which Jesus had embarked appears to have ended in failure. Even the women's report of the empty tomb is taken seriously only by Peter (Luke 24:1-12). The disciples' dejection and disappointment is revealed in the conversation of two of their number on the road to Emmaus:

---

65. *Contra* Fitzmyer (*Luke,* vol. 2, 1390–92), who interprets verses 19-20 as Luke's sacramental reinterpretation of verses 15-18.

66. Tannehill, *Narrative Unity,* vol. 1, 166.

"We had hoped that he would be the one to redeem Israel" (ἡμεῖς δὲ ἠλπί-ζομεν ὅτι αὐτός ἐστιν ὁ μέλλων λυτροῦσθαι τὸν Ἰσραήλ; Luke 24:21a).

Disappointment quickly turns to joy, however, when Jesus appears to them and, after interpreting the scriptures, breaks bread with them. In the performance of this symbolic act, their eyes are opened in a flood of recognition (Luke 24:30-31). Then Jesus appears to the remaining disciples and, after giving them similar instruction regarding the true meaning of the scriptures, charges them to become witnesses for the proclamation of the gospel in his name (Luke 24:47). The assurance of Jesus' exaltation and enthronement (Luke 24:26; Acts 1:9-11) launches a new phase of the mission, in which God's plan will continue to unfold through the work and witness of the disciples. The second half of the Lukan epic narrates the continued development of the mission from Jerusalem, the symbolic epicenter of the salvation drama, and its inexorable progress to Rome, symbolically identified with salvation's outermost reaches.

CONTINUATION OF THE MISSION BY THE TWELVE: ACTS 1–15

Although the authenticity of Luke 24:50-53 and Acts 1:1-5 has never been widely contested,[67] the longer Alexandrian reading of these verses has continued to be questioned by some. Despite the high regard in which the

---

67. Although the history of scholarship relating to this general problem has many variations and complexities that cannot be discussed here in detail, the basic outlines of that history may be summarized as follows: Although the issue had already been raised before the end of the preceding century (A. Gercke, *Hermes* 29 [1894]: 373–74), it did not become widely known until it was raised by E. Norden (*Agnostos Theos: Untersuchungen zur Formengeschichte religiöser Rede* [1913; reprint, Darmstadt: Wissenschaft, 1974], 312–13). It was subsequently developed by Alfred Loisy (*Les Actes des apôtres* [Paris: F. Rieder, 1925], 14). Although Kirsopp Lake (*Beginnings*, vol. 5, 3), along with many other scholars, reacted against the rather extreme interpretations that accompanied the hypotheses of Norden and Loisy, he did, nevertheless, express his suspicion that Luke 24:50-53 was secondary. In the study of Harald Sahlin (*Der Messias und das Gottesvolk: Studien zur protolukanischen Theologie* [Uppsala: Almqvist & Wiksell, 1945], 11–18, passim), discussion was again linked to an unfortunate interpretation, from which it was subsequently separated and redefined by Philippe Menoud ("Remarques sur les textes de l'ascension dans Luc-Actes," in *Neutestamentliche Studien für Rudolf Bultmann*, ed. W. Eltester [Berlin: Töpelmann, 1954], 148–56). Subsequently, however, even Menoud ("During Forty Days," in *Jesus Christ and the Faith: A Collection of Studies by Philippe Menoud* [Pittsburgh, Pa.: Pickwick, 1978], 167–79) retreated from his previous challenge of the authenticity of Acts 1:1-5.

Alexandrian text type is generally held, ever since the work of Westcott and Hort, textual critics have generally conceded that in cases in which the Alexandrian text conflicted with shorter readings in the Western text ("Western non-interpolations"), these Western readings should be granted the greater likelihood of priority, particularly when these shorter readings are corroborated by any of the Latin fathers. The relatively recent discovery of P[75], a papyrus of the Alexandrian text type dated to around the turn of the third century, ought not change the presumption of priority concerning the shorter Western reading, because this papyrus only brings the longer Alexandrian readings to within approximately a hundred years of the writing of Luke-Acts.[68]

Moreover, as Eldon Jay Epp's comparatively recent text-critical analysis of these passages has shown,[69] if one follows the shorter Western readings, a unified and, from a dramatic perspective, consistent composition emerges. What follows is Epp's reconstruction of these passages. In the case of the second passage, however, I have slightly modified Epp's translation.

Ἐξήγαγεν δὲ αὐτοὺς ἔξω ἕως πρὸς Βηθανίαν, καὶ ἐπάρας τὰς χεῖρας αὐτοῦ εὐλόγησεν αὐτούς. καὶ ἐγένετο ἐν τῷ εὐλογεῖν αὐτὸν αὐτοὺς ἀπέστη ἀπ' αὐτῶν. καὶ ὑπέστρεψαν εἰς Ἰερουσαλὴμ μετὰ χαρᾶς μεγάλης, καὶ ἦσαν διὰ παντὸς ἐν τῷ ἱερῷ εὐλογοῦντες τὸν θεόν.

Then he led them out as far as Bethany, and lifting up his hands he blessed them. While he was blessing them, he went away from them. And they returned to Jerusalem with great joy, and were continually in the temple praising God.

Luke 24:50-53

τὸν μὲν πρῶτον λόγον ἐποιησάμην περὶ πάντων, ὦ Θεόφιλε, ὧν ἤρξατο ὁ Ἰησοῦς ποιεῖν τε καὶ διδάσκειν, ἐν ᾗ ἡμέρα τοὺς ἀποστόλους ἐξελέξατο διὰ πνεύματος ἁγίου καὶ ἐκέλευσε κηρύσσειν τὸ εὐαγγέλιον.

In the first book, O Theophilus, I have dealt with all that Jesus began to do and to teach during the time[70] when he chose the apostles through the Holy Spirit and commanded them to preach the gospel.

Acts 1:1-2[71]

---

68. As has already been argued in more detail by Mikeal C. Parsons, *The Departure of Jesus in Luke-Acts*, JSNTSup 21 (Sheffield: Sheffield Academic Press, 1987), 34–51.

69. Eldon Jay Epp, "The Ascension in the Textual Tradition of Luke-Acts," in *New Testament Textual Criticism: Its Significance for Exegesis*, ed. E. J. Epp and G. D. Fee (Oxford: Clarendon, 1981), 131–45.

Based upon Epp's reconstruction of the shorter readings of the Western text in these bridge passages, the original unity of Luke-Acts is revealed with simplicity and clarity. Jesus' ascension does not occur until Acts 1:9, and the participle ἀναλημφθείς ("taken up") is applied to Jesus only in Acts 1:11. Indeed, from a historical critical standpoint, it is much more reasonable to assume that Luke's composition was originally a unity, which very early in its transmission history was split in half. This earliest phase of textual unity is still reflected in the shorter readings of the Western manuscripts. As a result of the early editorial decision to split the work and circulate each half independently, a more definitive ending was required for the Gospel half. The longer Alexandrian readings represent these early editorial interpolations.[72] Likewise, the resump-

70. This phrase definitely represents the "harder reading," as Metzger (*Textual Commentary*, 275) rightly observes. However, in view of the fact that Jesus' inaugural sermon and initial healing miracle (Luke 4) are followed immediately by the choosing of the first disciples (Luke 5:1-11), it is certainly not an impossible reading. What is most difficult about this Western reading is that the phrase ἐν ἡμέρᾳ places the emphasis of the Gospel on the launching of an ongoing mission of evangelization, rather than exclusively on the person of Jesus himself. But this broader perspective of the divine plan may indeed reflect the perspective of the author of Luke-Acts. On the other hand, it is also possible that the textual inconsistency evident in the Augustine and Old Latin manuscripts, from which (with the help of Codex Bezae) the Greek reconstruction of the shorter Western reading is derived, points to scribal error. Although the manuscripts that James H. Ropes (*The Text of Acts*, vol. 3, in F. J. Foakes-Jackson and Kirsopp Lake, eds., *The Beginnings of Christianity* [London: MacMillan, 1926] 256-57) considers to be most reflective of the original Western reading have the phrase in the ablative (*in die*; ablative of time within which), Ropes does note two Old Latin manuscripts (p. 258) that attest to the phrase in the accusative (*in diem*; accusative of extent or duration). Although Ropes himself seems inclined to discount this variant reading as having been influenced by the later Alexandrian manuscripts, if this variant reading of the Western text is accepted, then, of course, the phrase could be translated as "until the time." Whichever way the Western text is reconstructed, however, its shorter reading seems preferable to the longer Alexandrian readings for these passages. If one accepts the Alexandrian readings, then one is faced with defending the far more problematic authenticity of Jesus' double ascension: once in Bethany, at the end of the Gospel, and again in Jerusalem, some forty days later.

71. Epp, "Ascension," 142–43; see also, Ropes, *Beginnings*, vol. 3, 256–61.

72. Ironically, this need for a proper ending to the Gospel is precisely the argument that Jean-Marie Guillaumé (*Luc interprète des anciennes traditions sur la Résurrection de Jésus*, Études Bibliques [Paris: J. Gabalda et Cie, 1979], 226) uses for affirming the authenticity of the longer Alexandrian reading of Luke 24:50-53. But this argument requires a complete reversal in the text's transmission history.

tive prologue (Acts 1:1-5)[73] had to be revised to incorporate references to the prior ascension of Jesus, which, in the Alexandrian readings, takes place twice and in differing circumstances.

Finally, if any doubt remains as to the original unity of Luke-Acts, those doubts may be laid to rest on purely artistic grounds, inasmuch as several key elements of the narrative of Acts 1:6-12 indicate that Luke intended them as the completion of the preceding resurrection scenes recorded in Luke 24. Three elements of correspondence are most often mentioned: the reiteration of concern for the future of Israel (Luke 24:21/Acts 1:6), Jesus' command that the disciples be his witnesses (μάρτυρες, Luke 24:48/Acts 1:8), and Jesus' promise of the Holy Spirit (Luke 24:49/Acts 1:8).

In addition to these examples, however, the element that most clearly exhibits Luke's intentional literary artistry is the theme of "the two men" who appear in dazzling/white clothing, with which the resurrection narrative begins (Luke 24:4) and with which the ascension narrative concludes (Acts 1:9-11).[74] In Luke 24:4, the evangelist describes the appearance of two angels to the women at the tomb: καὶ ἰδοὺ ἄνδρες δύο ἐπέστησαν αὐταῖς ἐν ἐσθῆτι ἀστραπτούσῃ ("and behold, two men stood before them in dazzling apparel"). Likewise, after Jesus is taken up in a cloud, Luke draws the ascension narrative to a close by again describing the appearance of two angels, this time to the disciples (Acts 1:10): καὶ ἰδοὺ ἄνδρες δύο παρειστήκεισαν αὐτοῖς ἐν ἐσθήσεσι λευκαῖς ("and behold, two men stood beside them in white clothing").

Thus, Luke appears to have designed the momentous events of Jesus' resurrection and ascension to form a literary *inclusio*, marked at either end by the appearance of two angels in dazzling/white raiment. Furthermore, in his narrative of the transfiguration, Luke has deliberately modified his source to prefigure this theme of the two men (καὶ ἰδοὺ ἄνδρες δύο; Luke 9:30), just as he has doubtless incorporated the detail of the cloud (Acts 1:9) to create a further correspondence between his account of the ascension and the description

---

73. Beyond a considerable degree of textual corruption, which has been discussed in some detail by J. H. Ropes (*Beginnings*, vol. 3, 256–61) and, more recently, by Parsons (*Departure of Jesus*, 126–27), there is no evidence that the original text may have lacked verses 1-5. Because of the comparative lateness of the earliest textual witnesses, however, this silence cannot be considered definitive. Nor can Guillaumé's detailed style analysis be considered conclusive (*Luc interprète*, 234–37), especially when verses 3-4 contain a whopping four *hapax legomena* (terms that occur only once).

74. According to Parsons (*Departure of Jesus*, 60), the references to the two men of otherworldly appearance in Luke 24 and Acts 1 are further distinguished from other angelic appearances marking important events, because these two instances are the only ones in which the human witnesses exit first.

of the transfiguration already established in the tradition that he has inherited. Moreover, there is no need for the extended prologue, particularly verses 3-5, beyond the necessity of bridging the narrative gap caused by the division of the text into two parts.[75]

In any event, as was previously noted, verse 8 of this opening segment sets forth, with greater clarity than was articulated in Luke 24:47, the phase of the mission yet to be completed. The promise of the Father is further clarified in the anticipated power of the Holy Spirit; the scope of the mission is now described as a series of concentric circles (Judea, Samaria, the end of the earth) radiating out from Jerusalem, the eschatological epicenter.

Thematic Unity

With a brief account of the reconstitution of the twelve, the narrative resumes (Acts 1:12-26). In its present context, the function of the twelve is to be present at the birth of the church and to preside over its earliest formative mission, thus providing a critical affirmation of unity with the original mission of Jesus. Indeed, as the concrete expression of the gradual fulfillment of the divine plan, the unity of the mission is the central theme of Luke-Acts. That Luke understood Jesus' death and resurrection as a vital part of this more inclusive mission and not in itself as the sum and totality of that mission is exemplified in the unified structure of his literary composition. Indeed, Luke's perception that the overriding goal of God's plan was the formation of a new people provides the key for understanding the work in its originally intended unity.

As with Jesus' inaugural proclamation in Nazareth, Luke's narration of the first Christian Pentecost is programmatic for his entire composition. Luke begins with a dramatic narration of the event itself (Acts 2:1-13). The Holy Spirit with tongues of fire descends as promised upon the praying disciples. Instead of inspiring them to utter incomprehensible speech, however, this supernatural force empowers the disciples to proclaim the divine message in a multiplicity of ethnic languages, thereby proleptically and symbolically drawing together representatives of every nation of the known world—the miracle of mutual understanding being complemented by the subsequent miracle of spiritual harmony, as exemplified in the mutuality of possessions.

The initial event is followed by Peter's speech (Acts 2:14-36). Although it is rather long, this speech is amazingly concise, when one considers the variety of themes it sets forth and the literary and structural importance of its con-

---

75. It bears repeating that the extraordinarily high number of *hapax legomena* in verses 3-4, and the formulaic quality of verse 5 ought to give exegetes more cause for concern than they usually do.

tent. To begin with, verses 15-21 establish the narrative present as the time of eschatological promise, indeed, as the beginning of the time of fulfillment.[76] The prophetic pronouncement of verse 17 again signals the universal scope of the mission. Yet the text quickly moves to a deliberately misleading concentration on the descendants of the Israelites as the intended recipients of the divine promise. Prophecies, visions, dreams, and miraculous healings will all be experienced by God's true servants. Verses 22-36, however, suggest that not all of Israel may be counted within this circle of salvation. At present, Peter warns, Israelites stand in defiance of God. This situation was brought about by the events portrayed in the Gospel, events that reached their climax in Jesus' final rejection and execution. As a result, Jerusalem and the entire house of Israel stand under the threat of divine condemnation. It is on this note of warning that Luke has Peter's speech conclude.

The effects of this first proclamation are, nonetheless, positive, and Acts begins on a falsely encouraging note with respect to both the city and the people, as thousands repent and are baptized into the Spirit-filled community of Jerusalem believers (Acts 2:37-41). This idyllic picture of peaceful beginnings continues through the closing summary of the second chapter (Acts 2:42-47). In chapters 2–5, the mutual sharing of material goods is stressed, but primarily in the sense of its bearing witness to the harmony and mutuality of heart and mind in this Spirit-filled community.[77]

Within this opening segment of Acts, which describes the peace and harmony of the earliest disciples, Luke incorporates two edifying tales, one positive and one negative. The positive tale relates the story of Joseph/Barnabas, the Levite who sold a field and gave all of the proceeds to the church (Acts 4:37-38). This exemplary story is followed immediately by the double tale of Ananias

76. Conzelmann, *Acts,* 20.

77. Indeed, Eckhard Plümacher (*Lukas als hellenistischer Schriftsteller: Studien zur Apostelgeschichte*, SUNT 9 [Göttingen: Vandenhoeck & Ruprecht, 1972], 17–18) may be correct in suggesting that Luke incorporated these idealized descriptions of early Christian communal life in order to conform to Greco-Roman philosophical depictions of utopian societies. According to Bovon (*L'Évangile 1–9,* 292–93), the Gospel's exclusive concentration on the poor is translated into an ethic of mutuality and sharing in Acts. Alan C. Mitchell ("The Social Function of Friendship in Acts 2:22-47 and 4:32-37," *JBL* 111 [1992]: 255–72) also stresses the ethical and edifying aspects of the summaries on sharing in Acts. Moreover, since the promised renewal of the paradisial Golden Age—the mythological archetype for utopian concepts—was a perennial element of imperial propaganda, beginning with Augustus and continuing through Domitian, Luke may well have determined that allusion to this popular social ideal would enable him to adapt it for his own theological ends. See also, the more detailed discussion in chapter 4.

and Sapphira (Acts 5:1-11), who, in an effort to deceive the community and its leadership, hold back some money from the sale of their property for themselves.[78] In relating these tales, Luke's primary purpose is to emphasize the radical nature of the unity and harmony of the early Jerusalem church, under the extraordinary power and presence of the Spirit.

After these edifying asides, Luke returns to the main theme of the plot, the spread of the gospel at divine behest and its implementation through miraculous healings, divine interventions, and the bold proclamation of the word. In chapters 5–7, Luke begins to illustrate the countervailing tendencies of continuity and reversal that the spread of the gospel throws into dramatic relief. The apostles are cast into prison by the Jerusalem authorities, only to be released at night by an angel (Acts 5:17-20). Frustrated by their inability to curb the disciples' behavior, the religious establishment wants to kill them but is warned of the possible consequences of its actions by one of its own members, Gamaliel.

Gamaliel's warning (Acts 5:34-39) is twofold and thus functions as one of the book's ambiguous prophecies. On one level, it warns Israel's leaders that if this work is divinely inspired, as the disciples claim, the opposition of the religious authorities is futile. The truth of this warning is immediately borne out in the story that follows of the trial of Stephen and the persecution, scattering, and spread of the mission that follows in the wake of his martyrdom. The consequences of the second and more ominous element of Gamaliel's prophetic warning—that the actions of the religious establishment could place the people in opposition to God—is realized irretrievably only at the end of the book, when Luke has Paul deliver Isaiah's dismissive words as God's final judgment on those who have chosen to remain in the fallen house of Israel.

In his earlier narration of the prayer, which the congregation made in unison and which caused a new eruption of the Holy Spirit, specifically empowering the community to speak the word of God with boldness (Acts 4:23-31), Luke not only establishes the basis for the apostles' works of healing but also the basis of their ability to proclaim the word boldly. This new apostolic boldness subsequently reaches its climax in Stephen's lengthy and powerful indictment of faithless Israel (Acts 7:1-53). Unlike the missionary proclamations of Peter, Stephen's speech is simply an indictment of a rebellious people who, from the very beginning, were resistant to God's plan.[79] The implication is

---

78. One literary model for such an edifying insertion into the main body of the text is found in *Aeneid* 3.89–90, also cited by Conzelmann (*Acts,* 35).

79. Other commentators frame this observation in the positive. Stephen's speech is the justification for asserting the Christians as the rightful heirs to the promises of the Scriptures; for example, Helmut Koester, *Introduction to the New Testament,* vol. 2

that as it always has been, thus it always will be. Perhaps for this reason, therefore, Stephen does not include any call to repentance, nor does he hold out any hope of divine forgiveness and reconciliation. Not surprisingly, his scathing indictment prompts Jerusalem's religious leaders to oppose the disciples with new vigor. And at the moment of Stephen's martyrdom, Luke depicts him as a perfect servant of Jesus,[80] just as in the passion narrative of Luke's Gospel, Jesus is depicted as a perfect servant of God.[81]

After the harsh tone of his indictment against the people, Stephen's dying words of forgiveness at first appear out of place. Yet they serve as more than a reminder of Jesus, for Luke has placed them in between two references to Saul. In Luke's dramatic scheme, Saul/Paul becomes the ironic embodiment of the important theme of divinely inspired reversal. The persecutor Saul, who becomes the believer Paul, is living proof that God gave Israel every chance for repentance and forgiveness. When, therefore, it is Paul himself who finally pronounces Isaiah's judgmental prophecy as fulfilled, and for the requisite third time announces his intention to preach to the gentiles (Acts 28:26-28), Luke is clearly and dramatically implying that no future reconciliation with the unconverted house of Israel is possible.

With his vivid depiction of Stephen's death, the keystone section of Luke's two-part epic comes to a dramatic close. Although the founding Christian community will remain in Jerusalem throughout the narrative of Acts, the death of Stephen and the ensuing persecution prompt the dynamic power of the Holy Spirit to depart from the city, leading the scattered disciples to new mission fields. Indeed, from the Lukan perspective, Jerusalem's role as the city of destiny and the occurrence therein of the momentous events constituting the center of salvation history are now consigned to the narrative past.

Divided Action and Interlacement

Functioning as an artistic reprise to the story of the ten lepers, in which only the Samaritan returns to give thanks (Luke 17:11-19), the stubbornness of the Judeans in rejecting the gospel is dramatically juxtaposed with the whole-hearted acceptance with which the Samaritans greet Philip's preaching (Acts 8:5-8). Their initial acceptance of the proclamation on the basis of Philip's mir-

---

(Philadelphia: Fortress Press, 1982), 320. Conzelmann (*Acts*, 56–57), however, emphasizes Stephen's negative portrayal of Israel. Voicing yet another perspective, Tannehill (*Narrative Unity,* vol. 2, 86–95) sees this speech as positive until it reaches the closing verses.

80. To whom Stephen refers as ὁ δικαίος and ὁ υἱὸς τοῦ ἀνθρώπου.

81. The parallels have often been noted, esp. 7:59-60. However, the authenticity of Luke 23:35 is generally regarded as doubtful.

acles is subsequently reinforced when, through prayer and the laying on of hands, the apostles Peter and John convey to them the Holy Spirit (Acts 8:14-17). Although there has been much debate as to whether Philip's conversion of the Ethiopian eunuch is intended as an inauguration of the mission to the gentiles, the story clearly serves this function proleptically, even as it also gives a foretaste of the fulfillment of Jesus' initial missionary command to witness to the ends of the earth.[82] Indeed, in his careful placement of the story of Stephen, followed by Philip's conversion of the Samaritans and the Ethiopian official, Luke has successfully structured a narrative unit in which Jesus' words (Acts 1:8) are fulfilled *in nuce* (in a nutshell).

It is Paul's call/conversion, however, that is the climax of the dramatic sequence that begins with Stephen's speech and martyrdom. The current consensus of biblical commentators regards Luke's portrayal of Saul's encounter with an auditory vision of the risen Jesus on the Damascus road as a call or commission modeled on the famous prophetic calls of Israelite tradition.[83] Many of these commentators further argue that, insofar as any elements of a conversion do exist, they merely reflect the view of the source, which Luke has been insufficiently skillful in transforming.[84]

Yet such a reading ignores the way in which Luke consciously shapes this incident to reflect and enhance all of his major narrative themes. In reality, Saul's encounter with the risen Jesus, his divine blinding, and his subsequent healing and baptism includes the formal and stylistic elements of prophetic call,

---

82. Conzelmann (*Acts*, 67–68) argues that Luke deliberately leaves the Ethiopian's religious status vague so as *not* to preempt Peter's mission. Haenchen (*Acts*, 314) is even more emphatic on this point. Tannehill (*Narrative Unity,* vol. 2, 109–12), however, disagrees, arguing that his description as both an Ethiopian and a eunuch suggest his gentile identity.

83. For example, Moses (Exod 3:4-12); Ezekiel (Ezek 2:1-3); Samuel (1 Sam 3:10-11). Hans Windisch, "Die Christusepiphanie vor Damaskus (Act 9, 22 und 26) und ihre religionsgeschichtlichen Parallelen," *ZNW* 31 (1932): 1–23; Martin Dibelius, "Die Reden der Apostelgeschichte und die antike Geschichtsschreibung," in *Aufsätz zur Apostelgeschichte* (Göttingen: Vandenhoeck & Ruprecht, 1951), 137–38; Benjamin J. Hubbard, "The Role of Commissioning Accounts in Acts," in *Perspectives on Luke-Acts*, ed. C. H. Talbert (Edinburgh: T & T Clark, 1978), 187–98; Christoph Burchard, *Der dreizehnte Zeuge: Traditions-und kompositionsgeschichtliche Untersuchungen zu Lukas' Darstellung der Frühzeit des Paulus* (Göttingen: Vandenhoeck & Ruprecht, 1970), 59–88; Charles W. Hedrick, "Paul's Conversion/Call: A Comparative Analysis of the Three Reports in Acts," *JBL* 100 (1981): 415–32.

84. Dibelius, "Die Reden," 137–38; Burchard, *Der dreizehnte Zeuge,* 120–21; Hedrick, "Paul's Conversion/Call," 427–28.

punishment of a persecutor,[85] *and* conversion. Benjamin Hubbard's study of the commissioning accounts in Acts notes the similarities between the commission of Saul/Paul and the commissionings found in connection with Philip (Acts 8:26-30) and with Peter (Acts 10:1-33), even mentioning that, in the case of Peter, commission is linked with conversion.[86]

Indeed, Luke clearly views the conversion aspects of these apostolic stories as of equal importance to the divine commissionings with which they are linked. Furthermore, he uses the stylistic technique of divided action and interlacement to pair the characters of Philip with the Ethiopian and Peter with Cornelius, as well as to show how in each instance the Holy Spirit guides the least likely of protagonists into cooperation with the overarching divine plan. In Acts, this divine plan is accomplished as much through conversions as it is through commissionings. The linking of Saul's conversion to the commissioning of Ananias also applies the same stylistic devices of divided action and interlacement found in the two previously mentioned literary pairings.[87] Thus, Ananias is commissioned to bring about Saul's baptism into the faith through the laying on of hands, which, in turn, activates the gift of the Spirit.

On the other hand, Saul/Paul's case is clearly unique in that he is commissioned by God for his important task even before he is properly converted.[88] His commissioning stresses the Lukan theme of continuity, but his conversion enhances the equally important motif of divine reversal, which confounds the wisdom of the world by reversing the fortunes and destinies of the seemingly comfortable and the manifestly afflicted, of those who appear free and those who are held captive, of those who appear sighted and those believed to be blind. Leaving the historical merits of his interpretation aside, it must be recognized that from Luke's narrative perspective, the persecuting Saul represents the stubborn blindness of unrepentant Israel. In his conversion to an obedient

---

85. Regarding the presentation of the punishment of a persecutor, see the story of Heliodorus, 2 Maccabees 3.

86. Benjamin Hubbard, "Commissioning Accounts," 196.

87. According to A. Wikenhauser ("Doppelträume," *Bib* 29 [1948]: 100–117), the literary device of paired visions, in which the divine command imparted to one character is complemented by an answering revelation or vision imparted to another, is taken over by Luke from Greco-Roman literature, both historical writings and fiction. Among the examples that Wikenhauser cites are the following: Dionysius of Halicarnassus *Roman Antiquities* 1.56.1–4; Josephus *Antiquities* 11.8.4–5; and Apuleius *Metamorphoses* 11.1–3, 21–22, 26–27. Also of interest, however, are the two inscriptions from the Sarapeum at Thessaliniki, regarding the spread of the cult to Opus, as a result of paired dream visions; see R. Merkelbach, "Zwei Texte aus dem Sarapeum zu Thessalonike," *ZPE* 10 (1973): 45–54.

88. Hubbard, "Commissioning Accounts," 187–98.

and zealous defender of the church, the Paul of Luke-Acts becomes the definitive reproach to those Israelites who continue to reject the gospel.

The third and final part of this narrative series of commission/conversions (Acts 8, 9, and 10) comes to a climax with the dramatic revelation that salvation is to be offered to gentiles on terms equal with those of Jews. The story involves the conversion of a godfearing Roman centurion named Cornelius and Peter's acceptance of God's changing of the rules regarding the importance of the ceremonial law. Here again, Luke appears to have combined a relatively straightforward story of conversion with a commissioning account. Moreover, this commissioning story includes a startling revelation, which signals a significant reversal in divine judgment in that a major premise of Mosaic law is revealed to be null and void.

In Luke's narrative, therefore, Cornelius's visitation by an angel in Caesarea is set in juxtaposition with Peter's divine vision on a rooftop in Joppa. Subsequently, when Peter responds to the summons of the men sent by Cornelius and, together with his companions, is received into the centurion's household, Peter confesses before the joint company of Jews and gentiles that God's salvation is open to all who request the forgiveness of their sins through Jesus, God's anointed (Acts 10:43). Cornelius's piety and Peter's obedience to God's will are immediately and climactically rewarded by an outpouring of the Spirit upon the entire company, both Jews and gentiles (Acts 10:44-45). Luke depicts this effusion of divine grace as a second Pentecost, in which the recipients speak in tongues and praise God. With this literary reprise of the Pentecost event, Luke dramatizes the fulfillment of another phase of the mission, the creation of a church encompassing both Jews and gentiles.

Poetic Use of the Supernatural

With the repetition of the Pentecost event in Acts 10, Luke's narrative enters a new phase of the mission in which the word is still proclaimed to Israel first, but increasingly it is also proclaimed and accepted by gentiles. Indeed, the divine legitimation and dramatic success of the nascent mission to the gentiles becomes the central focus of the next segment of the narrative. Peter returns to the Jerusalem church to justify his actions and to win the church's approval (Acts 11:1-18), thus enabling a new teaching mission to be undertaken by the recently converted Saul and the Jerusalem disciple Barnabas, under the auspices of the Antioch church (Acts 11:19-26). That Peter's interpretation of the Holy Spirit's directive was indeed the correct one is dramatically verified in his miraculous escape from prison (Acts 12:6-11) and his instructions that the verifying miracle be reported back to "James and the believers" (Acts 12:17).

Peter's miraculous prison escape, although perhaps the most vivid example, is nonetheless just one of many narrative incidents that are dramatically enhanced by aid and guidance from supernatural beings. In Luke's Gospel, angels deliver the annunciation prophecies (Luke 1:11-20, 26-38), they herald Jesus' birth and its saving significance (Luke 2:9-14), and at Jesus' empty tomb (Luke 24:4) their number is doubled from that found in Mark and Matthew. It is in these instances of divine proclamation, particularly with respect to the birth narratives, that Luke's use of angels most closely resembles that found in the Septuagint.

The angelic appearances in Luke 1 are intentionally evocative of prophetic birth announcements depicted, for example, in Genesis, Judges, and 1 Samuel. Indeed, Raymond Brown has shown convincingly that biblical annunciation stories had achieved a well-defined form at a relatively early compositional phase in the development of Israel's scriptures, and this form included five basic literary elements, the first of which always featured the appearance of an angel of the Lord.[89] But Luke makes no deliberate attempt to pattern either of his annunciation stories on any one specific scriptural account. Elements from the scene in Genesis 16 are combined with elements from other biblical scenes and distributed between the two annunciation stories of Luke 1. For example, in the first annunciation story (Luke 1:11-20), Luke uses the term ἄγγελος κυρίου to describe the angel issuing the birth prophecy (cf. Gen 16:7, 9-10; Judg 13:3). Only later is this angel identified as Gabriel. In this first annunciation scene in Luke, however, the angel does not appear directly to the woman in question, as was the case in Genesis 16:7. Instead, Luke reserves this detail of an angel appearing to a woman of lowly station for the annunciation story regarding Mary. In this second annunciation story also, the angel is not merely an "angel of the Lord" but the angel Gabriel.

Likewise, the prohibition against drinking wine or strong drink (Luke 1:15), which is part of the angel's prophecy regarding John, is a common biblical command for those chosen to serve God in some special capacity. And although it appears in a number of biblical narratives (cf. Num 6:3; Lev 10:9; and 1 Sam 1:11 LXX), including the annunciation of Samson (Judg 13:4, 7 LXX), this prohibition is not found in the annunciation scene of Genesis 16. Indeed, the prophecy that Gabriel imparts to Mary in order to convey the special importance of Jesus' birth announcement is patterned after the Davidic royal prophecies, especially 2 Samuel 7:16 LXX. Thus, the angelic appearances

---

89. Raymond E. Brown, *The Birth of the Messiah: A Commentary on the Infancy Narratives in the Gospels of Matthew and Luke* (New York: Doubleday, 1993), 156, 256–329.

in Luke 1 are part of a larger pastiche of biblical allusions crafted to evoke images of the birth of a hero and the destiny of a future king.

In a similar manner, Luke's theme of the two men of marvelous or other-worldly appearance (Luke 24:4; Acts 1:10) that marks both the beginning and end of the resurrection/ascension narrative also appears to be a conscious Lukan adaptation of biblical style and idiom. In the Genesis stories in partic-ular, references to angelic beings and divine representatives frequently occur using the word ἄνερ rather than ἄγγελος. Moreover, these divine emissaries frequently travel in twos or threes.[90]

Throughout most of Acts, however, as the story of the Christian mission begins its movement toward the gentile world, not only does the interaction between the human characters and angelic beings increase, but the nature of these encounters and their function in the story also change significantly as well. With the possible exception of the role of angelic messengers in Genesis 19, there are no biblical narratives that can serve as literary parallels for the numerous angelic encounters in Acts. Although the active role that angels play both in Daniel and in 2 Maccabees has been cited as a possible precedent, these literary models are quite inadequate. For example, the two angelic rescuers in Dan 3:28 and 6:22 are both silent and invisible, and the reference in Daniel 8:17-26 is part of a standard revelatory appearance. Conversely, the divine avengers that make such dramatic visual impressions in 2 Maccabees (2 Macc 3:25-26; 9:5; 11:8) are all described explicitly as personifications of God's power, not as discrete, heavenly emissaries from the divine realm. Nor do the divine warrior personifications of 2 Maccabees interact with the human char-acters of the drama as do the angels in Acts.

To say, therefore, that the angelology in Luke-Acts can only be explained adequately by acknowledging that its author is drawing on a wider Hellenistic background is to belabor the obvious.[91] But it is important to bear in mind that Luke is writing at the end of the first century CE, and in the early Roman imperial period there is only one genre in which audiences might expect to find supernatural beings intermingling with human characters in historical stories. That genre is epic, and a brief summary of Luke's use of supernatural beings will illustrate the manner in which this gentile-oriented segment of his story reflects the Greco-Roman epic convention of divine encounters with the human world.

Already in chapter 5, when the apostles have been thrown into prison by the Jerusalem authorities, an angel opens the prison doors, brings the disciples

90. Gen 18–19, esp. Gen 18:2.
91. See, for example, Brawley, *Centering on God*, 173.

out, and then tells them where to go next and even what to say (Acts 5:19-20). In chapter 8, an angel commands Philip to travel south on the road leading from Jerusalem to Gaza (Acts 8:26). After completing his missionary task, Philip is suddenly whisked away by the Spirit (Acts 8:39). Again in chapter 12, when Peter has been thrown into prison by Herod, an angel enters his cell, removes his chains, tells him to rise and dress, and then instructs Peter to follow him as he weaves his way past guards and through an iron city gate (Acts 12:7-10). As if for good measure, another angel is busy striking down Peter's persecutor, the wicked king Herod (Acts 12:23).

Moreover, the Spirit serves as travel consultant for Paul's missionary journeys, forbidding him and Silas to preach in Asia (Acts 16:6) or even to enter Bithynia (Acts 16:7), and enabling him (through a vision) to see that he is needed in Macedonia (Acts 16:9). When Paul is thrown into prison in Philippi, an earthquake of supernatural origins leads to his release (Acts 16:26). Moreover, when he encounters trouble from Jews in Corinth, the risen Jesus appears in a vision to assure Paul that he will not be harmed (Acts 18:9-10), thus enabling him to remain in that city for another year and a half. Likewise, in chapter 19, the Spirit advises Paul on the rest of his travel itinerary, which, for the first time, now specifies Rome as its destination (Acts 19:21). As Paul approaches Jerusalem for the last time, the Spirit (through the voice of the prophet Agabus) warns him that he will be arrested. Moreover, even after he has been arrested and imprisoned in Jerusalem, the risen Jesus visits him in his prison cell to assure him that he will live to testify in Rome (Acts 23:11), a message that is repeated by an angel on the storm-tossed sea of the Adriatic (Acts 27:23-24).

Luke's use of supernatural beings as a narrative device employed at critical junctures to shape the direction and further the movement of the plot finds its closest parallel in Greek and Roman epic. Originally introduced by Homer, supernatural interaction with the central characters of the narrative remained a signature characteristic of the epic genre from Apollonius Rhodius's *Argonautica* (mid–third century BCE), to Virgil's *Aeneid* (late first century BCE), to Silius Italicus's *Punica* (late first century CE). Unlike the closest biblical parallels, therefore, which were written hundreds of years earlier, the *Punica* is a true literary contemporary of Luke-Acts.

Prelude to the Pauline Mission: Acts 13–15

After the brief interlude created by the presentation of the paired stories of Peter's escape and Herod's death, the narrative resumes its central theme of the spread of the gospel. In the Antioch church, the believers are portrayed as praying and fasting when the Spirit directs them to commission Saul and

Barnabas for a special mission (Acts 13:2-3). Luke depicts the two disciples as being sent out by the Spirit on an extended missionary journey, first to Cyprus and then to cities in southern and central Asia Minor. Although the Spirit does not specify whether this mission is to be directed only to Jews or to both Jews and gentiles, Saul and Barnabas initially assume the priority of the house of Israel. Thus, in Paphos, Perge, and Pisidian Antioch, they preach in the synagogue.

Paul's lengthy sermon preached in the synagogue of Pisidian Antioch (Acts 13:16-41), however, is addressed to both Israelites and godfearers (Acts 13:16). In this speech, which stresses Jesus' descent from David and also his role as savior of his people, Paul is careful to blame only "those dwelling in Jerusalem" and their leaders (Acts 13:27)[92] for Jesus' crucifixion. Moreover, Paul adds that God's having raised Jesus from the dead has secured one last chance for the people to repent and be forgiven.

Although Paul's words meet with an initially favorable response among his Jewish audience, as more and more gentiles flock to hear his message, "the Jews" respond by rejecting it (Acts 13:44-45). This rejection in turn prompts the first of three fateful pronouncements by Paul that Jewish rejection merely accelerates the progress of the divinely willed mission to the gentiles (Acts 13:46-47). The remainder of the journey incurs mixed results, both in Iconium (Acts 14:4) and in Lystra, where Paul delivers his first sermon directed primarily to a gentile audience (Acts 14:15-18). Despite continued opposition from Jews, who also attempt to dissuade gentiles, Paul and Barnabas complete their journey and return to the Antioch church, celebrating the divinely inspired miracle of numerous gentile conversions (Acts 14:27-28).

Luke's narration of the Jerusalem Council and its results (Acts 15:1-35) represents the dramatic center of the second half of his composition.[93] In this meeting, however, the work that the Spirit has accomplished—first through Peter and then through Paul and Barnabas—is affirmed after each of these

---

92. In Acts 2:5, 14, however, the phrase [οἱ] κατοικοῦντες [εἰς] Ἰερουσαλήμ was applied to diasporan Jews, those who had come from every nation (Acts 2:5). The limitation of guilt implied in Acts 13:27, therefore, is ambiguous at best.

93. For a summary of older opinions, see Philippe Menoud, "Le plan des Acts des apôtres," *NTS* (1954): 44–51. A more recent survey may be found in Jacques Dupont, "La question du plan des Actes des apôtres à la lumière d'un texte de Lucien de Samosate," *NovT* 21 (1979): 220–31. Both Haenchen (*Acts*, 461–62) and Conzelmann (*Acts*, 115) argue strongly for this structural division. Charles H. Talbert (*Literary Patterns, Theological Themes and the Genre of Luke-Acts*, SBLMS 20 [Missoula: Scholars Press, 1974], 23–24), however, argues just as insistently for a dramatic break between chapters 12–13.

principals has told his story before the Jerusalem congregation. Despite the position accorded to Paul's and Barnabas's report of their mission (Acts 15:12), it is the words of Peter (Acts 15:7-11) and James (Acts 15:14-21) that convey the true significance of this event in Luke's eyes. That is because Peter is made to declare the priority of grace over law (Acts 15:10-11) and James paraphrases the prophet Amos in declaring that the engrafting of gentiles into the eschatological people of God constitutes a new creation, rebuilt out of the ruins of the former house of Israel, which is now marked for destruction (Acts 15:16-18).

The Jerusalem Council occupies the position of central importance in the Lukan narrative, not simply because it provides the apostolic sanction necessary for Paul's mission to begin in earnest,[94] but because it represents the moment of equipoise, when the mission to the Jews and the mission to the gentiles are held in perfect balance. Indeed, it is in this scene that the ultimate meaning of the biblical prophecies forewarning a profound program of divine reversal remains truly ambiguous for the last narrative moment. Moreover, this scene also marks the end of the missionary phase that began with the repetition of Pentecost (Acts 10:44) and that concretely inaugurated the incorporation of gentiles into the reconstituted people of God. With the completion of the Jerusalem Council, gentiles are admitted into the community of believers on equal terms and with only minimal restrictions on their way of life (Acts 15:28-29).

Thus, it is the Jerusalem Council which, in retrospect, ensures that the community of Christian believers will indeed be a new community, eclectic and inclusive, and, from Luke's perspective, the true Israel of the already dawning eschatological age. By the time the next missionary phase draws to a close at the beginning of chapter 19, the mission to the decaying house of Israel will all but have ended, and the Christian communities will be increasingly gentile, with only a relatively small remnant of those formerly designated as the chosen people having followed Paul's example.

THE WITNESSING OF PAUL AND THE SUCCESSFUL ADVANCEMENT OF THE MISSION: ACTS 16–28

After separating from Barnabas, Paul, now accompanied by Silas, begins a new missionary journey extending through four chapters. This new missionary phase is heralded by an intense amount of guidance and direction from the Holy Spirit as well as other divine manifestations (Acts 16:6-9). Moreover,

---

94. Conzelmann, *Acts,* xlii, xlv–xlvi, 115–22.

although Paul will not receive instructions to go to Rome until the end of the journey, this segment of the narrative is clearly structured to illuminate this new direction as the ultimate intention of the divine plan. With the exception of chapter 17, which focuses on Athens and Paul's encounter with that center of Greek culture, Paul's missionary efforts are concentrated on three provincial cities: Philippi, Corinth, and Ephesus. In the narrative's time, as well as in Luke's own time, Corinth and Philippi each had the status of Roman colonies, and Ephesus was the seat of the Roman governor for the wealthy and important senatorial province of Asia. Furthermore, it is in his conflict with authorities at Philippi that Paul first reveals his Roman citizenship. Even the brief account of Paul's stay in Thessalonica (Acts 17:1-9) has the Jews accuse the local believers of preaching a gospel that is politically seditious with respect to Roman authority.

This gradual movement toward Rome also reflects the progression of the mission toward the locus of imperial power, prestige, and affluence. As the Spirit directs the Pauline mission toward Rome, the center of world power, its converts begin to include a number of gentiles with a degree of wealth or social position. One early example of this phenomenon is Lydia, the dealer in purple cloth from Thyatira (Acts 16:14) whose felicitous combination of name, occupation, and place of origin suggests that Luke is presenting the reader with a symbolic character.[95] Rather than representing a historical person, therefore, Lydia is almost certainly a Lukan literary creation; she epitomizes a type of convert that Luke wishes to introduce at this point in his portrayal of the historical development of the mission, a convert who, although relatively low in social status, is somewhat well-to-do nonetheless.[96]

In Thessalonica, Luke notes that Paul's converts number "not a few of the leading women" (Acts 17:4), and in Beroea, both men and women of high standing are added to the company of believers (Acts 17:12). Although Luke does not claim great success for Paul in Athens, some Athenians are converted. One of these converts is Dionysius the Areopagite (Acts 17:33), who doubtless also represents a type of convert rather than a historical person.[97] Moreover,

---

95. A felicitous combination in the sense that Lydia is the name of a region of western Asia Minor fabled for its wealth ever since the days of its sixth-century BCE king Croesus. Thyatira is a city within the region of Lydia that was famous for its purple dye industry.

96. Although this occupation is generally associated with slaves or freed people, it could be quite lucrative. See John H. D'Arms, *Commerce and Social Standing in Ancient Rome* (Cambridge: Harvard Univ. Press, 1981), 97–120.

97. The theater and temple of Dionysos, in addition to the Areopagus, are prominently connected with the Athenian Acropolis, and Areopagites were members of the Council

although some converts—and indeed Paul himself—are depicted as craftsmen or skilled laborers, Paul is also depicted as befriended by Asiarchs in Ephesus (Acts 19:31), extremely wealthy provincial officials, whose status approaches the highest summit of the social and political hierarchy.[98]

This depiction of the church as it takes root and grows in the Greek provinces of the Roman empire does not make sense if one interprets the gospel's prophecies and blessings for the poor and hungry simply on a literal level. If, however, one understands Luke's literary and theological task as that of deliberate ambiguity, leading toward progressive revelation, then the development of these themes becomes clear. Jesus preaches good news to the poor and heals the blind (literally and figuratively). He warns the rich that they will one day hunger, just as he consoles the poor and hungry that they will one day be satisfied.

As the drama of Luke-Acts progressively unfolds, it becomes increasingly clear that the religious leaders and many of the members of the house of Israel, who consider themselves to be morally and spiritually superior, are to be cut off from salvation because of their rebellious pride and their blind obstinacy. Conversely, it is primarily the gentiles, who, viewed from the perspective of Israel's scriptures, are considered to be morally and spiritually lost. Nevertheless, it is these very gentiles—those who were formerly considered to be far removed from, or, at best, tangential to the promises of scripture[99]—who are accepting the invitation into the kingdom in record numbers. Thus Luke's preoccupation with the poor and the hungry is as much motivated by literary and theological concerns as it is fueled by his sense of social justice. More precisely, for this presumably gentile Christian author, it *is* an important element of the divine justice that so many members of the former house of Israel have finally been disinherited as a consequence of their hostility to and obstruction of the dynamic progression of God's plan of salvation.

---

of the Areopagus, the traditional council of elders at Athens. "Dionysius the Areopagite," therefore, is probably another Lukan cipher, this one symbolizing wealthy Athenian converts, men from the Greek provincial social and political elite.

98. Mainly attested in Greek inscriptional evidence, Asiarchs were holders or former holders of a yearly office in the prestigious *Koinon* of Asia. This league of cities of the Roman province of Asia was responsible for the festivities connected with the imperial cult within its important provincial jurisdiction. Asiarchs were chosen from the wealthiest and most influential citizens of the *Koinon's* member cities, and they wielded great power on a provincial level.

99. Second Isaiah offers a more universalized perspective of human destiny. Even in Second Isaiah, however, God's plan for salvation centers on the role of his servant Israel, repeatedly described as God's chosen, in implied contrast to the nations; cf. Isa 42:1, 6-7; 43:1, 3-4, 10; 44:1, 3; 45:14-17, passim.

Finally, within these chapters of Paul's main missionary journey, Luke depicts the movement from a Jewish/gentile equipoise to a mission that is increasingly directed toward gentiles. Paul preaches in Thessalonica and converts some Jews but many more godfearing Greeks (Acts 17:4). In Beroea, however, many Jews become believers (Acts 17:12), and initially also in Corinth. Indeed, Paul even converts Crispus, who is described as the synagogue president (ἀρχισυνά-γωγος), together with his entire household (Acts 18:8).

Nevertheless, with the passage of time, Luke depicts a progressive "harden-ing"[100] of Jews toward the Christian message. Thus, even in Corinth, sometime after the conversion of Crispus, the Jews are reported by Luke as having made a concerted attack upon Paul, even dragging him before the Roman author-ities (Acts 18:12).[101] As is characteristic of his literary technique, Luke thereby gives a vivid narrative preview of a theme that will be developed in far greater detail in a succeeding segment of the book, when Paul returns to Jerusalem and is attacked by the mob and arrested. Moreover, it is significant that it is no longer merely Jewish leaders but the Jews as a unified community who become hostile to Paul in Corinth and who seek to bring him to trial.

A further sign that the Christian mission in general and Paul's work in par-ticular is about to enter a new and final phase is Luke's depiction of a third reprise of Pentecost. Upon Paul's arrival in Ephesus, he finds that there are believers in that city who know only the baptism of John (Acts 19:2-3). Paul rebaptizes them in the name of Jesus and performs the laying on of hands. Immediately they receive the Holy Spirit, speaking in tongues and prophesy-ing (Acts 19:5-6). According to Helmut Koester, this Lukan reference is prob-ably based on information from Luke's source concerning followers of John the Baptist in first-century Ephesus and indicates Luke's approval of the incorpo-ration of these pious and repentant Jews into the Ephesian Christian commu-nity.[102] Even if this is the case, and even if such information is reliable histori-cally, however, Luke's inclusion of this pericope functions primarily on a metaphorical level in that it further illustrates his literary and theological

100. This "hardening" is mentioned explicitly in Acts 19:9.

101. This is just one of a number of instances in which Luke's literary requirements directly conflict with any presumed historiographical agenda. If Paul had indeed been a Roman citizen, it is highly unlikely that Jewish noncitizens would have presumed to drag him before local Roman authorities. Likewise, as Richard I. Pervo has so elo-quently observed, it is absurd to claim (as Luke does) that Paul was a tentmaker who somehow gained the favor of Ephesian Asiarchs (*Profit with Delight: The Literary Genre of the Acts of the Apostles* [Philadelphia: Fortress Press, 1987], 10).

102. Helmut Koester, "Ephesos in Early Christian Literature," in *Ephesos: Metropolis of Asia*, HTS, ed. H. Koester (Valley Forge, Pa.: Trinity Press International, 1995), 126.

emphasis on John's special prefatory role in the divine mission that is accomplished by Jesus and by the disciples who subsequently minister in his name.

With this final Pentecost experience, Luke marks the completion of another phase in the mission: the Christian community as the reconstituted people of God is finally achieved. This new people, which in Luke's eyes constitutes the true Israel, is created from the merging of a faithful remnant of Jewish Christian believers with an ever increasing majority of gentile converts. This new community affirms its now wholly separate existence from Jewish social and religious structures, even as it celebrates its continuity with the still unfolding plan of God. Paul began his stay in Ephesus by speaking in the synagogue; within a matter of months, however, he had withdrawn, taking his disciples with him. For the following two years, he preached in a public place to "both Jew and Greek" (Acts 19:9-10).

The "We" Passages: Symbolic and Proleptic Inclusion of the Pauline Churches
The problem of the "we" passages that occur in segments of progressive length, beginning in the second half of Acts (16:10-17; 20:5-15; 21:1-18; and 27:1—28:16), remains essentially unresolved. Although the old and largely discredited theory that these passages reflect authentic, eyewitness accounts by a companion of Paul has been revived in recent years,[103] it does not enjoy wide acceptance. Nor does the theory that Luke created these passages to enhance the verisimilitude of his narrative withstand careful scrutiny.[104] Likewise, the theory that Luke is simply employing a common literary convention characteristic of sea-voyage narratives[105] has proven an inadequate explanation for the full range of "we" passages in Acts.

Recently, however, Dennis R. MacDonald has offered an intriguing explanation of the literary inspiration for the "we" pasages, focusing especially on the sea voyage and shipwreck of Acts 27–28. He argues that this passage, and all of the "we" passages, derive from a single literary influence, Homer's *Odyssey*.[106] As in the *Odyssey*, these narratives of sea-voyage journeys in the lat-

103. For the most recent revival of this theory, see Kurz, *Reading Luke-Acts*, 111–24, esp. 123.

104. Conzelmann, *Acts*, xxxix–xl; Plümacher, "Lukas als Griechischer Historiker," PW Sup 14 (Munich: Alfred Druckenmüller, 1974), 235–63.

105. Vernon K. Robbins, "By Land and By Sea: The We-Passages and Ancient Sea Voyages," in *Perspectives on Luke-Acts*, ed. C. H. Talbert (Edinburgh: T & T Clark, 1978), 215–42.

106. Although a number of other authors had previously cited the *Odyessy* as a likely literary model, Dennis R. MacDonald ("The Shipwrecks of Odysseus and Paul," *NTS* 45 [1999]: 88–107) is the first to present a detailed literary analyis showing the exten-

ter part of Acts focus on themes of homecoming from the general vicinity of ancient Troy. Along with the storm scene in book 5, arguably the most famous of the Homeric sea-voyage journeys occurs in books 9–12 of the *Odyssey*. As in the voyages of Acts, first-person narrative is entwined with the more predominant third-person narrative. And, although Virgil's narration of Aeneas's sea voyage from Troy is also patterned on the Homeric model and also interjects first-person narration within the more pervasive third-person format, MacDonald makes a compelling case for Luke's having used the earlier Homeric epic as the primary literary inspiration for these voyages that ultimately bring Paul to Rome.[107]

As with the vast majority of examples of literary mimesis, Luke's allusions to the storm scenes in the *Odyssey* are introduced so that the audience will both recognize the model *and* note the divergences. According to Luke, these divergences are both social and theological. For example, whereas the Homeric gods grant the hero Odysseus alone salvation from the perils of the storm, Paul is assured that God will save everyone who has sailed with him. Thus, MacDonald concludes that the journeys involving sea voyages in the latter part of Acts are a skillful blending of artistic medium with religious message. The message of Acts 27 in particular is that God is more powerful and more benevolent than the divinities of Odysseus's world, and the artistic medium from which Luke draws that message is the medium of Greek fiction.

Although MacDonald's work sheds intriguing new light on the perplexing problem of the "we" passages, certain difficulties remain unresolved. Indeed, two anomalies characteristic of the Lukan passages as articulated by Susan Marie Praeder over ten years ago remain a challenge for interpreters of Luke-Acts:[108] (1) the anonymity of the first-person narrator, and (2) the plurality of the first-person participants.[109] Praeder's own literary analysis reveals two other interesting elements characteristic of the "we" passages: (1) when the "we" participants are prominent, Paul's own presence is peripheral, and when the "we" participants are peripheral, Paul's presence is central; and (2) whereas the "we"

---

sive number of points of comparison, as well as providing a convincing explanation of function of this extensive allusion to Homer in terms of Luke's broader theological concerns.

107. See also Dennis R. MacDonald, "Young Men Falling to Their Deaths" (unpublished paper) for additional evidence that Luke is creating an extended allusion to Odyssean plot elements in Paul's adventurous and eventful journey to Rome.

108. Susan Marie Praeder, "The Problem of the First Person Narration in Acts," *NovT* 29 (1987): 193–218.

109. Ibid., 214.

participants are featured in the connecting travelogues, Paul is featured in the dramatic scenes embedded in those travelogues.[110]

Therefore, despite MacDonald's important contribution in explaining the literary inspiration for the narrative framework of the Lukan "we" passages, Praeder's observations still demand a solution for the idiosyncratic meaning of the Lukan term *we*. To begin with, the "we" passages occur only after the resolutions of the Jerusalem Council assuming the full equality of the gentile mission (Acts 15:22-29). Moreover, Acts 15 ends with Paul's embarking on a new mission to strengthen those churches that he had established on his first missionary journey (Acts 15:36, 41).

Accordingly, the new missionary journey begins with stops along the route of the former journey. However, Paul is soon confronted by a vision urging him to go west into Macedonia. It is at this point that the first "we" passage occurs. The "we" group accompanies Paul as he travels from north-central Asia Minor to Philippi (Acts 16:4); it proclaims the word to women gathered outside its city gates (Acts 16:13), and its members are named along with Paul as servants of God (Acts 16:17).

The "we" group is not heard from again until the end of Paul's public ministry when, traveling from Philippi to Troas, it reunites with Paul to witness the miraculous recovery of Eutychus (Acts 20:9-12). The group continues to accompany Paul to Assos, Mitylene, Chios, Samos, and Miletus (Acts 20:13-15). Although it is not mentioned among those whom Paul addresses in Miletus, the group's presence in the city implies its vicarious participation in—or at the very least, its vicarious knowledge of—Paul's farewell message. The group then continues with Paul aboard ship, traveling to eastern ports and, ultimately, to Jerusalem itself (Acts 21:1-16), where it accompanies Paul on a visit to James and is warmly embraced by the elders of the Jerusalem church (Acts 21:17-18).

Again there is a substantial interruption in the "we" narrative as Paul undergoes his series of trials. The narrative resumes again, however, for the climactic journey to Rome. This final "we" passage embraces an entire chapter and half of the text (Acts 27:1—28:16), not leaving Paul on his own again until the final scene of the narrative. During this passage to Rome, as with the stay in Miletus in Acts 21, the "we" group functions primarily as a vicarious witness to Paul's encounter with the soldiers and crew. Upon arrival in Rome, the group is greeted warmly by other Christians (ἀδελφοί) already living there. The uniting of earlier Christian communities with this newly arrived group of Pauline Christians serves as the penultimate climax of the book (Acts 28:14b-15b).

---

110. Ibid., 205. This observation was, of course, made previously by Dibelius, *Studies in the Acts of the Apostles*, ed. Heinrich Greeven (London: SCM, 1956), 105.

In summary, the "we" passages begin only after the conclusion of the Jerusalem Council, which functions as the end point for the Jerusalem phase of the story as well as the starting point of the gentile-oriented narrative focus. Once introduced, the "we" group serves as a peripheral or vicarious participant in all of the elements of Paul's active ministry: proclamation, the breaking of bread and its salvific results—even acceptance by James and the body of Jerusalem elders. Most importantly, the group accompanies Paul to Rome, the dramatic climax of the narrative journey and the geographical and theological symbol of the fulfillment of the missionary prophecy.

The "we" passages do not represent historical, eyewitness accounts. But while they are, therefore, rhetorical, they were not created to add verisimilitude to Luke's historical narrative. Nor was Luke merely attempting to follow a literary convention for certain types of adventurous voyages. Rather, the "we" references serve as rhetorical shorthand for the Pauline Christians—those who are vicariously privy to Paul's example and who, as heirs to his legacy, have been called by him to continue his unfinished mission. They are Luke's intended audience, whose participation in the ongoing drama of God's salvation plan is signaled by the words of the Lukan prologue: "concerning the events that have been fulfilled *among us*" (περὶ τῶν πεπληροφορημέϛων ἐν ἡμῖν πραγμάτων).

The Journey to Rome: Proleptic Symbol for the Ends of the Earth

Although Conzelmann attaches no literary or theological significance to Rome as the mission's ultimate geographical objective, beyond the observation that it is the stereotypical destination of missionaries and wonder workers,[111] his interpretation has been challenged indirectly by Jacques Dupont.[112] Indeed, Rome's importance as the goal of the mission is the Spirit's final clarification of the risen Jesus' initial missionary charge. Jesus' first command to his disciples is made at the end of Luke's Gospel. It emphasizes Jerusalem as the starting point of the mission and somewhat ambiguously refers to the gentiles or "nations" (πάντα τὰ ἔθνη) as its ultimate objective (Luke 24:47). In the beginning of Acts (Acts 1:8), the risen Jesus repeats this missionary charge in seemingly equally imprecise terms: "in Jerusalem, and in all Judea and Samaria, and to the end of the earth" (ἔν τε Ἰερουσαλὴμ καὶ ἐν πάσῃ τῇ Ἰουδαίᾳ καὶ Σαμαρείᾳ καὶ ἕως ἐσχάτου τῆς γῆς).

The missionary charge of Acts 1:8, therefore, also functions as ambiguous prophecy, which is clarified only gradually as the narrative progresses and as the

---

111. Conzelmann, *Acts*, 164.
112. See the discussion in chapter 4.

characters increasingly yield to the guidance of the Spirit. Each of the major stops of the Pauline itinerary—Philippi, Corinth, and Ephesus—brings the mission closer to the influence and power of Rome.[113] Moreover, it is the Ephesian elders who are called together by Paul and to whom he delivers his farewell address (Acts 20:17-35). Thus, these symbols of a gentile-dominated Christianity become the guardians of the future generations of the church. Jerusalem and the apostolic church founded there have all but passed into historical memory.

The Spirit does direct Paul to Jerusalem one last time, but only to emphasize that this city no longer bears any fruit for the Christian mission. That Paul is pursued in Jerusalem by Jews from Asia serves to expand the coming judgment to include even diasporan Jews. Paul is seized in the temple, whose gates are symbolically closed once he has been violently dragged from its once-sacred precincts (Acts 21:30). With this dramatic scene, Luke draws to a definitive and dramatic conclusion any lingering relationship between the Jerusalem temple and the true Israel.

Temple and Trial: Luke's Programmatic Use of Balance and Repetition
Although Luke's skillful use of the stylistic techniques of balance and repetition were duly noted by Cadbury, the pervasive and programmatic integration of these stylistic techniques into the unified structure of Luke's composition goes well beyond any literary parallels in Hellenistic historiography. Only in Greco-Roman epic, in fact, is the programmatic use of balance and repetition a defining characteristic of the genre. Two themes that Luke employs to impose structural unity upon his composition are the temple and the trials.

Throughout his narrative, Luke has linked the theme of the temple to the central question of the ultimate status of the house of Israel and the fate of its people. In Luke-Acts there are more than forty references to the temple, most of which are concentrated into four narrative clusters. The first of these clusters occurs in chapters 1–2 of the Gospel, Luke's extended prologue (Luke 1:8; 2:27, 37, 46).[114] These references serve to place John and Jesus, their births, and the divine prophecies concerning their future roles within the continuing

---

113. Although Philippi and Corinth were Roman colonies located in Greece, Ephesus was the home of the governor of one of Rome's wealthiest and most important senatorial provinces, and it was also the site of a major new temple to the imperial cult. Dedicated in 89/90 CE, this temple remained the most prominent temple in Asia dedicated to the imperial cult, until an even more impressive temple was built in nearby Pergamon, late in Trajan's reign. Thus, Ephesus's proximity to imperial power is not measured by Luke in geographical terms, but rather in political and religious terms.

114. The reference to the temple in Luke 1:8 is only implied.

story of Israel. Indeed, Luke's use of the temple as the legitimating backdrop for the opening narrative segment of his story is appropriate because, as Klaus Baltzer has pointed out, even in Jesus' time the temple continued to represent the center of Israel's social, economic, judicial, and religious life.[115] This cluster of temple references, therefore, establishes a vital element of continuity between the events that Luke's narrative seeks to interpret and the foundational institution of Israel's sacred and secular life.

The second major cluster of references to the temple occurs in Luke 19–22, chapters narrating the final phase of Jesus' public ministry and the circumstances surrounding his arrest and trial (Luke 19:45, 46, 47; 20:1, 5, 37, 38; 22:52, 53). Although Conzelmann originally noted the singularity of Luke's description of Jesus' movements back and forth between the temple and the Mt. of Olives, Baltzer has provided insight into the true meaning of these movements. Baltzer has suggested that Jesus' entrance into the temple from the Mt. of Olives and his subsequent retreat from the temple back to the Mt. of Olives appears to be a conscious Lukan allusion to a complex of passages from Ezekiel (Ezek 10:18; 11:23; 43:4, 7). In Ezekiel 10:18 and 11:23, the departure of the divine *kavod* (glory) from the temple for a mountain to the east (that is, the Mt. of Olives) signals judgment against Israel. Conversely, Ezekiel 43:4 envisions the return of the divine *kavod* from the east to the temple, an eschatological event that inaugurates the time of salvation (Ezek 43:7).[116]

Luke's depiction of Jesus' moving back and forth between the Mt. of Olives and the temple, therefore, may be a dramatic device intended to emphasize the crucial nature of this narrative segment, wherein Israel's fate hangs in the balance. The tension between the existential possibilities of salvation and judgment is further dramatized by Jesus' dire warnings and admonitions (Luke 20:9-18, 45-47; 21:5-36), juxtaposed with repeated references to the people's favorable response to his teaching (Luke 19:48; 20:26; 21:37-38). In the account of Jesus' subsequent arrest and trial, in which the people are now depicted as aligning themselves with their leaders against him (Luke 23:13-23), Luke implies that Israel's guilt has placed it under the divine judgment foretold in Ezekiel's prophecy.

The third and largest cluster of temple references, however, occurs in Acts 3–5, chapters narrating the healing of the lame man, a second major speech by Peter, and scattered incidents involving the apostles' conflicts with temple authorities (Acts 3:1, 2-3, 8, 10; 4:1; 5:20-21, 24, 25).[117] The apostles claim the

---

115. Klaus Baltzer, "The Meaning of the Temple in the Lukan Writings," *HTR* 58 (1965): 264.

116. Ibid., 267.

117. This segment of Acts is also preceded and concluded with narrative summaries that incorporate two additional temple references (Acts 2:46; 5:42).

authority to minister to and instruct the people in Jesus' name. Thus, in essence, the conflict with authorities that dominates these chapters is a reprise of the conflict that led to Jesus' crucifixion: the issue of whether God's specially appointed emissaries can be prohibited by the Jerusalem religious establishment from teaching and ministering to God's people. For this reason, Peter's speech deliberately refers to the details of Jesus' trial (Acts 3:13-15), and the apostles respond to their own persecution by the authorities with a verbal attack on the temple leaders for the killing of Jesus (Acts 5:28).[118] In this conflict between the religious authorities and the apostles, as in the original conflict between the religious authorities and Jesus, a dramatic tension is maintained by the initially favorable response of the people (Acts 4:21; 5:13, 26).

Just as the temple ministry of the apostles (Acts 3–5) is crafted as a reprise of Jesus' temple ministry, so also is Stephen's trial and execution crafted as a reflection of Jesus' trial and execution. The mass of the people, who had initially been favorable to the apostles' ministry, now align themselves with their leaders against Stephen (Acts 6:12),[119] whose death is depicted by Luke in an evocatively similar fashion to Jesus' death. Israel's second major confrontation with God's emissaries ends dramatically, therefore, with a deepening of Israel's guilt and the beginning of the mission's movement beyond its immediate borders.

The last major cluster of temple references occurs with Paul's arrest and the subsequent speeches that he makes in defense of his own actions and in defense of the gospel (Acts 21:26, 27, 28, 29, 30; 22:17; 24:6, 12, 18; 25:8; 26:21). Unlike the previous temple confrontations, however, Paul is actually seized inside the temple, and not just by temple authorities but by representatives of the entire people. In this last narrative indictment, Luke implicates those dwelling in Jerusalem (Acts 21:30) as well as those who have arrived from Paul's mission field in the diaspora (Acts 21:27). This third and final confrontation between representatives of Israel and one of God's chosen emissaries ends, as was noted above, with the literal and metaphorical slamming of the temple doors. Indeed, the risen Jesus himself has already appeared to Paul in a dream and instructed him to leave Jerusalem for more fruitful missionary work among the gentiles (Acts 22:17-21). With this third and final abandonment of the temple and the city by God's chosen emissaries, Luke dramatically and definitively sets forth the circumstances justifying the eventual destruction of these foremost symbols of the house of Israel and its historical claim to chosen status.

---

118. Tannehill, *Narrative Unity*, vol. 2, 58–59.
119. Ibid., 59–60.

After his arrest and before his incarceration, Paul persuades the Roman soldiers to let him address the people of Jerusalem one last time. In this speech he offers his own experience as an example of God's continuing concern for the salvation of the people of Israel, even after the death of Jesus and the persecution of the first disciples. Yet the speech ends on a note of pessimism, if not utter doom, when Paul acknowledges that God has urged him to abandon Jerusalem, a city that, when all is said and done, will be unresponsive to his witness. From now on, therefore, Paul will set his sights on proclaiming the Word to the gentiles "far away" (Acts 22:17-21).

Although Conzelmann understands Paul's reference to his complicity in the death of Stephen as a Lukan means of setting forth "the continuity between the original congregation in Jerusalem and the present church,"[120] it is also and more profoundly a means by which Luke is able to show the working of divine reversal, a theme that is central to his understanding of salvation history. Paul, the quintessential descendant of Abraham and early persecutor of the church, in a dramatic reversal of destiny is chosen by the risen Jesus to bear witness to his work and message and to suffer persecution, even death, for the sake of Jesus' name.

With the arrest and subsequent trials of Paul, the divine verdict against the Jews is nearing finality. The temple doors have indeed closed, but it is the unbelieving majority of the former house of Israel who are ultimately left outside the sacred precincts of the Messiah's kingdom. Those who were once designated as God's chosen are about to be turned away empty, replaced to a great degree by the formerly disinherited descendants of Adam. In a marvelous reversal of the divine plan (as it was once humanly perceived), those formerly considered to be disinherited now find that the outer reaches of God's concern have become its new center.

Accordingly, Luke draws Paul's final persecution in a broadly defined parallelism to that of Jesus,[121] thereby suggesting that, from the author's perspective, the Jews are not convicted and sentenced until they have refused the proclamation of Jesus three times.[122] Paul appears in four trials: before the Sanhedrin (Acts 22:30—23:10), before the Roman governor Felix (Acts 24:1-23), before Felix's successor Festus (Acts 25:6-12), and before the Judean client king Agrippa (Acts 26:1-32). As is widely acknowledged, this sequence consciously parallels Jesus' sequence of trial appearances: before the temple author-

---

120. Conzelmann, *Acts,* 187.

121. For example, Walter Radl, *Paulus und Jesus im lukanischen Doppelwerk,* Europäische Hochschulschriften (Bern: Peter Lang, 1975), 295–324.

122. Stephen's martyrdom, which was also drawn with elements of parallelism to Jesus' death, represents the Jews' second refusal of the proclamation.

ities (Luke 22:54-71), before the Roman procurator Pilate (Luke 23:1-5); before the Judean client king Herod (Luke 23:6-11); and before Pilate, the Jewish leaders, and all the Jewish people (Luke 23:13-25).

On the other hand, even though Luke emphasizes the consistency of Jewish rejection and blindness by creating Jesus' and Paul's trials in parallel structure, he also emphasizes the reversal in fortune that the proclamation undergoes, at least from the perspective of human perception unaided by divine insight. Thus, Jesus' disciples scatter and deny him, and Jesus himself is serenely quiescent throughout his trials (Luke 22:63-65, 67-71; 23:3, 34, 46-47). Paul, however, responds to his unjust arrest and series of trials with vigorous, articulate, and indignant speech (Acts 21:39; 22:21, 25; 23:3-6; 24:10-21; 25:8-11; 26:2-23).

Even though Paul's ordeal begins in Jerusalem, it must clearly end in Rome. Luke depicts Paul as the divinely chosen Christian witness par excellence, the only one who, in his person, fulfills the initial missionary command to witness to the gospel from Jerusalem to the end of the earth. After Paul's initial hearing before the Sanhedrin, the risen Lord appears to Paul in his prison cell and commands him to bear witness in Rome, even as he has done in Jerusalem (Acts 23:11). When he is brought before Festus, Paul refuses the governor's offer to be tried in Jerusalem and appeals directly to the emperor (Acts 25:9-11), a request that Festus reluctantly grants.

In Paul's defense before King Agrippa, Luke presents the third and last narration of the apostle's call/conversion experience. This final trial speech provides yet another forum for the reiteration of the Lukan theme of reversal, particularly as it pertains to Israel. Paul recalls the risen Lord's warning that resistance to the divine plan will only lead to pain and peril for the resister (Acts 26:14), an observation already made to Jewish leaders by Gamaliel (Acts 5:34-39).[123] Moreover, Jesus' initial missionary claim of having been sent to bring sight to the blind, freedom to the captives, and restoration of the disinherited to a place in the kingdom of God (Luke 4:18; 6:20) is revealed by Paul as God's intention, which, in conjunction with Jewish rejection, is primarily to be accomplished among the gentiles (Acts 26:17-18).

Sea Voyage and Arrival in Rome: Acts 27:1—28:31
In his creation of Paul's perilous voyage to Rome, particularly the storm at sea and shipwreck (Acts 27:13-44), Luke presents a more fanciful metaphor for the salvation of the gentiles. According to Susan Praeder, the storm scene of Acts 27 shows both a literary relationship to this characteristic motif of Greco-

---

123. Although this prophecy is not fulfilled within the narrative, it is doubtless another oblique reference to the destruction of Jerusalem and its temple.

Roman literature[124] and a theological relationship to one of the dominant themes of Luke-Acts: "Luke has chosen what could be called a characteristically Gentile story to conclude his Christian story of the sending of salvation to the Gentiles."[125] In Luke's narration of the dangerous storm that threatens both the ship and its passengers, Paul receives divine assurance that all will be saved (Acts 27:23-24), an assurance that has many parallels in Greco-Roman storm scenes.[126]

Most interpreters, however, are in agreement that the action and adventure of Luke's storm scene is a thinly veiled presentation of the inevitable victory of God's plan for salvation, against which the deviant machinations of human beings are ultimately powerless.[127] According to Praeder, however, the most striking deviation of Luke's storm scene from that of typical ancient accounts is his introduction of the invitation to eat and his description of the meal itself (Acts 27:33-38). Although she is mindful of the idiosyncrasies of this particular account, Praeder insists that Luke's description of the meal has been styled to suggest a Christian meal.[128] Moreover, despite the objections of some interpreters, Praeder believes that some level of Jesus/Paul parallel is intended by Luke.[129] At a minimum, Luke's intention is to emphasize Paul's legitimate mediation of the divine powers and saving message of Jesus.

Nevertheless, Paul would not have been able to bring about the safety of the passengers and crew without the help of the Roman centurion assigned to guard him. Indeed, this centurion, who is even mentioned by name (Acts 27:1, 3), is a very important character in the story. In the beginning of the sea-

124. Particularly Greco-Roman epic, of which genre it is far more characteristic than it is of the ancient novel. Susan Marie Praeder, "Acts 27:1—28:16: Sea Voyages in Ancient Literature and the Theology of Luke-Acts," *CBQ* 46 (1984): 693–94. As previously noted, Dennis MacDonald ("Sea Voyages") has argued persuasively that Luke had consciously styled this passage to evoke the famous sea storms in Homer's *Odyssey*.

125. Praeder, "Acts," 704.

126. Ibid., 695–96; see also, MacDonald, "Sea Voyages," 100, 105.

127. Marion L. Soards, *The Speeches in Acts: Their Content, Context, and Concerns* (Louisville: Westminster John Knox, 1994), 128–30; see also, Paul Schubert, "The Final Cycle of Speeches in the Book of Acts," *JBL* 87 (1968): 1–16.

128. Praeder appears to be steering a middle course between scholars such as Conzelmann (*Acts,* 220) and Haenchen (*Acts,* 707), who deny any such interest, and scholars such as Bo Reicke ("Die Mahlzeit mit Paulus auf den Wellen des Mittelmeers Act. 27,33–39," *ThZ* 4 [1948]: 401–10) and Philippe Menoud ("Les Actes des apôtres et l'eucharistie," *RHPhR* 33 [1953]: 21–35), who do see eucharistic overtones. The dispute is best resolved by recognizing that Acts 27:33-36 is another example of Luke's propensity to suggest a theme without insisting upon it.

129. Ibid., 699.

voyage narrative, he is presented as having been assigned to guard Paul and several other prisoners aboard the ship. Although basically kind to Paul (Acts 27:3), the centurion is at first more solicitous of the opinions of the ship's captain and owner (Acts 27:11). Later, however, he heeds Paul's warnings and foils the attempts of the crew to abandon ship (Acts 27:31). Moreover, because the centurion saves Paul's life by protecting him from those who want to have the prisoners killed, Paul is able to bring all of the ship's passengers and crew safely to shore (Acts 27:43-44).

The sea voyage of chapter 27 appears to be another example of the Lukan literary technique of providing a proleptic narrative tableau of themes that the author plans to address more thoroughly at a later point in the story.[130] In this instance, however, the full implication of this proleptic summary must remain conjecture.[131] Nevertheless, it would seem that Luke is suggesting or anticipating the conversion of certain key elements of Roman society, particularly those placed within the provincial or imperial chain of authority. It is therefore likely that the fulfillment of this final proleptic narrative tableau is being realized in the historical situation of Luke's own community.

When Paul finally arrives in Rome (Acts 28:11), he makes one last attempt to preach to the Jews. Although Luke reports that some were convinced, others disbelieved (Acts 28:24). This mixed level of acceptance is misleadingly optimistic, in view of the preceding assertion that "everywhere" this sect is being spoken against (Acts 28:22).[132] Paul's final quotation of the prophet Isaiah again emphasizes the reversal of the fate of Israel with respect to its salvation status; the words of the prophet speak of a people who once saw, heard, and understood but do so no longer (Acts 28:26-28).

As Luke's narrative draws to a close, God's judgment against the fallen house of Israel has become final. A faithful remnant of its number will merge with an increasing majority of gentiles to form a new people with a new name. The ambiguous prophecies that formerly veiled God's true salvation plan have all been revealed and fulfilled. The gospel has been proclaimed in Rome, signaling the symbolic completion of the divine mission and setting forth the new city of destiny for the true Israel, the reconstituted people of God. The mission is complete, and the angel's prophecy to Mary is fulfilled, at least symbolically. Inasmuch as Luke's contemporary audience affirms the successful continuation of the spread of the gospel in his own day, it is indeed only a mat-

---

130. For example, Luke 9:1-6; 10:1-12; Acts 2:5-11; 10:44-46.

131. However, Acts 28:30-31 provides a further indication of the preaching of the gospel to the gentiles of Rome.

132. See the discussion of ἀντιλέγω in chapter 4.

ter of time until the glorified Messiah will preside over a kingdom without temporal or spatial limits.

The Kingdom of God versus Rome's World Dominion

Over the years, students of Luke-Acts have ascribed to it every shade of political bias, from abject apology, to principled accommodation, to revolutionary opposition.[133] And it should be acknowledged that there are elements of truth in nearly all of these opinions. Indeed, given the total integration of religion and politics in antiquity, the only completely erroneous assertion regarding Luke's attitude toward Rome would be that he was utterly indifferent to its power, influence, and future.

Likewise, recent studies have emphasized the inherently political (as well as religious) nature of the major epics of antiquity. According to John Alvis, for example, Homer attempts to transform Zeus from a mere philanderer of superhuman proportions to the author of a divine plan, whereby heroes will no longer be allowed to disrupt the human landscape with their excessive ambitions.[134] Indeed, Zeus's providential oversight of the human world becomes a precondition for life in the Greek city-state: "Homer's portrayal of the war with Achilles' wrath prepares a Panhellenic audience for political life by shifting the focus of poetry from the glorification of heroes to the analysis of moral responsibility."[135]

The blending of political and religious authority is even more complete in Virgil's *Aeneid*, as is widely acknowledged. Furthermore, the political order that

---

133. Both Haenchen (*Acts*, 102–3) and Conzelmann (*St. Luke*, 138–44) stress Luke's apologetic concerns. More recent interpretations, which emphasize that Luke-Acts was written primarily for Christian readers, also tend to stress accommodation rather than apologetic as a more accurate assessment of the author's political perspective. Representative of this viewpoint is Stephen G. Wilson, *Related Strangers: Jews and Christians, 70–170 CE* (Minneapolis: Fortress Press, 1995), 67–71. On the other hand, Gregory E. Sterling ("'Athletes of Virtue': An Analysis of the Summaries in Acts [2:41–47; 4:32-35; 5:12-16]" *JBL* 113 [1994]: 696; *Historiography and Self-Definition: Josephos, Luke-Acts, and the Apologetic Historiography* [Leiden: E. J. Brill, 1992], 313), while agreeing that Luke-Acts was written primarily for Christians, still favors an apologetic motive for its author, arguing that Luke wrote directly for his Christian audience but indirectly for the outside world. Richard Cassidy (*Jesus, Politics, and Society: A Study of Luke's Gospel* [Maryknoll, N.Y.: Orbis, 1978]) is one of the few Lukan interpreters who, albeit for the wrong reasons, actually argues that Luke's motives are politically subversive with regard to the Roman empire.

134. John Alvis, *Divine Purpose and Heroic Response in Homer and Virgil: The Political Plan of Zeus* (Landover, Md.: Rowman & Littlefield, 1995), 6–12.

135. Ibid., 78–79.

this epic celebrates is both universal and eternal. Indeed, despite the struggles and setbacks that the story relates, all of these sufferings are perceived by its audience against a backdrop of the assurance of Jupiter's prophecy for his chosen people. "Explicitly, the *Aeneid* supports the right of Roman power by invoking Jupiter's express word. . . . [But], of course, it settles things *only for those disposed to acknowledge Virgil's Jupiter.*"[136]

This last point—that Rome's eternal rule has been granted in accordance with divine will only if one accepts the divine legitimacy of Virgil's Jupiter—brings one directly to a consideration of the motives behind the composition of Luke-Acts in narrative epic style. If imitation is indeed a genuine form of flattery, then one must acknowledge a definite admiration for Rome on the part of Luke. Nevertheless, Luke-Acts presents a rival vision of empire, with a rival deity issuing an alternative plan for universal human salvation. Furthermore, Luke-Acts names a very different sort of hero as the primary instrument for the implementation of that plan, a different concept of the chosen people, and a very different means by which conquest leads to inevitable victory. To assume, therefore, that Luke's vision is exclusively spiritual, or even that its only implied rival is the diasporan synagogue, is to ignore both the external historical evidence regarding religion and politics in antiquity and the internal evidence of the text itself.

Just as the implicit claim of Luke-Acts regarding the church as the true Israel and sole legitimate heir to the history and scriptures of ancient Israel had profound social and religious implications for diasporan Judaism, so also did it implicitly address the religious and political claims of polytheistic Rome. If Jupiter does not exist, then Rome's eternal rule is by no means assured. Indeed, according to Luke, the divine plan ultimately calls for the eternal reign of the risen Jesus over a universally chosen community of believers. Thus, while it is true that Jesus' birth takes place in the humblest of circumstances and against the backdrop of the power and majesty of the Roman *imperium*,[137] the annunciation prophecy of Luke 1:32-33, and the use of the civic and political term *savior* (σωτήρ) in the angelic proclamation in Luke 2:11 assures Luke's audience that some kind of divinely orchestrated reversal will ultimately take place.

Accordingly, the beginning of the story presents the following question: how will it take place? Through the narrative development of the ministry, death, resurrection, and ascension of Jesus—followed by the outpouring of the Spirit, the continuation of the mission by the disciples, and the spread of the

---

136. Ibid., 143, my emphasis.

137. Paul W. Walaskay, *"And So We Came to Rome": The Political Perspective of St. Luke* (Cambridge: Cambridge Univ. Press, 1983), 25.

Pauline mission to Rome itself—the answer gradually emerges. As in the *Aeneid*, the divine plan revealed in Luke-Acts will require toil, suffering, and sacrifice. But, whereas in the *Aeneid* conquest was envisioned and accomplished in traditional military terms, in Luke-Acts conquest is achieved through religious conversion.[138]

As Paul's encounters with Roman officials suggest, particularly in Acts 25–27, Luke's vision of peaceful internal conquest does not exclude members of the imperial bureaucracy, perhaps not even the emperor himself (cf. Acts 25:10-12; 27:24). And as with the *Aeneid*, which ends well before the historical completion of Jupiter's plan, so also does Luke-Acts end long before the full terms of the divine plan are accomplished. In each of these works, however, all of the major obstacles to fulfillment (at least from the author's perspective) have been addressed and overcome by the conclusion of the narrative. To determine whether Luke-Acts should be considered politically subversive in its late-first-century context, therefore, depends upon whether the Christian emperors of late antiquity are viewed as a continuation or a reversal of Roman imperial hegemony.

LUKE-ACTS AND THE IMPORTANCE OF GENRE TO INTERPRETATION

Why does there continue to be such controversy over the literary genre of Luke-Acts? Because genre is fundamental to interpretation.[139] Genre provides the initial key to understanding what an author actually means by what he has written. Are his words to be taken literally, figuratively, satirically, or hyperbolically? For example, a politely distant tone would have one meaning if employed in a business letter, but quite a different meaning in correspondence exchanged between lovers. Therefore, genre matters, as does the historical situation out of which a particular text arose.

Both historiography and historical epic seek to interpret history, but they do so in very different ways. The present consensus among New Testament scholars that Luke-Acts must be classified as historiography is based primarily on the rarely articulated but widely accepted premise that it is somehow inap-

138. Ibid., 58. But Walaskay fails to note the politically subversive consequences of conversion. Nevertheless, it is highly likely that Luke knew exactly what he was implying, which is why he chose to write his composition in the particular style and genre that he did.

139. Indeed, as Brawley ironically observed, "the first constraint that qualifies interpretation is genre" (*Centering on God*, 37).

propriate to presume a New Testament author to be "in imaginative control of a fictional world which he or she creates."[140] This predilection on the part of many New Testament scholars may help to explain why even an extremely skillful and perceptive narrative critic, such as Robert Tannehill, nonetheless accepts as a given the classification of Luke-Acts as historiography, despite the high degree of literary creativity and control that his thoughtful analysis of Lukan composition reveals. Indeed, the manifest weakness of the narrative-critical method is its misguided attempt to obviate critical questions of genre and historical particularity.[141]

The continuing preference among New Testament scholars for classifying Luke-Acts as historiography has received new vigor with the relatively recent publication of Gregory E. Sterling's impressive study, which presents one of the most thorough and compelling cases to date for viewing Luke-Acts as historiography. He argues that Luke-Acts should be considered within the sub-genre of apologetic historiography,[142] stipulating at the outset that, for the historians of "subject nations," a certain amount of literary creativity was both permissible and necessary,[143] and designating Josephus's *Antiquities* as the most instructive example. Sterling further contends that the *Antiquities* is an appropriate literary model for Luke-Acts because it strives to achieve both Hellenistic style and historical reliability.[144] Moreover, whereas Josephus saw his monumental work as a replacement for the Septuagintal biblical narrative, Luke wrote his work as the fulfillment of that narrative.[145] Thus, according to Sterling, as with the much longer and more detailed work of Josephus, Luke's history is also extremely comprehensive in scope. "It is, therefore, not the story of Jesus nor of Paul. It is the story of Christianity, that is, of a people."[146]

140. Pheme Perkins, "Crisis in Jerusalem? Narrative Criticism in New Testament Studies," *TS* 50 (1989): 299.

141. The more problematic aspects of the narrative-critical method can be seen more readily in the work of Kurz, *Reading Luke-Acts*, 5 and passim.

142. According to Sterling (*Historiography and Self-Definition*, 17), "Apologetic historiography is the story of a subgroup of people in an extended prose narrative written by a member of the group who follows the group's own traditions but Hellenizes them in an effort to establish the identity of the group within the setting of the larger world."

143. Ibid., 11.

144. With regard to style, Sterling (ibid., 244–50) cites recent studies that have noted a bipartite division in the formal structure of the *Antiquities* (books 1–10 covering the beginning of Jewish history to the exile; books 11–20 covering the postexilic period to the Jewish War).

145. Ibid., 346.

146. Ibid., 349.

On the other hand, Sterling argues, if Josephus is Luke's primary contemporary literary model, the influence of the Septuagint is nonetheless critical in several respects. Indeed, the numerous allusions to the Greek version of the scriptures are not just to create local color, as it were. On the contrary, Sterling affirms that biblical narratives have provided Luke with his standard of what history *is*.[147] And what is unique for Luke-Acts among New Testament writers "is the writing of history from the perspective of the fulfillment of both the promises and prophecies."[148] Moreover, whereas the Old Testament authors saw fulfillment of the promises in terms of Israel and Judah alone, "the story of Luke-Acts . . . is the record of salvation for all the world."[149]

On balance, however, Sterling points out that, from a purely literary standpoint, Luke-Acts has more in common with its immediate Greco-Roman cultural milieu than it does with biblical narrative. Literary elements, such as the pervasive use of speeches to serve as transitions, and a number of characteristic Lukan literary patterns have more numerous and direct affinities with the secular histories of the Greco-Roman world, even though they can be found also in the narratives of the Septuagint.[150]

Near the end of his analysis, however, Sterling makes the surprising acknowledgment that the historical picture of early Christianity presented in Luke-Acts is false—that Luke has imposed an artificial unity upon the church in order to present his readers as heirs to the unbroken chain of apostolic tradition.[151] According to Sterling, this breach of faith with the reliable transmission of tradition is justified by Luke's apologetic aims.[152] And whereas Josephus made his apologetic case directly to the Greco-Roman world, Sterling suggests that Luke made his case indirectly, by addressing Christians in the expectation that they, in turn, would address the world at large. Sterling concludes that Luke-Acts is an indirect plea for respectability and rights that, in both its literary and functional characteristics, belongs to the subgenre of apologetic historiography. "I would not go so far as to call it an *Antiquitates Christianae* . . . . It does, however, use the same conventions *to relate the full story of a new group.*"[153]

---

147. Ibid., 358.

148. Ibid.

149. Ibid., 360.

150. Ibid., 357–61.

151. Ibid., 379–80.

152. "Luke-Acts served to help Christians understand their place in the Roman Empire. . . . The claim that Christianity was a continuator of Judaism was a way of claiming the standing of Judaism." Ibid., 385.

153. Ibid., 387, my emphasis.

Sterling's study is impressive, both in its erudition and in its detail. It makes a complete, balanced, and articulate case for characterizing Luke-Acts as a unified, historical work. Nevertheless, his analysis at once claims too much and too little for Luke-Acts. It claims too much because Luke-Acts does not even come close to telling the "full story" of the origins and early development of the church—and not only as modern scholarship has begun to understand that history in all of its complexity. Indeed, Luke himself was in a position to have learned a great deal regarding the "full story" on the basis of contemporary historical sources available to him.[154]

At the same time, Sterling's analysis also claims too little for this important early Christian composition. In forcing Luke-Acts into the genre of Hellenistic historiography and limiting its underlying message to "the story of a new people" and their plea for respectability and rights, Sterling loses sight of the Lukan sense of miracle and the inspired drama of eschatological fulfillment, a drama that is heightened by Luke's skillfully condensed presentation of the events of Jesus' death, resurrection, ascension, and bestowal of the Spirit upon the waiting disciples, and by his conscious placement of these events in the center of his composition. Likewise, by characterizing the Lukan presentation of early Christian origins as a linear development of the chain of apostolic tradition, Sterling fails to credit Luke's composition with capturing the essence of the whole of Christian history, even as it narrates only one significant segment of that history. Finally, Sterling's recourse to a historiographical literary model does not allow him to discern and address crucial theological issues, such as Luke's attitude toward the ultimate fate of the Jews or the meaning behind the seeming lack of closure to Paul's ministry in Rome. Indeed, despite the reluctance of many NT interpreters to acknowledge a very high degree of Lukan creativity, the numerous examples of this author's artistic overriding of the historical "facts" make it increasingly difficult to accept the verdict of Sterling and others that Luke's composition merits placement in any subgenre of ancient historiography.

Nor is it simply a matter of Luke's dependence upon historically inaccurate sources, as is frequently alleged. On the contrary, in instance upon instance Luke can be seen creating seemingly plausible historical details for much the same reason that he simulates Septuagintal biblical language, namely, to advance his literary and theological themes. One of the more impressive examples of Luke's ability to create scenes with history-like precision and detail is the well-

154. Luke's blatant contradiction of the authentic Pauline letters is the best-known example of valuable historical evidence deliberately ignored in his own imaginative presentation.

known scene from the introductory section of Luke-Acts, the scene that sets the stage for nearly every Christmas pageant held in America:

> In those days a decree went out from Caesar Augustus that all the world should be registered. This was the first registration and was taken while Quirinius was governor of Syria. All went to their own towns to be registered. Joseph also went from the town of Nazareth in Galilee to Judea, to the city of David called Bethlehem, because he was descended from the house and family of David. He went to be registered with Mary, to whom he was engaged and who was expecting a child. While they were there, the time came for her to deliver her child. And she gave birth to her firstborn son and wrapped him in bands of cloth and laid him in a manger, because there was no room for them in the inn.
>
> Luke 2:1–7 RSV

As John Dominic Crossan so eloquently argues, despite Luke's seemingly impressive mastery of historical detail, the account is clearly a product of Luke's literary imagination.

> First, there never was a worldwide census under Augustus. Second, the Palestinian census was undertaken by the Syrian legate, P. Sulpicius Quirinius, in 6 to 7 CE. . . . Third, and above all, even if Augustus had ordained a complete census of the Roman world, and even if Quirinius had overseen its administration in Archelaus' territories, the Roman custom was to count you in the place of your domicile or work and not in that of your ancestry or birth.[155]

The scope of Luke's literary creativity, although somewhat limited within the body of the Gospel itself, can nonetheless be documented throughout Luke-Acts. In Acts it includes his idiosyncratic portrayal of the principal historical figures of Peter and Paul,[156] the recasting of the twelve apostles as guarantors of the tradition and the prototype for church officials,[157] the miraculous unity in

---

155. John Dominic Crossan, *The Historical Jesus: The Life of a Mediterranean Jewish Peasant* (San Francisco: HarperSanFrancisco, 1992), 372.

156. See, for example, 2 Cor 11:1-15; Gal 1:6-9 for Paul's rivalry with other Christian apostles; Gal 2:11-13 for Peter in conflict with Paul, even after the Jerusalem Council, and so forth.

157. For the fluidity of the term *apostle* in early Christian parlance, there are numerous examples in the letters of Paul. See 1 Cor 9:1; 15:5, 7; and Rom 16:7. The limitation of the term *apostle* to the twelve appears for the first time in the Gospel of Mark; but it is only in Luke-Acts that the tradition of the twelve is reshaped specifically to serve as the model for an ecumenical presbytery.

heart and mind of the early church,[158] and, most especially, the linear development of the spread of the proclamation in an orderly progression from Jerusalem, to Antioch, and across the Aegean to Rome.[159] As only a third-generation Christian, Luke was certainly in a position to know that from the very beginning there had existed diverse communities of believers, apparently not all of whom even considered the resurrection significant.[160] In the Gospel half of his own work, Luke had exercised considerable skill in combining at least three early Christian sources (Mark, Q, and L), each reflecting a diverse body of traditions. Furthermore, at least two of these second-generation sources (Mark and Q) are themselves the product of the merging of differing earlier views of Jesus,[161] thus placing the phenomenon of conflicting perceptions directly into the very earliest historical stratum.

Accordingly, it must be acknowledged that, had Luke decided to do so, he certainly could have written an informed history of Christian origins. Indeed, had he done so, it would be quite legitimate to compare his work to that of Josephus, who clearly does acknowledge the existence of various sects in the Judaism of his time. Luke, however, did not chose to write that kind of history. Instead, he presented both Jesus and the richly diverse movement Jesus inspired as an orderly historical typology—an idealized and, from the perspective of extant historical evidence, largely mythologized version of the origins and early development of the church.

Luke sought to convey what he perceived to be the underlying truth of Christian origins: its divinely mandated mission, earthly trials, and divinely ordained destiny of continued growth within the largely pagan empire of Rome. Viewed from the perspective of Christian faith, Luke's composition is both profound and truthful. The church's historic problems, from the death of its founder, the persecution of the apostles, the internal rivalry between Jewish

---

158. Although some studies have argued for the historicity of the sharing of possessions in the early church (see, for example, S. Scott Bartchy, "Community of Goods in Acts: Idealization or Social Reality?" in *The Future of Early Christianity: Essays in Honor of Helmut Koester*, ed. B. A. Pearson [Minneapolis: Fortress Press, 1991], 309–18), most interpreters assume that this is an idealization on the part of Luke. In any event, 1 Cor 1:10-13 and 1 Cor 11:17-22 indicate that factionalism was certainly a problem in the communities founded somewhat later by Paul.

159. Although Acts 28:14-15 presupposes an earlier Christian mission to Rome, Luke's story makes no allowance for such a reality.

160. If the existence of Q as the product of an early Christian community is accepted.

161. See, for example, Koester, *Ancient Christian Gospels*, 149–71, 286–302; and John S. Kloppenborg, *The Formation of Q: Trajectories in Ancient Wisdom Collections*, Studies in Antiquity and Christianity (Philadelphia: Fortress Press, 1987), passim.

and gentile adherents, which subsequently gives way to a more single-minded concern with the rivalry between an emerging orthodoxy and a variety of heresies—all of these authentically historical problems are simplified within typologies and are concisely arranged within an overarching focus on the gradual and inevitable fulfillment of the divinely prophesied plan of God. And although the origin and intention of this plan can be glimpsed in the sacred scriptures of ancient Israel, the final chapters are being written only in the historical and eschatological present of Luke and his readers/hearers.

LUKE-ACTS: AN EPIC PRESENTATION OF CHRISTIAN ORIGINS

Of all the literary forms that were popular in the late-first-century Greco-Roman world, only epic could truly bridge the gulf between the seriousness of high literature and the accessibility of popular literature. This had clearly been the case for the Homeric epics,[162] and it appears to have been equally true for Virgil's *Aeneid*. Because epics lent themselves to oral performance, their audience and appeal transcended the relatively small number of the educated elite. On the other hand, heroic epics, whether historical or mythological, were serious works addressing the most profound issues of human destiny in ways that both inspired and entertained their audiences. At its best, heroic epic could provide a powerful synthesis of prophecy and history, wherein the recent events of the audience's own time were interpreted by the poet as the fulfillment of divine prophecy, part of a providential plan with universal implications.

Although this oldest and most revered narrative form had first regained a measure of its archaic glory in Apollonius Rhodius's *Argonautica,* it achieved perfection in Virgil's *Aeneid*. In this truly famous and widely popular work, the signature characteristics of the epic genre were skillfully and successfully marshaled to celebrate Roman virtues, Roman achievements, and Roman destiny. Moreover, this literary effort on behalf of Rome was continued in a series of epics by lesser poets of Luke's own day. Although one can no longer be certain what, if any, influence these later works may have had on Rome's provincial subjects, it is quite certain that the *Aeneid*'s fame continued to be widespread.

If, therefore, Luke was seeking an effective and widely appealing literary means of presenting the profound significance of the Christian kerygma and its connection with the creation of a newly constituted people in the further-

---

162. Bowersock (*Fiction as History: Nero to Julian*, Sather Classical Lectures 58 [Berkeley: Univ. of California Press, 1994], 11, 23) notes the extreme popularity of the Homeric legacy with Greeks and non-Greeks alike, as evidenced in the widespread rewriting of the Homeric stories throughout the Roman period.

ance of God's plan for a universal human destiny, then a Christian prose adaptation of heroic epic, in the form of a response to its most famous Roman imperial example, may have presented itself as a uniquely promising form of proclamation. Because of his need to evoke the language and style of Israel's scriptures, however, Luke would not have wanted to compose his work in heroic hexameter, even had he possessed the leisure and literary skill to accomplish such a task.[163] Moreover, as has already been noted in chapters 1 and 3, the Greek version of the *Aeneid* that Luke is most likely to have known would have been the imperial slave Polybius's prose translation.

With the important exception of its lack of poetic form and the inclusion of minor literary elements primarily characteristic of other literary genres,[164] Luke's narrative has nevertheless incorporated with evident skill, if not real polish, a number of the stylistic and dramatic devices characteristic of Greco-Roman epic in general and emblematic of the *Aeneid* and its successors in particular. The plot of Luke-Acts is structured around a central action, in the form of a divinely willed mission to proclaim the kingdom of God and to establish the composition of its chosen people. The accomplishment of the divine plan, which includes the death of the hero and the continuance of the mission by his followers, involves the pervasive use of divine guidance and supernatural intervention.

This interpenetrating of the mundane and supramundane worlds not only validates the protagonists and their mission, it also provides dramatic narrative interludes and, occasionally, critical forward momentum for the development of the plot. Luke-Acts even betrays the influence of the stylistic and structural refinements that had become characteristic of the epic genre as a result of the artistic reforms of the Alexandrian school: extensive use of parallelism, a programmatic reliance on the literary devices of ambiguity and reversal, and the carefully balanced structural divisions by which Luke's composition may be distinguished thematically in either bipartite or tripartite segments.

Furthermore, Luke appears to have been inspired by epic paradigms for a number of specific narrative techniques. For example, he begins his narrative proper with a prelude to calamity. Jesus' rejection by the people of Nazareth, which nearly results in his death, represents a major departure from Luke's Markan source and serves as a prelude to the crisis in Jerusalem in the same way that the perils of the storm in the *Aeneid*'s opening scene are a prelude to the crisis that will unfold when Aeneas and his followers reach Italy, and in the

---

163. As was noted in chapter 1, previous efforts to adapt the themes and linguistic flavor of the Septuagint to poetic meter had produced very little success.

164. Most notably, the genealogy of Luke 3 and the healing miracles throughout.

same way that the plague with which the *Iliad* begins is a prelude to the more profound crisis of the Trojan War. Likewise, Luke's frequently employed technique of creating vivid narrative tableaux that serve as dramatic preludes to the enactment of future events may well have been inspired by Virgil's effective use of this same technique.[165]

Moreover, as Brodie has observed, Virgil incorporates Homeric allusions with the same ubiquity and for essentially the same reasons that Luke employs allusions to the Septuagint. For Luke, as for writers of Greco-Roman epic, the programmatic use of literary allusion serves the dual purpose of appropriation of the authority and antiquity of the model and modification or even transformation of the model's message. Thus, Luke deliberately and skillfully evokes the language and thematic motifs of the Septuagint so that, from its inception, he may appropriate the authority of Israel's sacred scriptures for the Christian church and for it alone. Accordingly, through his skillful narration of the Christian story, he manages to transform the original intent of the prophetic messages concerning Israel.

Above all, however, Luke-Acts appears to have drawn inspiration from heroic epic in the manner in which it creates its story as the fulfillment of divine prophecy and the accomplishment of a divine plan. Not only in Virgil's *Aeneid,* but also in Valerius Flaccus's late-first-century version of the *Argonautica,* divine prophecies are incorporated that place Rome at the center of a saving history of cosmic dimensions. Whereas in his opening chapters Luke employs a series of prophecies delivered by a variety of characters both human and superhuman, in these Roman epics Jupiter himself proclaims one lengthy inaugural prophecy (*Aeneid* 1.257–79; *Argonautica* 1.498–593), which is then supplemented by a number of lesser prophesies and visions delivered by characters with some connection to the supernatural world.[166] In all of these examples, moreover, fulfillment is metaphorically or proleptically implied, rather than definitively achieved within the story line, a technique enabling the audience to assume a participatory role in the ongoing drama of the enactment of the divine plan.

---

165. For example, the brief descriptions of apostolic missions in Luke 9–10, the description of the nations present at the Pentecost event (Acts 2), and Paul's treatment by the Jews in Corinth (Acts 18); cf. the funeral games in *Aeneid* 5, which serve as prelude to the wars of *Aeneid* 9–12; the pageant of future Roman heroes in *Aeneid* 6; and the depiction of Aeneas's shield in *Aeneid* 8. These literary tableaux prefigure events that occur beyond the time of the narrative, and in this respect they are similar to the manner in which Luke narrates the storm scene of Acts 27.

166. For example, *Aeneid* 2.779–84; 8.36–84, and so forth.

Some Virgilian scholars, however, have detected a pessimistic undertone in the *Aeneid*'s prophesies concerning Rome's future. As James J. O'Hara has argued, for example, there is an element of benign duplicity in Jupiter's speech, fleetingly revealed in strategically placed hints of misrepresentation, which subtly suggest that all of the prophetic words of assurance and optimism are perhaps an illusion.[167] Part of the genius of Virgil's incorporation of prophecy and fulfillment, therefore, is that, despite the fact that all of the divine prophecies regarding Rome are proleptically fulfilled within the narrative, the reader is left to ponder the ambiguity of such divine blessings. Although Luke has also created ambiguity in the divine prophecies with which his narrative begins, in Luke-Acts this prophetic ambiguity centers on the true identity and composition of the eschatological Israel. The divine aura of blessing and protection for the historic house of Israel, with which Luke's opening chapters misleadingly begin, is ultimately revealed to be illusory for many of its people.

Despite their emphases on the fulfillment of a divine plan, however, in neither the *Aeneid* nor in Luke-Acts is the divine will allowed to completely overpower human freedom.[168] In both works, the characters must make moral choices; Fate's prophecies are fulfilled despite allowances for the vicissitudes of human response (cf. *Aeneid* 10.111–13; Acts 5:33-39).

In addition to the prophecies inaugurating the narratives of the *Aeneid* and Luke-Acts, a variety of other forms of divine guidance permeate both works, one of the most prominent of which is the appearance of supernatural beings. For example, the roles of Iris and Mercury, who bring the *Aeneid*'s various protagonists instructions and warnings from the supernatural world, are paralleled in Luke-Acts by the intervention of angels who, particularly in Acts, bring the protagonists instructions and warnings and who participate actively in the rescue of the protagonists from physical danger. Likewise, the unending stream of visions, omens, and oracles that successfully guide Aeneas's mission against great obstacles is matched by a similar stream of visions and oracles guiding the apostles in the successful progress of their mission, despite great opposition.

Above all, Luke appears to have been inspired by Virgil in his presentation of the church as the natural and, indeed, the only legitimate successor to ancient Israel. Seizing upon the divine origins of the Trojan people, long established in legend, Virgil's epic extends those claims to encompass Rome and its inhabitants. The promise of ancient Troy reaches its fulfillment in the creation

---

167. James J. O'Hara, *Death and the Optimistic Prophecy in Virgil's* Aeneid (Princeton: Princeton Univ. Press, 1990), 162.

168. *Contra* Siegfried Schulz, "Gottes Vorsehung bei Lukas," *ZNW* 54 (1963): 112.

of the Roman people, just as, in Luke's narrative, the promise of ancient Israel reaches its fulfillment in the establishment and growth of the new community of believers.

All of these elements of a coherently conceived and artistically executed literary composition strongly suggest that Luke's aim was not simply to improve upon Mark's collection and narration of early Christian tradition, but also to create for the Pauline churches and their ongoing mission a compelling and authoritative foundational story. For Luke, writing more than twenty years after Mark and living in a predominantly gentile Christian community, now wholly separate from the synagogue, Jesus' death and resurrection were no longer seen as the immediate prelude to the cataclysmic end of history or the eschatological turning of the ages. Rather, Jesus' death had triggered God's final judgment against unbelieving Israel, and Jesus' resurrection and ascension had signaled the transformation of the old ethnic ideal of the people of God into a newly universalized concept of community.

Thus, in essence, the coalescence of these momentous events symbolizes the Lukan equivalent of the inauguration of the eschatological turning of the ages. Although the final ingathering of the elect from the peoples of the empire still lay in the distant future, the true intention and full scope of God's plan was already fully revealed in the mission begun by Jesus, renewed by the apostles under the guidance of the Spirit, and taken to Rome by Paul.

That Luke intended to present a definitively different interpretation of the Christian message is indicated by the wording of the prologue. Although acknowledging his indebtedness to earlier written sources, Luke invites the reader to make a determination concerning the validity of the Christian claim based upon Luke's own ordering or interpretation "concerning the events which have come to fulfillment among us" (περὶ τῶν πεπληροφορημένων ἐν ἡμῖν πραγμάτων). Luke thereby signals that his interpretation has a corporate or communal focus that engages history in a far more comprehensive and relevant manner than did Mark's essentially christological and soteriological concerns. At the center of Luke's theological reflections is the conviction that the divine solution for human salvation involves not just the death of the beloved Son but also the rebirth of the people of God.

APPENDIX A

THE *AENEID* AND ITS
CRITICAL INTERPRETERS

Although William S. Anderson, like Richard Heinze, Viktor Pöschl, Elisabeth Henry, R. D. Williams, and others, finds Virgil's depiction of Aeneas generally positive,[1] a number of scholars, particularly American, have expressed doubts. Their skepticism centers not only on Virgil's characterization of Aeneas, but also on his depiction of the glorious future of Rome. They even question Virgil's faith in the ultimate justice of the divine order.

Their criticisms focus particularly on the last book of the poem, especially its abrupt ending, in which the defeated Turnus begs for his life, a clemency that an angry Aeneas denies. Wendell Clausen, although acknowledging the dramatic necessity of this ending, refers to Aeneas's killing of Turnus as a "terrible, final act of *pietas* . . . which the poet, for reasons sufficient to his imagination, will not mitigate, will not explain away."[2]

Although Rhona Beare also believes that, from a dramatic point of view, Turnus's death is required, she questions whether it is a very good ending for the story of Aeneas.[3] Recalling the generally sympathetic manner in which Virgil narrates the complementary tales of Dido and Turnus from the viewpoints of these antagonists, rather than from the viewpoint of the protagonist Aeneas, Beare concludes that Virgil's ambivalence toward his hero reflects an unspoken ambivalence toward Augustus himself. "The epic carries an implication equally unflattering to Augustus, that his victory also was won at too

---

1. Elisabeth Henry, *The Vigor of Prophecy: A Study of Virgil's Aeneid* (Bristol: Bristol Classical Press, 1989); R. D. Williams, *The Aeneid* (London: Allen & Unwin, 1987).

2. Wendell Clausen, *Virgil's* Aeneid *and the Tradition of Hellenistic Poetry* (Berkeley: Univ. of California Press, 1987), 100.

3. Rhona Beare, "Invidious Success: Some Thoughts on *Aeneid* XII," *Proceedings of the Virgilian Society* 64 (1963–64): 26.

high a price, and that the avenger of Caesar is as hard to admire as the avenger of Pallas."[4]

Far more cynical is Michael C. J. Putnam's powerful critique of Virgil's portrayal of Aeneas and its significance for the meaning of the poem. To begin with, Putnam rejects the notion that it would have been dramatically impossible for Aeneas to spare Turnus. Indeed, he argues that such a display of clemency and self-restraint would have been the only possible ending if Virgil had, in fact, intended to portray the empire in a favorable light.[5] As was noted in chapter 2, Anderson had interpreted Virgil's use of dramatic reversal positively: Aeneas is the Roman Achilles transforming the defeat and humiliation of Troy into the victory and power of Rome. By contrast, Putnam interprets the scheme of reversal as Virgil's devastatingly negative commentary on the long-term effect of violence and irrationality upon Aeneas's character. In diametric opposition to Heinze's interpretation, which had seen Aeneas's progressive movement toward Stoic perfection,[6] Putnam suggests that Aeneas's "progress" within the narrative is from the role of protector in the early books, to that of predator by the end of the poem.[7]

Putnam further argues that several significant parallelisms favor his interpretation over that of Heinze, Pöschl, Williams, Anderson, and others. In book 1, Aeneas weeps over the paintings of the destruction of Troy; in book 12, he plots the destruction of Latinus's city (*Aeneid* 12.554–55). As Aeneas battles the storm caused by Juno's wrath, his limbs shudder with cold (*Aeneid* 1.92); when Turnus has been mortally wounded by Aeneas's wrath, these same words are used to describe his dying (*solvuntur frigore membra; Aeneid* 12.951).[8]

According to Putnam, another artistic device that Virgil uses to depict Aeneas's gradual metamorphosis from protector to predator is the application of animal similes to Dido and Turnus and, eventually, to Aeneas himself. In book 4, Aeneas is a shepherd who hits a doe unintentionally and is unaware of the damage he has caused. In book 12, Turnus begins as a wounded but still raging lion. Then Aeneas and Turnus are pictured as bulls competing for the same heifer. Aeneas's brutalization and Turnus's victimization reach their conclusion as the epic draws to its devastating close. "Finally, as the end nears, Turnus has

4. Ibid., 30.

5. Michael C. J. Putnam, *The Poetry of the* Aeneid (Ithaca, N.Y.: Cornell Univ. Press, 1965), 193.

6. Richard Heinze, *Vergils epische Technik* (Leipzig/Berlin: Tübner, 1915), 271–80, esp. 279.

7. Putnam, *Poetry of the* Aeneid, 162, 187.

8. Ibid., 200–201.

become only the frightened stag, Aeneas its vicious hunter—a hound who has taken to himself all the violence he has felt from others."[9] Putnam concludes by suggesting that, with the killing of Turnus, Aeneas succumbs to the very *furor* that it was his mission to subdue. Far from describing Juno's capitulation to divine justice, therefore, Virgil has instead affirmed her triumph.

More recently, W. R. Johnson has taken Putnam's proposed triumph of Juno to its nihilistic conclusion. Johnson argues that the interventions of Juno in book 12, like her appearances in book 1 and especially book 7, constitute a violent and malevolent disruption of the natural order. Moreover, because it is Juno and her demonic minion Allecto who cause Turnus's *furor*, "the possibility that hell can triumph is found to be worth pondering."[10] In Johnson's opinion, Virgil's poetic vision had been irreversibly scarred by the traumatic experience of the long and bloody civil wars, and it is this profoundly disillusioned vision which has been objectified in his mythological characters.

Finally, scholars such as R. O. A. M. Lyne, D. C. Feeney, and most recently James J. O'Hara have questioned even the sincerity of the poem's great prophetic speeches and tableaux. Referring to Virgil's adroit use of the Callimachean devices of detail, allusion, ambiguity, and artifice, O'Hara argues that many of the prophecies in the *Aeneid* present a surface optimism, which Virgil then deliberately undercuts by the inclusion of grimmer material only partially suppressed.[11] The reader is thereby encouraged to read between the lines, as it were, to learn the poet's doubts and fears, which lie beneath the hopeful veneer of Augustan propaganda.

In this regard, O'Hara interprets as programmatic metaphor the scene in book 1 in which Aeneas is depicted as feigning optimism for the sake of his comrades while stifling his own inner fears and grief. O'Hara then applies this insight of benign duplicity to Jupiter's speech concerning the future of Rome (*Aeneid* 1.257–96), which he interprets as having been tailored by Jupiter in order to please Venus.[12] Once the reader grasps the strategically placed hints of misrepresentation, he or she will realize that all of the prophetic words of assurance and optimism are probably illusory.[13] O'Hara concludes that Virgil

---

9. Ibid., 189.

10. W. R. Johnson, *Darkness Visible: A Study of Virgil's* Aeneid (Princeton: Princeton Univ. Press, 1990), 148.

11. James J. O'Hara, *Death and the Optimistic Prophecy in Virgil's* Aeneid (Princeton: Princeton Univ. Press, 1990), 3.

12. Ibid., 132–33; R. O. A. M. Lyne, *Further Voices in Virgil's "Aeneid"* (Oxford: Oxford Univ. Press, 1987), 78–81.

13. O'Hara, *Death and the Optimistic Prophecy,* 162.

wrote on one level to fulfill the high expectations that Augustan society held for the prophetic vision of its *vates* (visionary, prophet). In an ironic fidelity to the traditionally duplicitous nature of that calling, however, Virgil deliberately undermined this optimistic level of his poetic vision, thereby revealing his own doubts and disillusionment.[14]

In its renewed emphasis on the importance of Virgil's use of Alexandrian literary devices[15] and its discovery of their critical role in creating layers of meaning, there is no question that this pessimistic school of interpretation has made a valuable contribution to understanding the depth, richness, and complexity of the *Aeneid*. In the hands of its more extreme practitioners, however, this hermeneutics of suspicion threatens to flatten and distort the epic even more than the earlier optimistic or imperialistic school of interpretation is supposed to have done.[16] It is, therefore, necessary to discuss briefly some of the ways in which the cynics have overstated their case.

Putnam has placed great emphasis on Virgil's use of animal similes to bolster his contention that the poet seeks to portray the moral deterioration of his hero as the ultimate result of the madness and violence to which he is subjected throughout the poem. These animal similes used in the later chapters of the *Aeneid*, particularly in books 9 through 12, draw heavily and parallel rather closely their corresponding use in the *Iliad*, which associates human fortunes and reactions in battle with a range of metaphors for the hunter and the hunted. Homer, for example, uses the wolf simile sparingly and always with connotations of extreme fury or viciousness (*Iliad* 11.73; 16.352). Virgil applies the wolf simile twice to Turnus (*Aeneid* 9.59, 566), both references retaining the Homeric connotation of fierce, predatory rage, if not viciousness. Significantly, Virgil never applies this simile to Aeneas.[17]

It is not as a wolf, however, but as a lion that Turnus is most frequently characterized (*Aeneid* 9.339, 792; 10.454; 12.6). Although the lion is also a ferocious wild beast, it lacks the malevolent connotations of the wolf. Not even the lion simile, however, is applied to Aeneas. As Putnam has mentioned, Virgil does use the simile of competing bulls to describe the pugnacious positioning between Turnus and Aeneas (*Aeneid* 12.103–9). This simile, which is drawn from Virgil's

14. Ibid., 177–78.

15. Viktor Pöschl was the first modern critic to concentrate on this aspect of Virgil's art.

16. Among the modern critics, the first and most respected authority of this optimistic school of interpretation was Richard Heinze.

17. Although Virgil does have Aeneas apply the term to his fellow Trojans in their final defense of Troy (*Aeneid* 2.355–60).

own poetic imagery (*Georgics* 3.209–41) is morally neutral. Furthermore, since he also likens the youthful and indisputably virtuous Pallas to a bull (*Aeneid* 10.455), the simile's application to Aeneas cannot be interpreted as contributing to the depiction of his moral degeneration.

Finally, in the *Iliad* similes of hounds and deer abound. They occur both separately (hounds: *Iliad* 8.338; 11.292) (deer: *Iliad* 13.104) and in paired sequence (*Iliad* 10.360; 15.579–80). In Homeric parlance, the hound is a domesticated animal, a trained hunter—relentless and unyielding perhaps, but never vicious. Conversely, the deer generally connotes helplessness and vulnerability, but it also may imply cowardice or a loss of fighting will (*Iliad* 13.104).

In the last scene of the *Aeneid*, Virgil uses the deer simile to show that Turnus has been rendered helpless, inasmuch as the gods have now abandoned him to his fate and he has lost the use of his sword. Nevertheless, he has also lost his fighting will and is pictured as running this way and that in an ignominious panic (*Aeneid* 12.752–53). Aeneas is the hound in relentless and vigorous pursuit, but he is hardly vicious, as Putnam suggests.

Although it clearly is Virgil's desire to arouse the reader's sympathy for the fall of Turnus, who begins as a raging Achilles and ends as a fallen Hector, this does not necessitate the moral disintegration of Aeneas. No doubt Virgil also intends the bitter irony that accompanies this dramatic reversal in Trojan fortunes, but irony should not be confused with disillusionment or disdain. Indeed, Putnam's interpretation of Aeneas's progressive moral degeneration from protector to predator is as artificial and ideologically driven as was Heinze's interpretation of Aeneas as progressively developing toward the virtuous embodiment of Stoic perfection.

Contrary to the opinions of both Heinze and Putnam, Virgil's characterization of Aeneas is at once complex and superficial. Unlike the poem's main antagonists, Dido and Turnus, the readers is never allowed to view Aeneas from within, so to speak.[18] The reader forms his or her opinion of him from the way he responds to other characters and to the relentless trials thrust upon him by the plot. Virtually from the beginning the reader's judgment is mixed, and it remains so throughout the poem. Unlike Apollonius's Jason, Aeneas does not knowingly or deliberately seek Dido's ruin for the sake of his own advantage, although this is the outcome. Nor does he deliberately foment war or seek to destroy Turnus, although the pursuit of his mission makes these results inevitable.

---

18. This observation has been made by others. Notably, Lyne (*Further Voices*) and D. C. Feeny ("The Taciturnity of Aeneas," in *Oxford Readings,* ed. S. J. Harrison [Oxford: Oxford Univ. Press, 1990], 167–90). They both interpret the technique as part of Virgil's overall effort to undermine the credibility and appeal of his hero.

On the other hand, Aeneas readily complies with Dido's desires, and the reader sees him approach Jason-like behavior in his efforts to extricate himself from a situation in which his own acts have made him a willing accomplice. Similarly, when Aeneas is provoked beyond endurance by the treachery of the Latin tribes and the brutality of the killing of Pallas, he does eventually respond in kind. In the end, he shows no mercy.

Williams has argued that Aeneas is depicted as a noble character who must act at times in less than noble ways because circumstances force such behavior upon him.[19] Yet this assessment also misses the mark. At least one of Virgil's objectives in creating the ambiguous prophecies is to allow his characters to make moral choices. Fate is not mechanistic or all-encompassing. Aeneas appears to misinterpret Creüsa's prophecy, thus entrapping himself with Dido and causing tragic consequences. Similarly, the ambiguity of the Sibyl's prophecy allows either Turnus or Aeneas to claim the somewhat dubious honor of becoming the new Achilles. Turnus initially lays claim to it but angers the gods with his arrogant behavior in the slaying of Pallas (*Aeneid* 10.503–5). Aeneas becomes the new Achilles only reluctantly, when events arouse his own latent capacity for wrath and vengeance.

In the *Aeneid*, circumstances do not mold character; they merely reveal it. Aeneas is portrayed as consistently brave and dutiful, but neither consistently wise nor consistently compassionate. Fate works with human beings as they are, and the miracle of the poem lies in the fact that, despite the somewhat flawed nature of its human participants, ultimately Fate's prophecies are fulfilled; in the end, cosmic order and justice are restored. Virgil laces his narrative with heavy doses of irony but never with nihilism.

Nor is Juno allowed to prevail. Although the Olympian divinities, particularly Venus and Juno, are capable of instigating more malevolent consequences than their Homeric counterparts, Jupiter is a more positive and effective force for good than is the Homeric Zeus. Nevertheless, it is not entirely accurate to identify his will with the plans determined by the Fates.[20] A close reading of the text seems to suggest that although Jupiter is a far more powerful and effective

---

19. R. D. Williams, "The *Aeneid*," in *Latin Literature,* vol. 2 of *Cambridge History of Classical Literature,* ed. E. J. Kenney and W. V. Clausen [Cambridge: Cambridge Univ. Press, 1982], 352–53.

20. As, for example, does Heinze (*Vergils epische Technik*, 293–302, esp. 293); Robert Coleman ("The Gods of the *Aeneid*," in *Virgil*, Greece and Rome Studies, ed. I. McAuslan and P. Walcot [Oxford: Oxford Univ. Press, 1990], 55); Lyne (*Further Voices*, 74); and N. M. Horsfall ("Virgil, History, and the Roman Tradition," *Prudentia* 8.2 [1976]: 75–76).

divine sovereign than was the Homeric Zeus, he tends to delegate important details to subordinates. To the Fates Jupiter has entrusted the task of drawing detailed outlines of historical events in accordance with his underlying interest in cosmic order and justice. That is why, in his first major speech on the founding of Rome and the future of its people, Jupiter has to consult the plans of the Fates in order to give a more detailed response to Venus (*Aeneid* 1.262).

The sometimes tragic consequences of Jupiter's delegation of authority to his subordinates is depicted with a touch of irony in the opening scene of book 10. Jupiter summons a council of the gods to review the disastrous situation in Italy, in which the Trojans are in danger of being crushed in the bloody war that has ensued. He complains that he had never intended this war to occur, that in *his* mind the "great war to be waged in Italy" (*Aeneid* 1.263) referred to future warfare between Italy and Carthage (*Aeneid* 10.8–15). Evidently the Fates had misunderstood or amended his intentions in this disastrous respect. Because this error in the execution of his will has been compounded further by the competing machinations of Venus and Juno, Jupiter wonders aloud whether all the prophecies that were issued to the Trojans have now been put in jeopardy (*Aeneid* 10.110). His decision is to let the Fates sort things out in conjunction with the merits of the individual human participants (*Aeneid* 10.111–13). In the end, partly as a result of Turnus's arrogant and impious treatment of Pallas's corpse, the prophecies to the Trojans are upheld by the Fates, signifying the eventual restoration of cosmic order and justice. Thus Virgil makes the actions of Fate ultimately dependent, at least to a degree, upon human conduct.

With the notable exception of the civil wars, from which he did not feel obliged to exonerate the divine powers,[21] Virgil seems to believe that Rome's election is a reflection of Jupiter's benign and providential concern. Seizing upon the divine origins of the Trojan people long established in legend, Virgil extends those claims to encompass Rome and its inhabitants. The poem abounds in references to this people as chosen or blessed. Not surprisingly, most references occur in books 5–8 (5.729; 6.757, 784, 834; 7.219–21, 255–58; 8.36; 11.305–6; 12.166–67). Most significant, however, is the unprecedented degree to which prophecy and other forms of divine guidance function within the story. Their role is not only to validate the claims of the Trojans to blessed and chosen status but also to enable the mission that has been entrusted to them gradually to be accomplished, even though ultimate fulfillment awaits the distant future.

---

21. Although Virgil has Jupiter deny that he intended it to happen (*Aeneid* 10.6–10).

Virgil stops short of political or religious chauvinism, however. Although Fate may single out certain individuals—or even an entire people—for extraordinary historical roles, these people nonetheless remain personally untransformed and ontologically undistinguished from those whom they conquer or whom they are called upon to rule. There is very little moral difference between the new Achilles and the new Hector. Furthermore, in the short run the conflicting passions hidden within the hearts of the gods (*Aeneid* 1.8–11) can impose immense suffering on all mortals. Ultimately, however, a divine providence, guided by principles of order and justice, does prevail.

APPENDIX B

THE DATING OF
VALERIUS FLACCUS'S *ARGONAUTICA*

Controversy concerning the precise dating of this late-first-century Latin epic centers on the interpretation of a eulogy to Vespasian and his sons (*Argonautica* 1.5–21), part of which is quoted below.

5. Phoebe, mone, . . .
    . . . tuque o, pelagi cui maior aperti
    fama, Caledonius postquam tua carbasa vexit,
    oceanus Phrygios prius indignatus Iulos,
    eripe me populis et habenti nubila terrae,
    sancte pater, . . .
    . . . versam proles tua pandet Idumen
    . . . Solymo ac nigrantem pulvere fratrem
    spargentemque faces et in omni turre furentem.
15. *ille* tibi cultusque deum delubraque genti
    instituet, cum iam, genitor, lucebis ab omni
    parte poli . . .

5. Phoebus, be my guide . . .
    . . . And you too, who won even greater glory for opening
    up the sea, after the Caledonian Ocean had borne your sails,
    the ocean that formerly deemed the Phrygian Julius unworthy,
    raise me, holy father, above the peoples and cloud-wrapped earth.
    . . . Your son shall recount the overthrow of Idumea
    . . . of his brother, blackened with Solyman dust
    as he hurls the brands and spreads havoc in every tower.
15. In your honor *he* will ordain sacred rites
    and will erect temples [or shrines] to his house
    when already, father, you shine from every part of the sky . . .[1]

1. Valerius Flaccus *Argonautica* 1.5–17, my emphasis.

Long ago, both Kenneth Scott and Ronald Syme argued that the references to an apotheosized Vespasian and the references to temples erected to honor him and his house indicate that the work was not begun until sometime during the reign of Domitian.[2] More recently, however, some scholars have concluded that there is nothing mentioned in the prologue that would dismiss categorically a dating as early as Vespasian's reign; indeed, they argue, there is much to recommend an earlier dating.[3] Disavowing the temple references as uncertain and discounting the references to apotheosis as pious flatteries, they assert that the strong dynastic theme of the prologue is far more characteristic of Vespasian's propaganda than it is to that of either of his sons.

Still others argue for Valerius's having begun his work during the reign of Titus.[4] The basic points for this third possibility are set forth succinctly as follows: (1) the references to an apotheosized Vespasian are too numerous to have been addressed to a living emperor; (2) Domitian actually *was* writing a poem commemorating the Roman victory in the Jewish War at the beginning of his brother's reign; and (3) on grammatical and stylistic grounds, it is more likely that the *ille* of line 15 refers to Titus than to Domitian.[5]

Moreover, if *delubra* (line 15) is interpreted as "shrines," rather than "temples," even this reference could be seen as consistent with the extant evidence as it relates to Titus, inasmuch as Titus deified not only his father, Vespasian, but also his sister, Domitilla.[6]

2. Kenneth Scott, "La data di composizione delle *Argonautica* di Valerio Flacco," *Revista di Filologia et di Istruzione Classica* 62 (1934): 474–81; Ronald Syme, "The *Argonautica* of Valerius Flaccus," *Classical Quarterly* 23 (1929): 129–37; both cited in Silvie Franchet d'Espèrey, "Vespasien, Titus et la littérature," *ANRW* 2.32.5 (1986): 3074.

3. Eckhard Lefèvre, *Das Prooemium der Argonautica des Valerius Flaccus: Ein Beitrag zur Typik epischer Prooemien der römischen Kaiserzeit* (Mainz/Wiesbaden: Akademie der Wissenschaften und der Literatur, 1971), 8–11; J. Strand, *Notes on Valerius Flaccus' Argonautica*, Studia Graeca et Latina 31 (Stockholm: Almquist & Wiksell, 1972), 12.

4. E. Mary Smallwood, "Valerius Flaccus: *Argonautica* 1.5–21," *Mnemosyne* 4.15 (1962): 172.

5. Robert J. Getty, "The Introduction to the *Argonautica* of Valerius Flaccus," *CP* 35 (1940): 267, 273.

6. Brian W. Jones, *The Emperor Titus* (New York: St. Martin's, 1984), 162.

APPENDIX C

STEFAN WEINSTOCK'S COMPARATIVE PRESENTATION OF THE GEOGRAPHICAL LISTS OF PAULUS ALEXANDRINUS AND LUKE (ACTS 2:9-11)

PAULUS ALEXANDRINUS		ACTS 2:9-11
Astrological Signs	*Geographical Regions, Peoples*	*Geographical Regions, Peoples**
Κριός	Περσίς	1. Parthi et Medi et Elamitae
Ταῦρος	Βαβυλών	2. et qui habitant Mesopotamiam
Δίδυμοι	Καππαδοκία	3. et Iudeam et Cappadociam
Καρκίνος	Ἀρμενία	4. Pontum
Λέων	Ἀσία	5. et Asiam
Παρθένος	Ἑλλὰς καὶ Ἰωνία	6. Phrygiam et Pamphyliam
Ζυγός	Λιβύη καὶ Κυρήνη	8. et partes Libyae, quae est circa Cyrenen
Σκορπίος	Ἰταλία	9. et advenae Romani (Iudaei quoque et Proselyti)
Τοξότης	Κιλικία καὶ Κρήτη	10. Cretes
Αἰγόκερως	Συρία	
Ὑδροχόος	Αἴγυπτος	7. Aegyptus
Ἰχθύες	Ἐρυθρὰ θάλασσα καὶ ἡ Ἰνδικὴ χώρα	11. et Arabes

*The geographical references from Luke retain the Latin form in which they were originally transcribed in F. C. Burkitt's notes.

SOURCES

Aelius Aristides *Complete Works*. 2 vols. Charles A. Behr, trans.; Leiden: E. J. Brill, 1981.

Apollonius Rhodius. *Argonautica*. R. C. Seaton, trans., LCL, 1912; reprinted Cambridge, Mass./London: Harvard Univ. Press/William Heinemann, 1988.

Aristotle. *Poetics*. W. Hamilton Fyfe and Rhys Roberts, trans., LCL, 1927; reprinted Cambridge, Mass.: Harvard Univ. Press, 1991.

Callimachus. *Aetia*. C. A. Trypanis, trans., LCL, 1958; reprinted Cambridge, Mass.: Harvard Univ. Press, 1989.

Cicero. *De re publica*. Clinton Walker Keyes, trans., LCL, 1938; reprinted Cambridge, Mass./London: Harvard Univ. Press/William Heinemann, 1988.

Dionysius of Halicarnassus. *Roman Antiquities*. I–III Earnest Cary, trans. and ed., LCL, 1936–37; reprinted Cambridge, Mass.: Harvard Univ. Press, 1990–93.

Eusebius of Caesarea. *De evangelica praeparatione*. VIII–X Guy Schroeder and Edouard des Places, trans. and ed., Sources Chrétiennes; Paris: Cerf, 1991.

Hesiod. *Works and Days; and Theogony*. Stanley Lombardo, trans.; Indianapolis, Ind.: Hackett, 1993.

Homer. *Iliad*. A. T. Murray, trans., LCL, 1924–25; reprinted Cambridge, Mass: Harvard Univ. Press, 1988–93.

Homer. *Odyssey*. A. T. Murray, trans., LCL, 1919; reprinted Cambridge, Mass.: Harvard Univ. Press, 1984.

Horace. *Carmina*. C. E. Bennett, trans., LCL, 1938; reprinted Cambridge, Mass./London: Harvard Univ. Press/William Heinemann, 1988.

Flavius Josephus. *Bellum Iudaicum*. H. St. J. Thackeray, trans., LCL, 3 vols., 1926–28; reprinted Cambridge, Mass./London: Harvard Univ. Press/William Heinemann, 1976–90.

Livy. *Ab urbe condita*. I–III B. O. Foster, trans., LCL, 1919–22; reprinted Cambridge, Mass./London: Harvard Univ. Press/William Heinemann, 1984–88.

Lucan. *De bello civili*. J. D. Duff, trans., LCL, 1928; reprinted Cambridge, Mass./London: Harvard Univ. Press/William Heinemann, 1988.

Martial. *Epigrammata*. 3 vols. D. R. Shackleton Bailey, trans. and ed.; Cambridge, Mass./London: Harvard Univ. Press, 1993.

Novum Testamentum Graece. Nestle-Aland eds., 1898; 26th ed., Stuttgart: Deutsche
Bibelgesellschaft, 1979.

*The Old Testament in Greek: According to the Text of Codex Vaticanus, Supplemented from
Other Uncial Manuscripts, with a Critical Apparatus Containing the Variants of the Chief
Ancient Authorities for the Text of the Septuagint*, vol. 2.1: *1 and 2 Samuel*. Alan E.
Brooke and Norman McLean, eds.; Cambridge: Cambridge Univ. Press, 1927.

Philo. *De decalogo*. F. H. Colson, trans., LCL 1934; reprinted Cambridge, Mass./
London: Harvard Univ. Press/William Heinemann, 1984.

Plato. *Phaedo*. H. N. Fowler, trans., LCL, 1914; reprinted Cambridge, Mass./London:
Harvard Univ. Press/William Heinemann, 1982.

Pliny. *Epistulae*. Betty Radice, trans., LCL, 1969; reprinted Cambridge, Mass./
London: Harvard Univ. Press/William Heinemann, 1976.

Plutarch. *Lysander*. Bernadette Perrin, trans., LCL, 1916; reprinted Cambridge,
Mass./London: Harvard Univ. Press/William Heinemann, 1986.

———. *Life of Demosthenes*. Bernadotte Perrin, trans., LCL, 1936; reprinted
Cambridge, Mass./London: Harvard Univ. Press/William Heinemann, 1984.

Quintilian. *Institutio oratoria*. X–XII H. E. Butler, trans., LCL, 1922; reprinted
Cambridge, Mass./London: Harvard Univ. Press/William Heinemann, 1979.

Seneca. *De consolatione ad Polybium*. John W. Basore, trans., LCL, 1932; reprinted
Cambridge, Mass./London: Harvard Univ. Press, 1990.

Septuaginta. Alfred Rahlfs, ed., 1935; reprinted Stuttgart: Deutsche Bibelgesellschaft,
1979.

Septuaginta, vol. 13: *Duodecim prophetae*. Joseph Ziegler, ed., Societatis Litterarum
Gottingensis; Göttingen: Vandenhoeck & Ruprecht, 1943.

Silius Italicus. *Punica*. J. D. Duff, trans., LCL, 1934; reprinted Cambridge, Mass./
London: Harvard Univ. Press/William Heinemann, 1983–89.

Silius Italicus. *Punica*. Joseph Delz, ed., Bibliotheca scriptorum Graecorum et
Romanorum Teubneriana; Stuttgart: Tübner, 1987.

Statius. *Silvae*. J. H. Mozley, trans., LCL, 1928; reprinted Cambridge, Mass./London:
Harvard Univ. Press/William Heinemann, 1982.

Statius. *Thebaid*. J. H. Mozley, trans., LCL, 1928; reprinted Cambridge, Mass./
London: Harvard Univ. Press/William Heinemann, 1982–89.

Suetonius. *De vita caesarum*. J. C. Rolfe, trans., LCL, 1913–14; reprinted Cambridge,
Mass./London: Harvard Univ. Press/William Heinemann, 1979–89.

Suetonius. *Vita Vergili*. J. C. Rolfe, trans., LCL, 1914; reprinted Cambridge, Mass./
London: Harvard Univ. Press/William Heinemann, 1979.

Tacitus. *Dialogus*. M. Winterbottom, rev. trans., LCL, 1970; reprinted Cambridge,
Mass./London: Harvard Univ. Press, 1992.

Tacitus. *Fragmenta historiarum*. C. H. Moore and J. Jackson, trans., LCL, 1931;
reprinted Cambridge, Mass./London: Harvard Univ. Press/William Heinemann,
1979.

Valerius Flaccus. *Argonautica*. J. H. Mozley, trans., LCL, 1934; reprinted Cambridge,
Mass./London: Harvard Univ. Press/William Heinemann, 1972.

Valerius Flaccus. *Argonautica*. Wolfgang Ehlers, ed., Bibliotheca scriptorum
Graecorum et Romanorum Teubneriana; Stuttgart: Tübner, 1980.

Varro. *De lingua Latina.* Roland G. Kent, trans., LCL, 2 vols., 1938; reprinted Cambridge, Mass./London: Harvard Univ. Press, 1993.

Virgil. *Aeneid.* H. R. Fairclough, trans., LCL, 1916–18; reprinted Cambridge, Mass./London: Harvard Univ. Press/William Heinemann, 1986.

Virgil. *Eclogues.* H. R. Fairclough, trans., LCL, 1916; reprinted Cambridge, Mass./London: Harvard Univ. Press/William Heinemann, 1986.

Virgil. *Georgics.* H. R. Fairclough, trans., LCL, 1916; reprinted Cambridge, Mass./London: Harvard Univ. Press/William Heinemann, 1986.

Virgil. *Opera.* R. A. B. Mynors, ed., Scriptorum classicorum bibliotheca Oxoniensis; Oxford: Clarendon, 1972.

WORKS CONSULTED

Ahl, Frederick. "The Rider and the Horse: Politics and Power in Roman Poetry from Horace to Statius." *ANRW* 2.32.1 (1984): 40–110.

———. "Statius' 'Thebaid': A Reconsideration." *ANRW* 2.32.5 (1986): 2883–912.

Ahl, Frederick, Martha Davis, and Arthur Pomeroy. "Silius Italicus." *ANRW* 2.32.4 (1986): 2492–549.

Alexander, Loveday. "Luke's Preface in the Context of Greek Preface-Writing." *NovT* 28 (1986): 48–74.

Alvis, John. *Divine Purpose and Heroic Response in Homer and Virgil: The Political Plan of Zeus.* Landover, Md.: Rowman & Littlefield, 1995.

Anderson, William S. "Virgil's Second Iliad." In *Oxford Readings in Virgil's* Aeneid, edited by S. J. Harrison, 239–52. Oxford/New York: Oxford Univ. Press, 1990.

Attridge, Harold A. "Philo the Epic Poet." In *The Old Testament Pseudepigrapha*, vol. 2, edited by James H. Charlesworth, 781–82. Garden City, N.Y.: Doubleday, 1985.

Aune, David. *The New Testament in Its Literary Environment.* Library of Early Christianity 8. Philadelphia: Westminster, 1987.

Bakhtin, Mikhail M. *The Dialogic Imagination.* Ed. M. Holquist; trans. by C. Emerson and M. Holquist. Austin: University of Texas Press, 1981.

Balch, David L. "The Genre of Luke-Acts: Individual Biography, Adventure Novel, or Political History?" SNTS Seminar Paper, Bethel, Germany, July 1991.

Baltzer, Klaus. "The Meaning of the Temple in the Lukan Writings." *HTR* 58 (1965): 263–77.

Bardon, H. "Le goût à l'époque des Flaviens." *Latomus* 21 (1962): 732–48.

Barrett, C. K. *The Acts of the Apostles.* ICC, 2 vols. Edinburgh: T & T Clark, 1994–98.

Bartchy, S. Scott. "Community of Goods in Acts: Idealization or Social Reality?" In *The Future of Early Christianity: Essays in Honor of Helmut Koester*, edited by Birger A. Pearson, 309–18. Minneapolis: Fortress Press, 1991.

Barthélemy, Dominique. *Études d'histoire du texte de l'Ancien Testament.* OBO 21. Göttingen: Vandenhoeck & Ruprecht, 1978.

Beare, Rhona. "Invidious Success: Some Thoughts on Aeneid XII." *Proceedings of the Virgilian Society* 64 (1963–64): 18–30.

Benoit, Pierre. "L'Ascension." *RB* 56 (1949): 161–208.

———. "L'enfance de Jean-Baptiste selon Luc I." *NTS* 3 (1957): 169–94.

Betz, Hans Dieter. *The Sermon on the Mount.* Hermeneia. Minneapolis: Fortress Press, 1995.

Beye, Charles Rowan. *Ancient Epic Poetry: Homer, Apollonius, Virgil.* Ithaca: Cornell Univ. Press, 1993.

Bickerman, Elias J. *The Jews in the Greek Age.* Cambridge, Mass./London: Harvard Univ. Press, 1988.

Bieder, Werner. "πνεῦμα, πνευματικός." *TDNT* 6 (1968): 368–75.

Billaut, A. *La création romanesque dans la littérature grecque a l'époque impériale.* Paris: Presses Universitaires de France, 1991.

Bonz, Marianne Palmer. "The Jewish Donor Inscriptions from Aphrodisias: Are They Both Third-Century, and Who Are the Theosebeis?" *HSCP* 96 (1994): 288–99.

Bovon, François. "The Effect of Realism and Prophetic Ambiguity in the Works of Luke." In *New Testament Traditions and Apocryphal Narratives.* Princeton Theological Monograph Series 36. Translated by Jane Haapiseva-Hunter, 97–104. Allison Park, Pa.: Pickwick, 1995. Originally published as "Effet de réel et flou prophé-tique dans l'oeuvre de Luc," in *A cause de l'Évangile: Études sur les synoptiques et les Actes offertes au P. Jacques Dupont, O.S.B. (Order of the Society of Benedict),* 349–59 (Paris: Cerf, 1985).

———. *L'Évangile selon Saint Luc 1–9.* CNT 3a. Geneva: Labor et Fides, 1991.

———. *L'Évangile selon Saint Luc 9,51–14,35.* CNT 3b. Geneva: Labor et Fides, 1996.

———. *L'Évangile selon Saint Luc 15–24,* CNT 3c. Geneva: Labor et Fides, 2000.

———. "Évangile de Luc et Actes des apôtres." In *Évangiles synoptiques et Actes des apôtres,* Nouveau Testament 4, edited by Joseph Auneau, François Bovon, Étienne Charpentier, Michael Gourgues, and Jean Radermakers. Paris: Desclée, 1981.

———. "Israel, the Church and the Gentiles in the Twofold Work of Luke." In *New Testament Traditions* (1995): 81–95. Originally published as "Israel, die Kirche und die Völker im lukanischen Doppelwerk," *ThLZ* 108 (1983): 403–14.

———. "The Life of the Apostles: Biblical Traditions and Apocryphal Narratives." In *New Testament Traditions* (1995): 159–75. Originally published as "La vie des apôtres: Traditions bibliques et narrations apocryphes," in *Les Actes apocryphes des apôtres. Christianism et monde païen,* Publications de la Faculté de théologie de l'Université de Genève 4, 141–58 (Geneva: Labor et Fides, 1981).

———. *Luke the Theologian: Thirty-Three Years of Research.* Allison Park, Pa.: Pickwick, 1987.

Bowersock, G. W. *Fiction as History: Nero to Julian.* Sather Classical Lectures 58. Berkeley: University of California Press, 1994.

Bowra, C. M. "Aeneas and the Stoic Ideal." In *Oxford Readings in Virgil's* Aeneid, edited by S. J. Harrison, 239–52. Oxford/New York: Oxford Univ. Press, 1990.

Boyle, A. J., ed. *Roman Epic.* London: Routledge, 1993.

Brawley, Robert L. *Centering on God: Method and Message in Luke-Acts.* Louisville: Westminster John Knox, 1990.

Brinkman, J. A., "The Literary Background of the 'Catalogue of the Nations.'" *CBQ* 25 (1963): 418–27.

Brodie, Thomas L. "Greco-Roman Imitation of Texts as a Partial Guide to Luke's Use of Sources." In *Luke-Acts: New Perspectives from the Society of Biblical Literature Seminar,* edited by C. H. Talbert, 17–46. New York: Crossroads, 1984.

————. *Luke the Literary Interpreter.* Rome: Pontifica Studiorum Universitas A. S. Thomas Aq. in Urbe, 1987.

Brown, Raymond E. *The Birth of the Messiah.* New York: Image Books, 1979.

Brown, Schuyler. *Apostasy and Perserverance in the Theology of Luke.* Analecta Biblica 36. Rome: Pontifical Biblical Institute, 1969.

Büchner, Karl. "P. Vergilius Maro." PW, 2d ser., 8.2 (1958): 1266–493.

Bullock, A. W. "Hellenistic Poetry." In *Greek Literature,* vol. 1 of *Cambridge History of Classical Literature,* edited by P. E. Easterling and B. M. W. Knox, 541–621. Cambridge: Cambridge Univ. Press, 1985.

Burchard, Christoph. *Der dreizehnte Zeuge: Traditions-und-kompositionsgeschichtliche Untersuchungen zu Lukas' Darstellung der Frühzeit des Paulus.* Göttingen: Vandenhoeck & Ruprecht, 1970.

Cadbury, Henry J. "Commentary on the Preface of Luke." In *The Beginnings of Christianity: Acts of the Apostles,* vol. 2, edited by F. J. Foakes-Jackson and Kirsopp Lake, 489–510. London: Macmillan, 1922.

————. *The Making of Luke-Acts.* 1927. Reprint, London: SPCK, 1958.

————. *The Style and Literary Method of Luke.* Cambridge, Mass.: Harvard Univ. Press, 1920.

Camps, W. A. *An Introduction to Virgil's Aeneid.* Oxford: Oxford Univ. Press, 1969.

Carlston, Charles. "Reminiscence and Redaction in Luke 15:11–32." *JBL* 94 (1975): 368–90.

Cassidy, Richard. *Jesus, Politics, and Society: A Study of Luke's Gospel.* Maryknoll, N.Y.: Orbis, 1978.

Cerfaux, L. "Le symbolisme attaché au miracle des langues." *EThL* 13 (1936): 256–59.

Charlesworth, James H., ed. *The Old Testament Pseudepigrapha.* 2 vols. Garden City, N.Y.: Doubleday, 1983–85.

Clarke, K. L. "The Use of the Septuagint in Acts." In *The Beginnings of Christianity: Acts of the Apostles,* vol. 2, edited by F. J. Foakes-Jackson and Kirsopp Lake, 66–105. London: Macmillan, 1922.

Clausen, Wendell. "An Interpretation of the *Aeneid.*" *HSCP* 68 (1964): 139–47.

————. "Theocritus and Virgil." In *Latin Literature,* vol. 2 of *Cambridge History of Classical Literature,* edited by E. J. Kenney and W. V. Clausen, 301–19. Cambridge: Cambridge Univ. Press, 1982.

————. *Virgil's Aeneid and the Tradition of Hellenistic Poetry.* Berkeley: University of California Press, 1987.

Cohen, Shaye J. D. "Adolf Harnack's 'Mission and Expansion of Judaism': Christianity Succeeds Where Judaism Fails." In *The Future of Early Christianity: Essays in Honor of Helmut Koester,* edited by Birger A. Pearson, 163–72. Minneapolis: Fortress Press, 1991.

————. "Was Judaism in Antiquity a Missionary Religion?" In *Jewish Assimilation, Acculturation and Accommodation,* edited by Menachem Mor, 14–23. Studies in Jewish Civilization 2, London/New York: Univ. Press of America, 1992.

Coleman, Kenneth M. "The Emperor Domitian and Literature." *ANRW* 2.32.5 (1986): 3087–115.

Coleman, Robert. "The Gods of the *Aeneid*." In *Virgil*, edited by Ian McAuslan and Peter Walcot, 39–60. Nashville: Abingdon, 1990.

Collins, Adela Yarbro. *The Beginning of the Gospel: Probings of Mark in Context*. Minneapolis: Fortress Press, 1992.

Conte, Gian Biagio. *Latin Literature: A History*. Baltimore: Johns Hopkins Univ. Press, 1994.

Conzelmann, Hans. *Acts of the Apostles*. Translated by J. Limburg et al. Hermeneia. Philadelphia: Fortress Press, 1972. Originally published as *Die Apostelgeschichte* (Tübingen: Mohr/Siebeck, 1963).

———. *The Theology of St. Luke*. 1961. Reprint, Philadelphia: Fortress Press, 1982. Originally published as *Die Mitte der Zeit: Studien zur Theologie des Lukas* (Tübingen: Mohr/Siebeck, 1954).

Cullmann, Oscar. *Salvation in History*. Translated by S. G. Sowers. New York: Harper & Row, 1967.

Cumont, Franz. "La plus ancienne géographie astrologique." *Klio* 9 (1909): 263–73.

Dahl, Nils A. "A People for His Name." *NTS* 4 (1957–58): 319–27.

Dahlmann, H. "Vates." *Philologus: Zeitschrift für das klassische Altertum* 97 (1948): 337–53.

D'Arms, John H. *Commerce and Social Standing in Ancient Rome*. Cambridge, Mass.: Harvard Univ. Press, 1981.

D'Espèrey, Silvie Franchet. "Vespasien, Titus et la littérature." *ANRW* 2.32.5 (1986): 3048–86.

De Zwann, J. "The Use of the Greek Language in Acts." In *The Beginnings of Christianity: Acts of the Apostles*, vol. 2, edited by F. J. Foakes-Jackson and Kirsopp Lake, 30–65. London: Macmillan, 1922.

Dibelius, Martin. *Aufsätz zur Apostelgeschichte*. Göttingen: Vandenhoeck & Ruprecht, 1951.

———. "Der erste christliche Historiker." In *Aufsätz zur Apostelgeschichte*, 108–19.

———. "Paulus auf dem Areopag." In *Aufsätz zur Apostelgeschichte*, 29–70.

———. "Die Reden der Apostelgeschichte und die antike Geschichtsschreibung." In *Aufsätz zur Apostelgeschichte*, 120–62.

———. *Studies in Acts of the Apostles*, edited by H. Greeven and translated by M. Ling. London: SCM, 1956.

Dihle, Albrecht. *Greek and Latin Literature of the Roman Empire: From Augustus to Justinian*. Translated by Manfred Malzahn. London/New York: Routledge, 1994. Translated from the German *Die griechische und lateinische Literatur der Kaiserzeit: von Augustus bis Justinian* (Munich: C. H. Beck, 1989).

Dominik, William J. "From Greece to Rome: Ennius' Annales." In *Roman Epic*, edited by A. J. Boyle, 37–58. London: Routledge, 1993.

Duckworth, George E. *Structural Patterns and Proportions in Vergil's Aeneid*. Ann Arbor: University of Michigan Press, 1962.

Duling, Dennis C. and Norman Perrin, *The New Testament: Proclamation and Parenesis, Myth and History*, 3d ed. New York: Harcourt Brace, 1994.

Dupont, Jacques. "Apologetic Use of the Old Testament." In *The Salvation of the Gentiles: Essays on the Acts of the Apostles,* 129–60. New York: Paulist Press, 1979.

———. *Les Béatitudes: Le problème littéraire,* vol. 1. Bruges/Louvain, Bel.: Abbaye de Saint-André/E. Nauwelaerts, 1958.

———. "The First Christian Pentecost." In *The Salvation of the Gentiles: Essays on the Acts of the Apostles,* 35–60. New York: Paulist Press, 1979.

———. "ΛΑΟΣ 'ΕΞ 'ΕΘΝΩΝ." *NTS* 3 (1956–57): 47–50.

———. "La question du plan des Actes des apôtres à la lumière d'un texte de Lucien de Samosate." *NovT* 21 (1979): 220–31.

———. *The Salvation of the Gentiles: Essays on the Acts of the Apostles.* Translated by J. R. Keating. New York: Paulist Press, 1979.

———. "Le salut des gentiles et la signification théologique du livre des Actes." *NTS* 6 (1959–60): 132–55.

———. *Les sources du livre des Actes: État de la question.* Paris: Desclée de Brouwer, 1960.

Enslin, Morton S. "The Ascension Story." *JBL* 47 (1928): 60–73.

Epp, Eldon Jay. *The Theological Tendency of Codex Bezae Catabrigiensis in Acts.* SNTSMS 3. Cambridge: Cambridge Univ. Press, 1966.

Fallon, F. "Theodotus." In *The Old Testament Pseudepigrapha,* vol. 2, edited by James H. Charlesworth, 785–89. Garden City, N.Y.: Doubleday, 1985.

Feeney, D. C. "The Reconciliation of Juno." In *Oxford Readings in Virgil's* Aeneid, edited by S. J. Harrison, 363–77. Oxford/New York: Oxford Univ. Press, 1990.

———. "The Taciturnity of Aeneas." In *Oxford Readings in Virgil's* Aeneid, edited by S. J. Harrison, 167–90. Oxford/New York: Oxford Univ. Press, 1990.

Feldman, Louis. *Jew and Gentile in the Ancient World.* Princeton: Princeton Univ. Press, 1993.

Fine, John V. A. *The Ancient Greeks: A Critical History.* Cambridge, Mass.: Harvard Univ. Press, 1983.

Finkelpearl, Ellen. "Psyche, Aeneas, and an Ass: Apuleius' *Metamorphoses* 6.10–6.21." *TAPA* 120 (1990): 333–47.

Finley, John H. Jr. *Homer's Odyssey.* Cambridge, Mass.: Harvard Univ. Press, 1978.

Fitzmyer, Joseph A. *The Gospel According to Luke.* 2 vols. Anchor Bible 28, 28A. Garden City, N.Y.: Doubleday, 1981–85.

Foakes-Jackson, F. J., and Kirsopp Lake, eds. *The Beginnings of Christianity: Acts of the Apostles.* 5 vols. London: MacMillan, 1919–33.

Fordyce, C. J. *Virgil:* Aeneid *VII–VIII.* Bristol: Bristol Classical Press, 1977.

Fortna, Robert T. *The Gospel of Signs: A Reconstruction of the Narrative Source Underlying the Fourth Gospel.* SNTSMS 11. Cambridge: Cambridge Univ. Press, 1970.

George, Augustin. "L'Esprit Saint dans l'oeuvre de Luc." *RB* 85 (1978): 500–542.

———. "La predication inaugurale de Jésus dans la synagogue de Nazareth, Luc 4, 16–30." *Bible et Vie Chrétienne* 55–60 (1964): 17–29.

———. "Le parallèle entre Jean-Baptiste et Jésus en Lc 1–2." In *Études sur l'oeuvre de Luc.* Paris: Gabalda, 1978.

Georgi, Dieter. *The Opponents of Paul in Second Corinthians.* Philadelphia: Fortress Press, 1986. Originally published as *Die Gegner des Paulus im 2. Korintherbrief:*

Studien zur Religiösen Propaganda in der Spätantike (Neukirchen-Vluyn: Neukirchener, 1964).

———. "Who Is the True Prophet?" In *Christians among Jews and Gentiles,* edited by G. W. E. Nickelsburg and G. W. MacRae, 100–126. Philadelphia: Fortress Press, 1986.

Getty, Robert J. "The Introduction to the *Argonautica* of Valerius Flaccus." *CP* 35 (1940): 259–73.

Goodman, Martin. "Jewish Proselytizing in the First Century." In *The Jews among Pagans and Christians,* edited by J. Lieu, J. North, and T. Rajak, 53–78. London: Routledge, 1992.

———. *Mission and Conversion: Proselytizing in the Religious History of the Roman Empire.* Oxford/New York: Clarendon, 1994.

———. "Nerva, the Fiscus Judaicus and Jewish Identity." *JRomS* 79 (1989): 40–44.

Goulder, M. D. *Midrash and Lection in Matthew.* London: SPCK, 1974.

Green, Peter. *Alexander to Actium: The Historical Evolution of the Hellenistic Age.* Berkeley: University of California Press, 1990.

Griffin, Jasper. "The Fourth Georgic, Virgil and Rome." In *Virgil,* edited by Ian McAuslan and Peter Walcot, 94–111. Oxford: Oxford Univ. Press, 1990.

———. "Virgil." In *The Roman World,* edited by J. Boardman, J. Griffin, and O. Murray, 206–25. Oxford: Oxford Univ. Press, 1988.

Gruen, Erich S. *Culture and National Identity in Republican Rome.* Ithaca: Cornell Univ. Press, 1992.

Guillaumé, Jean-Marie. *Luc interprete des anciennes traditions sur la Résurrection de Jésus. Études Bibliques.* Paris: J. Gabalda et Cie, 1979.

Haenchen, Ernst. *The Acts of the Apostles: A Commentary.* Translated by B. Noble, G. Shinn, and revised by R. McL. Wilson. Philadelphia: Westminster, 1971. Originally published as *Die Apostelgeschichte* (Göttingen: Vandenhoeck & Ruprecht, 1956).

Hainsworth, J. B. *The Idea of Epic.* Eidos. Berkeley: University of California Press, 1991.

Hannestad, Niels. *Roman Art and Imperial Policy.* Aarhus, Den.: Aarhus Univ. Press, 1988.

Hanson, K. C. "How Honorable! How Shameful! A Cultural Analysis of Matthew's Makarisms and Reproaches." *Semeia* 68 (1994–96): 81–111.

———. "Sin, Purification, and Group Process." In *Problems in Biblical Theology: Essays in Honor of Rolf Knierim,* edited by H. T. C. Sun and K. L. Eades, 167–91. Grand Rapids: Eerdmans, 1997.

Hardie, Philip R. *The Epic Successors of Virgil: A Study in the Dynamics of a Tradition.* Roman Literature and Its Contexts. Cambridge: Cambridge Univ. Press, 1993.

———. *Virgil's Aeneid: Cosmos and Imperium.* Oxford: Clarendon, 1986.

Harris, William V. *Ancient Literacy.* Cambridge, Mass.: Harvard Univ. Press, 1989.

Harrison, S. J., ed. *Oxford Readings in Vergil's Aeneid.* Oxford: Oxford Univ. Press, 1990.

Hedrick, Charles W. "Paul's Conversion/Call: A Comparative Analysis of the Three Reports in Acts." *JBL* 100 (1981): 415–32.

Heidel, Alexander. *The Gilgamesh Epic and Old Testament Parallels.* Chicago: Phoenix Books, 1963.

Heinze, Richard. *Vergils epische Technik.* Leipzig/Berlin: Tübner, 1915.

Henderson, John. "Form Remade: Statius' *Thebaid.*" In *Roman Epic,* edited by A. J. Boyle, 162–91. London: Routledge, 1993.

Henry, Elisabeth. *The Vigor of Prophecy: A Study of Virgil's* Aeneid. Bristol, U.K.: Bristol Classical Press, 1989.

Horsfall, N. M. "Virgil, History, and the Roman Tradition." *Prudentia* 8.2 (1976): 73–89.

Hubbard, Benjamin J. "The Role of Commissioning Accounts in Acts." In *Perspectives on Luke-Acts,* edited by C. H. Talbert, 187–98. Edinburgh: T & T Clark, 1978.

Irmscher, Johannes. "Vergil in der griechischen Antike." *Klio* 67 (1985): 281–85.

Jeremias, Joachim. "Tradition und Redaktion in Lukas 15." *ZNW* 62 (1971): 172–89.

Johnson, Luke T. *The Literary Function of Possessions in Luke-Acts.* SBLDS 39. Missoula, Mont.: Scholars Press, 1977.

Johnson, W. R. *Darkness Visible: A Study of Vergil's* Aeneid. Berkeley: University of California Press, 1976.

Jones, Brian W. *The Emperor Domitian.* London: Routledge, 1992.

———. *The Emperor Titus.* New York: St. Martins, 1984.

Kaestli, J.-D. *L'eschatologie dans l'oeuvre de Luc, ses caractéristiques et sa place dans le développement du christianisme primitif.* Geneva: Labor et Fides, 1969.

Keck, Leander E. and J. Louis Martyn, eds. *Studies in Luke-Acts: Essays Presented in Honor of Paul Schubert.* Nashville: Abingdon, 1966.

Kennedy, George A. *Classical Rhetoric and Its Christian and Secular Tradition from Ancient to Modern Times.* Chapel Hill: University of North Carolina Press, 1980.

Kirk, G. S. *Homer and Oral Tradition.* Cambridge: Cambridge Univ. Press, 1976.

Kloppenborg, John S. *The Formation of Q: Trajectories in Ancient Wisdom Collections.* Studies in Antiquity and Christianity. Philadelphia: Fortress Press, 1987.

———. *Q Parallels: Critical Notes & Concordance.* Sonoma, Calif.: Polebridge, 1988.

Knauer, George Nicolaus. *Die Aeneis und Homer: Studien zur poetischen Technik Vergils.* Göttingen: Vandenhoeck & Ruprecht, 1964.

Koester, Helmut. *Ancient Christian Gospels: Their History and Development.* London/ Philadelphia: SCM/Trinity Press International, 1991.

———. "Ephesos in Early Christian Literature." In *Ephesos: Metropolis of Asia,* HTS, edited by H. Koester, 119–40. Valley Forge, Pa.: Trinity Press International, 1995.

———. *Introduction to the New Testament.* 2 vols. Philadelphia: Fortress Press, 1982.

Kugel, James L., and Rowan A. Greer. *Early Biblical Interpretation.* Philadelphia: Westminster, 1986.

Kurz, William S. *Reading Luke-Acts: Dynamics of Biblical Narrative.* Louisville: Westminster John Knox, 1993.

Larranaga, Victorien. *L'Ascension de notre Seigneur dans le Nouveau Testament.* Rome: Institut Biblique Pontifical, 1938.

Lefèvre, Eckhard. *Das Prooemium der Argonautica des Valerius Flaccus: Ein Beitrag zur Typik epischer Prooemien der römischen Kaiserzeit.* Mainz/Wiesbaden: Akademie der Wissenschaften und der Literatur, 1971.

Lesky, Albin. *A History of Greek Literature.* Translated by J. Willis and C. de Heer. London: Methuen, 1966. Originally published as *Geschichte der griechischen Literatur.* Bern, Swi.: Francke, 1957–58.

Létoublon, F. *Les lieux communs de roman: Stéréotypes grecs d'aventure et d'amour.* Mnemosyne Supp. 123. Leiden: E. J. Brill, 1993.

Lohfink, Gerhard. *Die Sammlung Israels: Eine Untersuchung zur lukanischen Ekklesiologie.* SANT 39. Munich: Kösel, 1975.

Lohse, Eduard. "πεντηκοστή." *TDNT* 6 (1968): 46–52.

Loisy, Alfred. *Les Actes des apôtres.* Paris: F. Rieder, 1925.

Lyne, R. O. A. M. "Augustan Poetry and Society." In *The Roman World,* edited by J. Boardman, J. Griffin, and O. Murray, 188–205. Oxford: Oxford Univ. Press, 1988.

———. *Further Voices in Vergil's* Aeneid. Oxford: Oxford Univ. Press, 1987.

———. "Vergil and the Politics of War." In *Oxford Readings in Virgil's* Aeneid, edited by S. J. Harrison, 316–38. Oxford/New York: Oxford Univ. Press, 1990.

MacDonald, Dennis R. "The Shipwrecks of Odysseus and Paul." *NTS* 45 (1999): 88–107.

———. "The Ending of Luke and the Ending of the Odyssey." Unpublished paper.

———. "Earthquakes and Prison Breaks." Unpublished paper.

Mack, Burton L. *Who Wrote the New Testament?* San Francisco: HarperCollins, 1995.

Maddox, Robert. *The Purpose of Luke-Acts.* Göttingen: Vandenhoeck & Ruprecht, 1982.

Malamud, Martha M. and Donald T. McGuire Jr. "Flavian Variant: Myth. Valerius' Argonautica." In *Roman Epic,* edited by A. J. Boyle, 192–217. London: Routledge, 1993.

McAuslan, Ian and Peter Walcot. *Virgil.* Greece and Rome Studies. Oxford: Oxford Univ. Press, 1990.

McNight, Scott. *A Light among the Gentiles: Jewish Missionary Activity in the Second Temple Period.* Minneapolis: Fortress Press, 1991.

Menoud, Philippe. "Les Actes des apôtres et l'eucharistie." *RHPhR* 33 (1953): 21–35.

———. "During Forty Days." In *Jesus Christ and the Faith: A Collection of Studies by Philippe Menoud.* Translated by E. M. Paul, 167–79. Pittsburgh, Pa.: Pickwick, 1978.

———. "Le plan des Actes des apôtres." *NTS* (1954): 44–51.

———. "Remarques sur les textes de l'ascension dans Luc-Actes." In *Neutestament-liche Studien für Rudolf Bultmann,* edited by W. Eltester, 148–56. Berlin: Töpelmann, 1954.

Merkelbach, R. "Zwei Texte aus dem Sarapeum zu Thessalonike." *ZPE* 10 (1973): 45–54.

Metzger, Bruce M. *A Textual Commentary on the Greek New Testament.* Stuttgart: United Bible Societies, 1975.

Minear, Paul. "Luke's Use of the Birth Stories." In *Studies in Luke-Acts: Essays Presented in Honor of Paul Schubert,* edited by Leander E. Keck and J. Louis Martyn, 111–30. Nashville: Abingdon, 1966.

Mitchell, Alan C. "The Social Function of Friendship in Acts 2:22-47 and 4:32-37." *JBL* 111 (1992): 255–72.

Momigliano, Arnaldo. "Panegyricus Messellae and 'Panegyricus Vespasiani.'" *JRomS* 40 (1950): 39–42.

Moore, Clifford H. "Latin Exercises from a Greek Schoolroom." *CP* 19 (1924): 317–28.

Moreland, Milton C. and James M. Robinson, "The International Q Project: Work Sessions 23–27 May, 22–26 August, 17–18 November 1994." *JBL* 114 (1995): 475–85.

Morford, Mark. "Nero's Patronage and Participation in Literature and the Arts." *ANRW* 2.32.3 (1985): 2003–31.

Morgan, J. R. "The Greek Novel: Towards a Sociology of Production and Reception." In *The Greek World,* edited by A. Powell, 130–52. London: Routledge, 1995.

Morgan, J. R., and Richard Stoneman, eds. *Greek Fiction: The Greek Novel in Context.* London/New York: Routledge, 1994.

Nagy, Gregory. *The Best of the Achaeans: Concepts of the Hero in Archaic Greek Poetry.* Baltimore/London: Johns Hopkins Univ. Press, 1979.

———. *Pindar's Homer: The Lyric Possession of an Epic Past.* Baltimore: Johns Hopkins Univ. Press, 1990.

Newman, John Kevin. *Augustus and the New Poetry.* Brussels: Revue d'Études Latines, 1967.

———. *The Classical Epic Tradition.* Madison: University of Wisconsin Press, 1986.

Newmyer, Stephen Thomas. *The Silvae of Statius: Structure and Theme.* Mnemosyne Supp. 53. Leiden: E. J. Brill, 1979.

Nickelsburg, George W. E. "Hellenistic Jewish Poets." In *Jewish Writings of the Second Temple Period,* CRINT, edited by M. E. Stone, 118–29. Philadelphia: Fortress Press, 1984.

Norden, Eduard. *Agnostos Theos: Untersuchungen zur Formengeschichte religiöser Rede.* Leipzig: Tübner, 1913. Reprint, Darmstadt: Wissenschaftliche Buchgesellschaft, 1974.

O'Hara, James J. *Death and the Optimistic Prophecy in Vergil's Aeneid.* Princeton: Princeton Univ. Press, 1990.

Oliver, H. H. "The Lucan Birth Stories and the Purpose of Luke-Acts." *NTS* 10 (1963–64): 202–26.

O'Rourke, J. J. "Some Notes on Luke XV.11–32." *NTS* 18 (1971–72): 431–33.

Overbeck, Franz. "Über die Anfänge der patrischen Literatur." *HZ* 48 (1882; reprint, Darmstadt: Wissenschaftliche Buchgesellschaft, 1966).

Pack, Roger A. *The Greek and Latin Literary Texts from Greco-Roman Egypt.* 2d rev. ed. Ann Arbor: University of Michigan Press, 1965.

Parsons, Mikeal C. *The Departure of Jesus in Luke-Acts.* JSNTSup 21. Sheffield, U.K.: Sheffield Academic Press, 1987.

Parsons, Mikeal C., and Richard I. Pervo. *Rethinking the Unity of Luke and Acts.* Minneapolis: Fortress Press, 1993.

Paulo, Pierre-Antoine. *Le problème ecclésial des Actes à la lumière de deux prophéties d'Amos.* Paris: Cerf, 1985.

Penglase, Charles. *Greek Myths and Mesopotamia: Parallels and Influence on the Homeric Hymns and Hesiod.* London: Routledge, 1994.

Perkins, Pheme. "Crisis in Jerusalem? Narrative Criticism in New Testament Studies." *TS* 50 (1989): 296–313.

Pervo, Richard I. "Early Christian Fiction." In *Greek Fiction: The Greek Novel in Context*, edited by J. R. Morgan and R. Stoneman, 239–54. London/New York: Routledge, 1994.

———. *Profit with Delight: The Literary Genre of the Acts of the Apostles.* Philadelphia: Fortress Press, 1987.

Plümacher, Eckhard. "Die Apostelgeschichte als historische Monographie." In *Les Actes des apôtres*, BEThL 48, edited by J. Kremer, 457–66. Leuven: Leuven Univ. Press, 1979.

———. "Lukas als griechischer Historiker," 235–63. PW Sup 14. Munich: Alfred Druckenmüller, 1974.

———. *Lukas als hellenistischer Schriftsteller: Studien zur Apostelgeschichte.* SUNT 9. Göttingen: Vandenhoeck & Ruprecht, 1972.

———. "Wirklichkeitserfahrung und Geschichtsschreibung bei Lukas." *ZNW* 68 (1977): 2–22.

Pöschl, Viktor. *The Art of Virgil: Image and Symbol in the Aeneid.* Translated by G. Seligson. Ann Arbor, Mich.: Greenwood Press, 1986. Translated from the German *Die Dichtkunst Vergils: Bild und Symbol in der Aeneis,* 3d rev. ed. (Berlin/New York: de Gruyter, 1977).

Potter, David. *Prophets & Emperors: Human and Divine Authority from Augustus to Theodosius.* Cambridge, Mass.: Harvard Univ. Press, 1994.

Praeder, Susan Marie. "Acts 27:1—28:16: Sea Voyages in Ancient Literature and the Theology of Luke-Acts." *CBQ* 46 (1984): 683–706.

———. "The Problem of the First Person Narration in Acts." *NovT* 29 (1987): 193–218.

Putnam, Michael C. J. *The Poetry of the Aeneid.* Ithaca: Cornell Univ. Press, 1965.

Quint, David. *Epic and Empire: Politics and Generic Form from Virgil to Milton.* Princeton: Princeton Univ. Press, 1993.

Raaflaub, Kurt A., and Mark Toher, eds. *Between Republic and Empire: Interpretations of Augustus and His Principate.* Berkeley/London: University of California Press, 1990.

Radl, Walter. *Das Lukas-Evangelium.* Erträge der Forschung 261. Darmstadt: Wissenschaftliche Buchgesellschaft, 1988.

———. *Paulus und Jesus im lukanischen Doppelwerk.* Europäische Hochschulschriften. Bern: Peter Lang, 1975.

Räisänen, Heikki. "The Prodigal Gentile and His Jewish Christian Brother, Lk 15, 11–32." In *The Four Gospels: Festschrift for Frans Neirynck*, vol. 2, edited by Frans van Segbroeck, C. M. Tuckett, G. van Belle, and J. Verheyden. Leuven: Peeters, 1992.

Reardon, B. P. *The Form of Greek Romance.* Princeton: Princeton Univ. Press, 1991.

Rehkopf, Friedrich. *Die lukanische Sonderquelle: Ihr Umfang und Sprachgebrauch.* Tübingen: Mohr/Siebeck, 1959.

Reicke, Bo. "Die Mahlzeit mit Paulus auf den Wellen des Mittelmeers Act. 27.33-38." *ThZ* 4 (1948): 401–10.

Reynolds, Joyce and Robert Tannenbaum. *Jews and Godfearers at Aphrodisias: Greek Inscriptions with Commentary.* Cambridge Philological Society Supp. 12. Cambridge: Cambridge Philological Society, 1987.

Richard, Earl. "The Creative Use of Amos by the Author of Acts." *NovT* 24 (1982): 37–53.

Robertson, R. G. "Ezekiel the Tragedian." In *The Old Testament Pseudepigrapha,* vol. 2, Edited by James H. Charlesworth, 803–19. Garden City, N.Y.: Doubleday, 1985.

Robbins, Vernon K. "By Land and By Sea: The We-Passages and Ancient Sea Voyages." In *Luke-Acts: New Perspectives from the Society of Biblical Literature Seminar,* edited by C. H. Talbert, 216–28. New York: Crossroads, 1984.

Robinson, James M. "The International Q Project: Work Sessions 12–14 July, 22 November 1991." *JBL* 111 (1992): 500–508.

Robinson, William Childs. *Der Weg des Herrn: Studien zur Geschichte und Eschatologie im Lukas-Evangelium.* Theologische Forschung 36. Hamburg: 1964.

Rochette, Bruno. "Les traductions grecques de l'Énéide sur papyrus." *LEC* 58 (1990): 333–46.

Rosner, Brian S. "Acts and Biblical History." In *The Book of Acts in Its First Century Setting,* vol. 1: *The Book of Acts in Its Ancient Literary Setting,* edited by B. W. Winter and A. D. Clarke, 65–82. Grand Rapids: Eerdmans, 1993.

Sahlin, Harold. *Der Messias und das Gottesvolk: Studien zur protolukanischen Theologie.* Upsala: Acta Seminarii Neotestamentlici Upsaliensis, 1945.

Samain, Étienne. "Le discours-programme de Jésus à la synagogue de Nazareth." *Foi et Vie* 70 (November 1971): 25–43.

———. "Le récit de Pentecôte." *Foi et Vie* 70 (1971): 44–67.

Sanders, Jack T. "The Jewish People in Luke-Acts." In *Luke-Acts and the Jewish People,* edited by J. B. Tyson, 51–75. Minneapolis: Augsburg, 1988.

———. "Tradition and Redaction in Luke XV.11–32." *NTS* 15 (1968–69) 433–38.

Santini, Carlo. *Silius Italicus and His View of the Past.* Amsterdam: Gieben, 1991.

Sauter, Franz. *Der römische Kaiserkult bei Martial und Statius.* Stuttgart: Kohlhammer, 1935.

Schmidt, Karl Ludwig. "Die Stellung der Evangelien in der allgemeinen Literaturgeschichte." In *Eucharisterion,* edited by H. Schmidt, 50–134. Göttingen: Vandenhoeck & Ruprecht, 1923.

Schotroff, Luise. "Das Gleichnis vom verlorenen Sohn." *ZThK* 68 (1971): 27–52.

Schubert, Paul. "The Final Cycle of Speeches in the Book of Acts." *JBL* 87 (1968) 1–16.

Schweizer, Eduard. "Antwort." *ThZ* 5 (1949): 231–33.

Schulz, Siegfried. "Gottes Vorsehung bei Lukas." *ZNW* 54 (1963): 104–16.

Schürmann, Heinz. *Das Lukasevangelium,* vol. 1. Herders Theologischer Kommentar zum Neuen Testament. Freiburg/Basel: Herder, 1969.

Scott, Kenneth. *The Imperial Cult Under the Flavians.* 1936. Reprint, New York: Arno, 1975.

Segal, Alan F. *Rebecca's Children.* Cambridge, Mass.: Harvard Univ. Press, 1986.

Segal, Charles. "Bard and Audience in Homer." In *Homer's Ancient Readers: The Hermeneutics of Greek Epic's Earliest Exegetes,* edited by R. Lamberton and J. J. Keany. Princeton: Princeton Univ. Press, 1992.

Shepherd, William H. Jr. *The Narrative Function of the Holy Spirit as a Character in Luke-Acts*. SBLDS 147. Atlanta: Scholars Press, 1994.

Siegert, Folker. "Gottesfürchtige und Sympathisanten." *JSJ* 4 (1973): 109–64.

Simon, Marcel. *Verus Israel*. Oxford: Oxford Univ. Press, 1986.

Smallwood, E. Mary. *The Jews Under Roman Rule: From Pompey to Diocletian*. Studies in Judaism in Late Antiquity 20. 2d ed. Leiden: E. J. Brill, 1981.

Smid, H. R. *Protevangelium Jacobi: A Commentary*. Apocrypha Novi Testamenti. Assen: van Gorcum, 1965.

Snell, B. "Ezechiels Moses-Drama." *Antike und Abendland* 13 (1967): 150–64.

Soards, Marion L. *The Speeches in Acts: Their Content, Context, and Concerns*. Louisville: Westminster John Knox, 1994.

Soden, Hans von. *Geschichte der christlichen Kirche*, vol. 1: *Die Enstehung der christlichen Kirche*. Leipzig: Tübner, 1919.

Söder, Rosa. *Die apokryphen Apostelgeschichten und die romanhafte Literatur der Antike*. Stuttgart: Kohlhammer, 1932.

Solmsen Friedrich. "The World of the Dead in Book 6 of the *Aeneid*." In *Oxford Readings in Virgil's Aeneid*, edited by S. J. Harrison, 208–23. Oxford/New York: Oxford Univ. Press, 1990.

Spencer, F. Scott. "Acts and Modern Literary Approaches." In *The Book of Acts in Its First Century Setting*, vol. 1: *The Book of Acts in Its Ancient Literary Setting*, edited by B. W. Winter and A. D. Clarke, 381–414. Grand Rapids: Eerdmans, 1993.

Squires, John T. *The Plan of God in Luke-Acts*. SNTSMS 76. Cambridge: Cambridge Univ. Press, 1993.

Sterling, Gregory E. "'Athletes of Virtue': An Analysis of the Summaries in Acts (2:41–47; 4:32–35; 5:12–16)." *JBL* 113 (1994): 679–96.

———. *Historiography and Self-Definition: Josephos, Luke-Acts, and Apologetic Historiography*. NovTSup 64. Leiden: E. J. Brill, 1992.

Sternberg, Meir. *The Poetics of Biblical Narrative: Ideological Literature and the Drama of Reading*. Bloomington, Ind.: Indiana Univ. Press, 1987.

Stockton, David. "The Founding of the Empire." In *The Roman World*, edited by J. Boardman, J. Griffin, and O. Murray, 121–49. Oxford: Oxford Univ. Press, 1988.

Stone, Michael E., ed. *Jewish Writings of the Second Temple Period*. CRINT. Philadelphia: Fortress Press, 1984.

Strand, J. *Notes on Valerius Flaccus' Argonautica*. Studia Graeca et Latina Gothoburgensia 31. Stockholm: Almquist & Wiksell, 1972.

Strange, W. A. *The Problem of the Text of Acts*. Cambridge: Cambridge Univ. Press, 1992.

Strathmann, Hermann. "λαός." *TDNT* 4 (1967): 33–39, 50–57.

Strauss, Mark L. *The Davidic Messiah in Luke-Acts*. JSNTSup 110. Sheffield: Sheffield Academic Press, 1995.

Strugnell, John. "Notes on the Text and Metre of Ezekiel the Tragedian's 'Exagogé.'" *HTR* 60 (1967): 449–57.

Sullivan, J. P. *Martial: The Unexpected Classic*. Cambridge: Cambridge Univ. Press, 1991.

———. *The Satyricon of Petronius: A Literary Study*. London: Faber & Faber, 1968.

Syme, Ronald. *The Roman Revolution.* 1939. Reprint, Oxford: Oxford Univ. Press, 1992.

Talbert, Charles H. *Literary Patterns, Theological Themes and the Genre of Luke-Acts.* SBLMS 20. Missoula: Scholars Press, 1974.

———, ed. *Luke-Acts: New Perspectives from the Society of Biblical Literature Seminar.* New York: Crossroads, 1984.

———, ed. *Perspectives on Luke-Acts.* Edinburgh: T & T Clark, 1978.

———. "Promise and Fulfillment in Lucan Theology." In *Luke-Acts: New Perspectives from the Society of Biblical Literature Seminar,* edited by C. H. Talbert, 91–103. New York: Crossroads, 1984.

Tannehill, Robert. *The Narrative Unity of Luke-Acts: A Literary Interpretation.* 2 vols. Philadelphia/Minneapolis: Fortress Press, 1986–94.

Thomas, Christine Marie. "The Acts of Peter, the Ancient World, and Early Christian History." Ph.D. diss., Harvard University, 1995.

Thomas, Rosalind. "The Place of the Poet in Archaic Society." In *The Greek World,* edited by A. Powell. London: Routledge, 1995.

Tigay, Jeffrey H. *The Evolution of the Gilgamesh Epic.* Philadelphia: University of Pennsylvania Press, 1982.

Toohey, Peter. *Reading Epic: An Introduction to the Ancient Narratives.* London: Routledge, 1992.

Trebilco, Paul. *Jewish Communities in Asia Minor.* SNTSMS 69. Cambridge: Cambridge Univ. Press, 1991.

Trocmé, Étienne. *Le livre des Actes et l'histoire.* Études d'histoire et de philosophie religieuses 45. Paris: Presses Universitaires de France, 1957.

Van Nortwick, Thomas. *Somewhere I Have Never Travelled: The Second Self and the Hero's Journey in Ancient Epic.* New York: Oxford Univ. Press, 1992.

Van Seters, John. *In Search of History: Historiography in the Ancient World and the Origins of Biblical History.* New Haven: Yale Univ. Press, 1983.

———. *Prologue to History: The Yahwist as Historian in Genesis.* Louisville: Westminster John Knox, 1992.

Van Stempvoort, P. A. "The Interpretation of the Ascension in Luke and Acts." *NTS* 5 (1958–59): 30–42.

Van Unnik, W. C. "Luke-Acts: A Storm Center in Contemporary Scholarship." In *Studies in Luke-Acts: Essays Presented in Honor of Paul Schubert,* edited by L. E. Keck and J. L. Martyn, 15–32. Nashville: Abingdon, 1966.

———. "The Purpose of Luke's Historical Writing (Luke 1, 1–4)." In *Sparsa Collecta: The Collected Essays of W. C. van Unnik,* 6–15. Leiden: E. J. Brill, 1973. Originally published as "Opmerkingen over het doel van Lucas' Geschiedwerk (Luc. i, 1–4)," *NedThT* 9 (1955): 323–31.

Vermes, Geza. *The Dead Sea Scrolls: Qumran in Perspective.* Philadelphia: Fortress Press, 1977.

Vessey, D. W. T. "Flavian Epic." In *Latin Literature,* vol. 2 of *Cambridge History of Classical Literature,* edited by E. J. Kenney and W. V. Clausen, 558–96. Cambridge: Cambridge Univ. Press, 1982.

———. "Pierius menti calor incidit: Statius' Epic Style." *ANRW* 2.32.5 (1986): 2965–3019.

————. *Statius and the* Thebaid. Cambridge: Cambridge Univ. Press, 1973.

Veyne, Paul. *Did the Greeks Believe in Their Myths? An Essay on the Constitutive Imagination.* Chicago: University of Chicago Press, 1988.

Walaskay, Paul W. *"And So We Came to Rome": The Political Perspective of St. Luke.* SNTSMS 49. Cambridge: Cambridge Univ. Press, 1983.

Walsh, P. G. *The Roman Novel: The "Satyricon" of Petronius and the "Metamorphoses" of Apuleius.* Cambridge: Cambridge Univ. Press, 1970.

Warzawz, Hanna Szelest. "Martial: Eigentlicher Schöpfer und hervorragendster Vertreter des römischen Epigramms." *ANRW* 2.32.4 (1986): 2563–623.

Weinstock, Stefan. "The Geographical Catalogue in Acts II, 9–11." *JRomS* 38 (1948): 43–46.

West, D. A. "The Bough and the Gate." In *Oxford Readings in Virgil's* Aeneid, edited by S. J. Harrison, 224–38. Oxford/New York: Oxford Univ. Press, 1990.

————. "Cernere erat: The Shield of Aeneas." In *Oxford Readings in Virgil's* Aeneid, edited by S. J. Harrison, 295–304. Oxford/New York: Oxford Univ. Press, 1990.

White, Peter. "Amicitia and the Profession of Poetry in Early Imperial Rome." *JRomS* 68 (1978): 74–92.

White, Peter and J. Schmid. *Einleitung in das Neue Testament.* 6th ed. Freiburg: Herder, 1973.

Wikenhauser, A. "Doppelträume." *Bib* 29 (1948): 100–11.

Wilckens, Ulrich. *Die Missionsreden der Apostelgeschichte.* WMANT 5. 3d ed. Neukirchen-Vluyn: Neukirchener, 1974.

Wilder, Amos. "Variant Traditions of the Resurrection in Acts." *JBL* 62 (1943): 307–18.

Williams, George. "Did Maecenas 'Fall from Favor'? Augustan Literary Patronage." In *Between Republic and Empire,* edited by K. A. Raaflaub and M. Toher, 258–75. Berkeley: University of California Press, 1990.

Williams, R. D. *The* Aeneid. London: Allen & Unwin, 1987.

————. "The Opening Scenes of the *Aeneid.*" *Proceedings of the Virgilian Society* 5 (1965–66): 14–23.

————. "The Purpose of the *Aeneid.*" In *Oxford Readings in Virgil's* Aeneid, edited by S. J. Harrison, 21–36. Oxford/New York: Oxford Univ. Press, 1990.

————. "The Sixth Book of the *Aeneid.*" In *Oxford Readings in Virgil's* Aeneid, edited by S. J. Harrison, 191–207. Oxford/New York: Oxford Univ. Press, 1990.

Wills, Lawrence. *The Jewish Novel in the Ancient World.* Ithaca: Cornell Univ. Press, 1995.

————. "The Jewish Novellas." In *Greek Fiction: The Greek Novel in Context,* edited by J. R. Morgan and R. Stoneman, 223–38. London/New York: Routledge, 1994.

————. *The Quest of the Historical Gospel.* London: Routledge, 1997.

Wilson, Marcus. "Flavian Variant: History. Silius' *Punica.*" In *Roman Epic,* edited by A. J. Boyle, 218–36. London: Routledge, 1993.

Wilson, Stephen G. *Related Strangers: Jews and Christians, 70–170 CE.* Minneapolis: Fortress Press, 1995.

Windisch, Hans. "Die Christusepiphanie vor Damaskus (Act 9, 22 und 26) und ihre religionsgeschichtlichen Parallelen." *ZNW* 31 (1932): 1–23.

Yavetz, Z. "The Personality of Augustus: Reflections on Syme's Roman Revolution." In *Between Republic and Empire,* edited by K. A. Raaflaub and M. Toher, 21–41. Berkeley: University of California, 1990.

Zanker, Paul. *The Power of Images in the Age of Augustus.* Jerome Lectures 16. Translated by A. Shapiro. Ann Arbor: University of Michigan Press, 1990.

Zehnle, Richard. *Peter's Pentecost Discourse.* SBLMS 15. Nashville: Abingdon, 1971.

INDEX OF ANCIENT DOCUMENTS

I. INDEX OF BIBLICAL PASSAGES

223

II. INDEX OF OTHER JEWISH AND EARLY CHRISTIAN SOURCES

III. INDEX OF DEAD SEA SCROLLS

IV. INDEX OF OTHER ANCIENT SOURCES